Learning Exchange LRC
0151 252-3769

follow us on twitter

Find us on: facebook

Like

THE THINKER'S GUIDE TO

God

PETER VARDY & JULIE ARLISS

BOOKS

MediaCom
Education Inc.

Dedication

To the Franciscan sisters at Compton Durville, Somerset, England
whose lives an example present the reality of God to the world
more than any philosophy.

With thanks for their friendship, prayer and support.

First published by O-Books, 2003
O-Books is an imprint of John Hunt Publishing Ltd., Laurel House, Station Approach,
Alresford, Hants, SO24 9JH, UK
office1@jhpbooks.net
www.johnhuntpublishing.com

For distributor details and how to order please visit the 'Ordering' section on our website.

Text copyright: Peter Vardy and Julie Arliss 2003

ISBN: 978 1 90381 622 6

Design: Andrew Milne Design

Printed and bound by South China Printing Co. Ltd

We operate a distinctive and ethical publishing philosophy in all
areas of our business, from our global network of authors to
production and worldwide distribution.

CONTENTS

CHAPTER 1

THINKING ABOUT GOD - PLATO AND ARISTOTLE

This book will embark on a journey through our rich intellectual heritage with the modest aim of clarifying the past in order to illuminate the present. Goethe said that "Anyone who cannot draw on 3000 years of history is living from hand to mouth. It is the only thing that separates us from a naked ape." To understand the diversity of the present it is important to visit the past.

The picture below was painted by Raphael in 1514. It is called *The School of Athens* after the great school of philosophy in ancient Greece. Raphael has painted the figures to represent great Greek philosophers. Raphael conveys a

The School of Athens *by Raphael*

leisurely atmosphere at the school where philosophy was engaged in by those who were rich enough not to have to work and could spend their time sitting and talking and discussing the meaning of life. The slaves and the free citizens of Athens who had to work for a living were not counted among the philosophers. It is fascinating to work out who these philosophers were and why they were painted as they were.

Plato and Aristotle

The central figures in the painting are Plato and Aristotle. These two great thinkers have had more influence on the world than any great king or army general. Plato is pictured as being older than Aristotle and so he was – Plato headed the School of Philosophy, which he founded when he was 40 years old. Aristotle expected to take over from him when he died but was not appointed and as a result he left to found another School of Philosophy. It was Aristotle who tutored the young Alexander who became Alexander the Great, one of the greatest generals the world has ever known. Alexander was the most powerful man of his age and conquered lands throughout the known world from Greece and North Africa through to India. It was Aristotle who taught Alexander how to lead men into war, how to govern the empire he would one day create, and how best to create a just society. In the right hands philosophy has practical relevance to life in the real world and the choice to appoint the greatest thinker of the age to tutor Alexander had an impact on civilisation that no one could have imagined at the time. Ultimately philosophy lies beneath all that we do and sits in sovereignty over all others forms of learning.

PLATO

Plato was born in 427 B.C.E. and died in 347 B.C.E. He was born of a noble family and was highly educated. The painting of Plato on page 9 summarizes his philosophic position and everything about the figure in the painting can be taken to represent different themes in Plato's thought.

Plato was a dualist. He believed that every human being was made up of a rational soul and a body and that when a person died it was the soul that survived. In life, the soul was in the body but the soul was the real person and after death the soul left the body. The soul then went before 'the judges' who would decide, with the person who had died, how their life had been spent and the soul would then be re-born in a new body. The task of life was to care for the soul – hence it was important not to give in to the desires of the body – hence philosophers should aim to be rational by controlling the desires for, for instance, sex and food, which came from the body.

Plato

Plato considered that this world was a dance of shadows – true reality belonged to the perfect ideas of the Good, Justice, Beauty, and Truth which existed above all the material world.

Different things may be considered as beautiful:

- The beauty of a spring morning
- The beauty of a baby's first cry
- The beauty of a painting
- The beauty of a bird in flight
- The beauty of a young girl

Plato considered that these were all beautiful because they in some way resembled the perfect Form or Idea of Beauty (the Forms are always written with a capital letter so examples of beautiful things resemble the perfect Form of Beauty).

The same applies to Justice, Truth, and Goodness. For Plato, therefore, ultimate reality lies beyond the world of experience and the task of life is to see through the illusions of this world and to come, through philosophy, to a knowledge of the Forms.

The story of the cave

Plato tells the following story. Imagine that all human beings are in a cave, tied to chairs and facing the wall at the back of the cave. They had always been in this position and had never left the cave. Behind the people is a fire and between the fire and the backs of the people are figures moving backwards and forwards. The people on the seats would see the flickering shadows on the wall of the cave cast by the light of the fire and the movement of the figures between the fire and the wall. Because they had never been released from their seats they would assume the shadows were real.

The task of philosophy for Plato is to try to see the world as it really is and not as a dance of shadows. Through reason he believed it was possible to be released from the limits imposed by our sensory perceptions. This is done by a process of questioning everything. Once released from the bonds of perception a person should turn round, walk past the fire and out of the cave into the light of the Sun. For Plato, the Sun represents the Form of the Good.

So humans should seek to release themselves from the "dance of shadows," from the illusion which this world represents and to find that which truly endures and remains unchanged – represented by the perfect idea of the Forms. Hence Plato's hand pointed vertically upwards, away from the changing world to the perfect Forms.

Plato's book, 'The Timaeus' points vertically upwards as well. This indicates that the task of philosophy was to seek ultimate truth that was not to be found in this everyday world. Plato's philosophy points his reader beyond the day to day concerns of life to a heavenly realm that would be achieved after death.

The science fiction film, *The Matrix* has a similar theme. In it everyone goes about their day to day lives but what they take to be real is not. They have been deceived and they are living in an illusion. This is very similar to Plato's position.

By using philosophy, people could remember what they once knew – since everybody has lived many different lives in different bodies, they have forgotten the knowledge that they once had. He asked a slave boy who had no knowledge at all various mathematical questions. The process of questioning enabled the boy to solve a mathematical problem – this was interpreted as evidence that the boy really knew what he was being taught already, but needed to be helped to remember it. This process of questioning is called the Socratic method.

Plato's feet are in motion (very different from those of Aristotle that are stationary – compare the position of the feet of the two philosophers on the page 7!) indicating that this world is constantly moving, constantly changing. Plato argued that things in motion are either moving toward perfection or away from it: either way this means that things in motion are necessarily imperfect. The Universe is imperfect because it is always changing. This Plato contrasted with the unchanging Forms which were outside time and space and never altered at all.

It was the Forms that represented perfection and perfection could not be obtained in this world. For Plato, we may:

- See many beautiful things, but none of these represent perfect Beauty
- See many acts of justice, but none of them represent perfect Justice
- See many good things, but none of these are perfectly Good.

Only the timeless and spaceless world of the Forms represents true perfection. Human beings therefore have to live in a very imperfect world and are constrained in their perception of reality. Their souls are eternal and must be safeguarded from the physical world, which can take over and dominate them. This safeguarding is achieved, for Plato, by learning, through philosophy, what is good, right, and just. For Plato, bad behavior is a choice based on ignorance and once a person learns what is good they will do it. Plato could not comprehend of a person knowingly choosing to do something they knew was wrong.

Plato condemned art as he considered that art is imitation and it leads people away from what is real. He also condemned democracy as this is rule by the majority and the majority of people are generally ruled by their desires and not by reason. He therefore considered that countries should be governed by philosophers who would not own property or even have families as these things would lead to self-interest. Instead the philosophers should govern countries solely for the good of their citizens and without any thought of self-seeking.

Aristotle

Aristotle was born at Stagira, Thrace, in 384 B.C.E., fourteen years after the death of Socrates, and died in 322 B.C.E. His father was court physician to the King of Macedon. At the age of eighteen, he entered Plato's Academy at Athens (Plato was then 60 years old) and remained in the Academy until Plato's death. Aristotle became tutor to the son of the King of Macedon, a boy of 13 who became Alexander the Great. Aristotle rejected almost everything for which Plato has argued. In particular, he rejected Plato's idea of the existence of the Forms and considered that human beings had to work out what was good and bad, right and wrong not by appeal to some heavenly, perfect realm but by looking at the world as it was.

Although both Plato and Aristotle have been hugely influential throughout more than 2000 years of history, it is actually Aristotle who has had the greatest influence.

Aristotle

Aristotle's hand is, unlike that of Plato, straight out ahead of him with his hand flat, parallel to the ground. He is effectively saying to Plato 'Forget your heavenly realm of perfect ideas. This is the real world. This is the world where we have to work out how to live and what is good and bad.'

Aristotle was one of the first Western scientists (the Chinese had had advanced science long before it was discovered in Europe!) and the whole of Aristotle's approach is based on scientific evidence and observation.

Aristotle argued that if we want to work out what is good, we need to study good examples of the thing in question:

• If you want to find out what a good general is, then study generals.

• If you want to work out what makes a good doctor, then study doctors.

• If you want to work out what makes a good teacher, then study teachers.

The same, he argued, applies if we want to work out what makes anything good:

• If you want to work out what is a good seagull, then study seagulls.

• If you want to work out what is a good wombat, then study wombats.

• If you want to work out what is a good human being, then study human beings.

It is by studying things in the world that we can work out what they should be – not by looking for some heavenly realm of perfect goodness. Aristotle classified many types of animal and plant and considered that each member of different species of animal, plant, fish, bird, and every living thing shared a distinct nature. Something was good if it fulfilled its nature and it was defective if it was not what it was intended by its nature to be.

Aristotle's hand holds his book 'Ethics' flat to the ground. This is again indicating that ethics – the study of what is good and bad, right and wrong – is grounded in this world.

Aristotle considered that:

1. A good human being fulfills the nature which is shared by all human beings

2. Therefore, what it is to be good depends on knowing what it is to be human and

3. This can only be worked out by studying human beings to understand what human nature is.

Whereas Plato's philosophy in some ways turned its back on the world, Aristotle's philosophy is fully engaged with the world.

Aristotle not only examined living things but the stars as well. Aristotle's philosophy merged into science because of its emphasis on observation. He controversially held that the Earth was a sphere, because the shadow the Earth casts on the moon would be different if the Earth was flat. Aristotle saw the stars moving and considered that the Earth was fixed with the Sun, the moon, and the stars revolving around it. He thought that the stars were fixed in circular rings that revolved around the Earth in perfect circles.

This idea was accepted by scientists for more than 1600 years. It was not until the time of Copernicus and later Galileo that the Earth was held to move round the Sun and even then it was many years before this was accepted by most scientists.

Aristotle was the first person to show that truth can be found through scientific method and trusted observations. He was thus an EMPIRICIST – this is someone who relies on experience to underwrite claims to knowledge. All Aristotle's philosophic arguments start from experience.

Aristotle's feet, in marked contrast to those of Plato, are stationary. They are placed firmly on the ground and this too represents Aristotle's position – his philosophy has its roots in the world in which we live. There is no world of perfect Forms of which this world is a 'shadowland': this is the world we live in and this is the way it is. We do not need to reason to a world of perfect ideas to understand the world, instead we should use our rationality to understand the world in which we live. For Aristotle, human beings share many things with plants and animals:

• Plants can grow and reproduce

• Animals can grow, reproduce, and move

• Humans can grow, reproduce, move, and understand.

It is the ability to understand the nature of things that makes human beings distinctive and special. This world is not something to run away from in a search for a heavenly realm. It is a world to be lived in and understood.

For Aristotle, something was good if it fulfilled its nature. Evil, he held, is not a positive thing at all – evil is merely an absence of good. Something suffers evil if it is missing a good that should be present. For instance a seagull without a wing suffers the evil of not having a wing. Humans that are not good are evil because they choose to use their free will to fall short of what their nature is intended to be. Evil is, therefore, a privation of good. This is dealt with in more detail in a companion book to this *The Thinker's Guide To Evil*.

ARISTOTLE AND PLATO ON GOD

Just as Plato and Aristotle disagreed on the nature of goodness and the source of true reality, so they disagreed almost totally on what they meant by God. They both believed in God, but their meaning was so very different that effectively their two views had nothing in common with each other.

Plato on God

Plato considered that there were different levels of reality:

1. *Firstly there was the world of the perfect Ideas or Forms (see previous pages). The perfect Forms of The Good, Justice, and Truth exist beyond time and space. These Forms were not created by God nor do they do anything. They are just there.*

2. *Secondly there was raw, chaotic matter. This is matter without any ordering principle at all. It is chaotic matter which is always changing and is random and obeys no rules. It is simply there – it was not created and has always existed.*

3. *Thirdly there is Plato's God which he calls THE DEMIURGE.*

The DEMIURGE acts like a sculptor – he brings orders out of chaos. As a sculptor uses clay or bronze (matter which he does not create,) to form his work of art, so the Demiurge takes the raw matter [(2) above] which he did not create and fashions it to make the Universe. The Demiurge brings order out of chaos and when forming the Universe the Demiurge uses the perfect Forms [(1) above] as the model.

It is very important to recognise that neither the Forms nor the chaotic matter are created by the Demiurge. The Demiurge molds the chaotic matter using the

MATHEMATICS

Do we discover the rules of mathematics or do we make up mathematical rules? Is the claim that the circumference of a circle is $2\pi r$ something that could be discovered by intelligent aliens so that the language of mathematics could be used to communicate with them?

If your answer to this is that we discover the rules of maths, then you are probably a Platonist about numbers as you consider that the laws of mathematics are real and they exist – human beings do not make up mathematics. Great mathematicians down the ages have discovered the way numbers work and their work has shown the truth of maths. Basically, many hold, the laws of maths exist and are real and they do not depend on the existence of the Universe – they are discovered by mathematicians and have been proved to be true.

Just as the laws of mathematics are held to exist and are discovered, so Plato considered that the perfect Forms exist. Just as mathematicians can discover the rules of mathematics, so Plato argued that human beings can discover what is true about goodness, morality, and justice.

Forms as a model. However Plato considered that the Demiurge faced two problems:

1. The chaotic matter resisted the will of the Demiurge. Because of its very nature, the Universe from which the matter is formed can never be perfect or form a perfect Universe. The Universe, therefore, is always flawed because it is made of pre-existent chaotic matter.

2. The Universe is in space and time and therefore is constantly changing. Plato considered that only that which is unchanging can be perfect, so it follows that the Universe must be imperfect.

The Demiurge does not, therefore, create from nothing like the God of Christianity, Judaism, and Islam. The Demiurge works with pre-existent material which he did not create. Equally the Demiurge did not create the Forms. The Demiurge is not all powerful nor is he a loving, personal God. What is more important, the Demiurge is not supreme – it is the perfect Forms that are supreme and these provide the basis for all morality. The Demiurge can be described as morally good because he can be judged against the Form of the Good which he did not create. Christianity, Judaism and Islam would reject:

- *The idea of anything beyond God,*
- *The idea that there is anything that God did not create or*
- *The idea that there is any standard against which God could be judged.*

Aristotle on God

Aristotle not only had a completely different understanding of God – he also started from a different point.

Aristotle argued that the Universe was everlasting. It had no beginning and it would have no end. The Universe was not created: it has always existed. Aristotle held that the Earth was the center of the Universe and round the Earth, in forty concentric rings, were set the stars. He thought that the circle was the perfect shape and, therefore, the stars had to revolve in perfect, circular orbits. The first ring of stars was moved by the second ring, the second ring by the third ring, the third ring by the fourth ring and so on out to the fortieth ring. What, then, moved the fortieth ring?

Aristotle's answer was that this last ring of stars was caused to move by God – but Aristotle's God did nothing:

- *God did not create*

- *God did not sustain the Universe in existence*

- *God did not act in the Universe*

- *God had no interest in the Universe*

And yet Aristotle held that God caused the fortieth ring of stars to move!

This seems very odd but in fact it is not. God is the Great Attractor – God attracts the outer ring of stars and therefore causes movement in this outer ring even though God does nothing.

To explain Aristotle's idea of God's action, Fr. Gerry Hughes SJ uses the following example: Imagine that there is a room with a pink carpet and there is a cat at one side of the room. Now imagine that a bowl of milk is put into the room. The milk will cause the cat to cross the room – not by the milk doing anything, but just by its being there it will attract the cat. There is a real sense in which the milk causes the cat to move even though the milk does not act.

For Aristotle, God does nothing at all, yet God is supremely happy because God contemplates himself. Aristotle considered contemplation to be the highest end (he was a philosopher and he considered that for human beings contemplating the truths found in philosophy was the route to perfect happiness) and God, being supremely perfect, would have no interest at all in the Universe. Instead God thinks about and contemplates his own nature and since God is supremely perfect this would make God supremely happy.

The Universe is in space and time but Aristotle considered that God was outside space and outside time, God was spaceless and timeless. God was not another object in the Universe – instead God was radically different from anything in the Universe.

Aristotle held a very different view on what a soul was to Plato. Plato was a dualist holding that a human being had a disembodied soul that survived death but Aristotle considered that talk of a soul was to talk of the form or 'shape' or specification of what a thing is. A thing's form or soul is what makes it what it is. So the form or soul of an oak tree is what makes an oak tree what it is. Everything has a soul since everything is a thing of a particular kind and what makes it what it is, is its soul. Today, in the case of plants and animals, there might be a parallel with genetics which determines what a living thing is. Everything in the Universe is made up of form or soul and matter. To put it another way, everything consists of its specification and what makes it what it is. Form or soul and matter are closely linked and cannot be separated. Matter needs form to make it what it is, but form needs matter to become what it is intended to be. God, uniquely, has form but no matter – thus Aristotle considers God does not have a body and has no physical shape at all. It is impossible, therefore, to conceive what God is since we can only conceive of things which have bodies.

IN SPITE OF THEIR DIFFERENCES Aristotle's God and Plato's Form of the Good have similarities. Neither does anything; neither is created; neither creates; neither is in space and time; neither has any interest in the Universe and yet both are timeless, spaceless, and completely perfect.

QUESTIONS FOR CONSIDERATION

1) What are the main differences between Plato and Aristotle's view of the role of God in relation to the Universe?

2) Is Aristotle or Plato's idea of God closer to the God of religion? Why?

3) What sort of life does Plato's story of the cave point people to?

4) What sort of life does Aristotle's understanding of science point people to?

5) What, for Aristotle, would it mean to be a good human being?

6) Why do you think that the film and play about the life of C.S. Lewis was called *Shadowlands*?

7) What does the nature of mathematics have to do with Plato's philosophy?

8) Think of an example of how a beautiful woman or a handsome man could attract while doing nothing. What relevance does this have to Aristotle's idea of God's action?

CHAPTER 2

THE GOD OF THE PHILOSOPHERS

Two ideas of God have dominated the history of the great monotheistic religions – these can crudely be described as "The God of the Philosophers" and "The God of Revelation." Although this is too simple a distinction, there has been a debate between which shall have priority – philosophy or revelation – when deciding on how to conceive God. The two understandings of God are very different and whilst the God of philosophy can be explained in relation to sacred texts and the God of the sacred texts can be explained in terms of philosophy, it is nevertheless true that there is a tension between these two ideas of God which has been recognised for thousands of years. Within the Christian tradition, in general and simplistic terms, "the God of the Philosophers" is adopted by the Catholic Church and the "God of the Bible" by Protestant Churches, although most members of both churches are not aware of the differences.

After Jesus died, the early Church had various accounts of his life and various letters written by St. Paul and others. These were put together to form 'The New Testament' as it is known today. There were many arguments about which stories and letters to include and it was not until 367 C.E. that final agreement was reached on the 'CANON' of the New Testament ('canon' simply means the books and letters that the Church formally accepted because it was believed that they 'measured up' to the standard of sacred texts).

From the earliest years after the death and resurrection of Jesus the DOCTRINE of Christianity was developed. 'Doctrine' means the ideas about God, the Church, Jesus, Mary, and other matters which form the key beliefs of Christians. There were many fierce disagreements and great COUNCILS were held which brought together Church leaders (mainly Bishops) from Christian Churches all over the Roman Empire. They decided by vote which doctrines were true and which were false. The doctrines that were false were called HERESIES. A heresy is a position that the Christian Church has specifically rejected as not being faithful to the teaching of the Church and over the next thousand years many heretics were condemned to death, put in prison or persecuted because the beliefs they held were not considered to be correct. Martin Luther, who was in part responsible for the reformation, was condemned and considered as a heretic by the Catholic Church as he wished to return to the God of the Bible and a simple worship of God. He rejected the philosophy of the Middle Ages.

In many cultures ideas about God can be seen to have developed over the centuries. A typical pattern of development is:

1. At first gods were thought to live in the woods, rivers, and trees,

2. Then the gods were thought to be in Earth, fire, air, and water,

3. Then the gods were thought to live on the top of mountains,

4. Then the gods were thought to live in the sky,

5. Then the gods were thought to live in a wonderful place somewhere called Valhalla or 'The kingdom of the blessed.'

Do you believe that snarks exist?

"Just the place for a Snark!"
the Bellman cried,
As he landed his crew with care;
Supporting each man on the top
of the tide
By a finger entwined in his hair.
"Just the place for a Snark! I have
said it twice:
That alone should encourage the crew.
Just the place for a Snark! I have said
it thrice:
What I tell you three times is true."

(from Lewis Carrol's 'The Hunting of the Snark')

Imagine that someone asks you whether you believe that snarks exist. You might very reasonably reply:

"I don't know what a snark is. Tell me what it is and I will tell you whether I believe that snarks exist."

Now assume that someone says: "Do you believe that God exists?" Most people will reply "Yes," "No" or "I am not sure" but in reality most people have not thought deeply about what it means to talk of God or whether this God exists.

The God of the Philosophers and the God of the biblical tradition are very different just as the God of Plato and the God of Aristotle are very different and before anyone can decide whether God exists or not, it is necessary to decide what is meant by the word 'God'.

*Jesus portrays God
in human terms*

For the great thinkers in all monotheistic religions, however, these pictures of God are too Earth-bound or too anthropomorphic (many still picture gods as very like human beings – stronger, grander, more powerful, and sometimes better, but nevertheless like them). Each of the above stages picture God, or the gods, inside of space and time. However Jewish, Christian, and Muslim theologians – using the philosophy of Plato and Aristotle – quickly realized that these models of God were not adequate. God could not be another being in the Universe, subject to space and time like humans were, as then God would be limited. God would change and therefore either be getting better or getting worse and in either case would not be God.

One of the central questions to be considered by the Christian Church in the early centuries after the death of Jesus was the nature of God. In other words what does it mean to talk of God? This was not an easy question to answer and the Church wanted to avoid two dangers:

1. *God must not be seen as an idol. The Hebrew Scriptures had, above all, condemned idol worship and the great Christian teachers and leaders were very anxious that God should not be portrayed as an idol like the idols of Greek and Roman religion. In these religions the different gods were pictured as divine humans who fought amongst each other, had desires, caused hurt to people on Earth, and were like great tyrants. In addition many Roman emperors were worshiped as Gods and the Christian leaders were clear that their God was nothing at all like this.*

2. *As the creator of the Universe, God must be very different from anything in the created Universe. God must be perfect and therefore not subject to change. Plato and Aristotle had been clear that perfection and changelessness were closely related, so the Christian God had to be non-material and incapable of change.*

This led to the view that God must be TIMELESS and SPACELESS. Since everything in the Universe was in time and space, God had to be outside time and outside space. Support for this came from the philosophy of Aristotle which, with the philosophy of Plato, dominated the thinking of the day. Christian thinkers therefore appealed to Greek philosophy to help them formulate Christian ideas about God. The consequences of this were to be profound for the thinking about God which developed in the Christian Church.

THE WHOLLY SIMPLE GOD

Space and time exist everywhere in the Universe. The Universe may have had a beginning and one day may have an end. Time passes as the Universe expands, stars are created, and stars die. Light travels at enormous speed but it still takes time for light to travel from one place to another – the nearest star to Earth is about 5 light years away. This means that it takes light, travelling at 186,000 miles a second, about 5 years to reach Earth. Time and space are the bedrock of the Universe. They are like water to the goldfish and just as the goldfish can not imagine a world without water, so human beings cannot imagine a Universe without space and time.

The early Christian thinkers concluded that if God created time and space then God cannot be in time and space – God has to be outside space and outside time. In goldfish terms, God has to be neither wet nor fishy. God has to be very, very different from anything within the Universe God made.

Plato and Aristotle both argued that whatever was perfect could not be in space and time – Christian thinkers argued that as God is perfect this confirmed the idea that God is spaceless and timeless. God created the Universe and sustains it by keeping it in existence, but that does not mean that God is in a particular place in the Universe. God is spaceless and timeless but the whole Universe depends on God and has its origins in God. God is, therefore, present in God's creation since the whole of creation owes its existence entirely to God.

Imagine

Imagine you lived in a goldfish pond but you were a philosophic goldfish. Not for you the normal life of eating and breeding and eating. You wondered why there was a pond at all. Where had the pond come from? What kept it in existence? You might think that whilst everything in the pond was wet and fishy, whatever created the pond would not be like that or it would be part of the pond. The pond's creator, therefore, would be not wet and not fishy at all. Imagining that, for the goldfish would be very hard indeed.

The Eagle Nebula

Some modern biologists completely reject the idea of God. They argue that theology is ridiculous and should be banned as a University subject. They mock religious believers and consider that, given our knowledge of the Universe, the God of religious believers is too small and petty to be a real God. In the face of our knowledge of the billions of stars in this galaxy and the billions of galaxies in the Universe, they laugh at the idea of God as an old man with a white beard worshiped by thousands of millions of people all over the world. However, it is, in fact, their understanding that is limited, not the concept of God, and most believers would laugh alongside him at the idea that God is a man with a beard. The great philosophers of Christianity, Islam, and Judaism have always recognized that the idea of God is a much bigger idea than that of the Universe – God is held to have created the Universe and can hardly, therefore, be part of creation. The God who could create black holes and the Eagle nebula (see picture) is a very long way from an old man with a white beard. The more our knowledge of the Universe and its origins increases, the more persuasive becomes the idea of a God who is outside time and space. (These arguments are dealt with in more detail in Chapter 13.)

It is now widely agreed among scientists (although it has not yet been totally proved and there are some alternative theories) that time and space came into existence with the singularity that resulted in the Big Bang. The enormous explosion that created the Universe brought into existence time and space. It might be claimed that the Big Bang appears to explain the existence of the Universe without need for a God. However the Big Bang theory fits perfectly with the idea of a God who is outside time and space and who created space and time at the same time as the Universe.

The early Church Fathers concluded that God cannot be imagined or conceived, that God is beyond the human imagination. Nevertheless, they said that it was possible to talk about God and to say many things about God provided the difficulties of using language about a God who is so totally different from anything within the Universe is appreciated. However if God was literally outside of space and time, outside the Universe (although of course the Universe depends on God), how could God be talked about or known?

What can be said about a wholly simple God?

NEGATIVE STATEMENTS

Ultimately God is held to be a Mystery, but there are some things that can be said about God. In particular some negative things can be said as, if God is outside space and time, then nothing that involved space and time could truthfully be said to apply to God. In particular:

1. *God could not have a body (since bodies occupy space and time passes whilst these bodies exist).*

2. *God cannot change so God must be immutable which means incapable of change.*

3. *God could not be divided into parts (bodies can be divided into parts, but God has no body).*

4. *Nothing that involves time or space could truthfully be said about God.*

However there was one further point that was considered to be more important still – and from which everything else flowed – this was that God has no potential. This needs explanation.

POTENTIAL

Aristotle had held that everything in the Universe was both **actual** in that it existed, and had **potential** to change. So:

- *A cat is actual in that it exists, but it has the potential to catch a mouse or a bird.*

- *A leaf is actual in that exists, but it has the potential to fall from the tree or to be burnt.*

- *A cow is actual in that it exists, but has the potential to move or eat grass.*

Human beings have much potential

For Aristotle, everything in the Universe is actual but also has a wide range of potentialities and these potentialities depend on the sort of thing that it is. In some cases, the list of potentialities can be very long – for instance an adult human being has a whole range of potentialities including the potential to run, walk, swim, run, climb, fall, talk, eat, drink, communicate, learn, reproduce, show compassion, do evil, do good, become ill, and die. However there are clear potentialities that humans do not have – they cannot fly unaided or swim for very long underwater without breathing equipment. One can only have potential if there is the possibility of actualizing the potential. For instance the potential to swim only makes sense if someone can actualize the potential by getting in the water and swimming – a tree clearly does not have the potential to swim, although it may have the potential to float.

At a very obvious level the person who wants to realize their potential to swim must be able to move, or be moved, from dry land into some water – this process of moving into the water involves change and time passes as the change occurs. The realization of potential depends on the capacity to change and the passage of time. As God cannot change and is outside time he cannot have potential. This led the early Church Fathers to say that GOD IS FULLY ACTUAL and GOD HAS NO POTENTIAL – God is fully whatever it is to be God and cannot be other than this. The early Church Fathers found this confirmed in the Scriptures.

Yahweh – The Hebrew name for God

The book of Exodus in the Hebrew scriptures records that the people of Israel were slaves under the Egyptians in about 1300 B.C.E. At this time God appeared to Moses and told him that he had to go to the ruler of Egypt, the Pharaoh, and order him to "Let my people go." God appeared to Moses in the form of a burning bush and spoke to Moses giving him instructions. Moses was, naturally, terrified and was not sure the Pharaoh would take any notice of him. In particular Moses thought the people would not believe him and would ask who this God was who was ordering the Pharaoh to release them:

> **"Moses said to God, 'Who am I that I should go to Pharaoh and lead the Israelites out of Egypt?'"**
> **God answered, 'I will be with you; and this shall be your proof that it is I who have sent you: when you bring my people out of Egypt, you will worship God on this very mountain.'**
> **'But,' said Moses to God, 'when I go to the Israelites and say to them, "The God of your fathers has sent me to you," if they ask me, "What is his name?" what am I to tell them?'**
> **God replied, 'I am who I am.' Then he added, 'This is what you shall tell the Israelites: I AM sent me to you.'" (Exodus 3.11–14)**

God's reply suggests that god alone is the source of all that is. In Hebrew "I am" can be read as "I was" or "I will be" or "I am being." this is seen in Christian theology to support the idea of a wholly simple, timeless, and spaceless God who is the source of all creation and contains the essence of being.

Everything in the Universe is subject to change and this ability to change is indicated by talk of its potential. God alone is fully actual and has no potential at all.

NECESSITY AND CONTINGENCY

Everything in the Universe comes into existence and goes out of existence. Every plant and animal grows and dies. Even stars come into existence and after billions of years go through various stages until they cease to exist. This state of being is known as CONTINGENCY. Everything in the Universe may exist or may not exist and is dependent on other things for existence. Everything in the Universe is contingent.

Every human being is dependent on their parents for their existence but also on many other factors – food, water, air, their body's immune system protecting them from disease and illness, car drivers driving on the correct side of the road so that they do not crash into those who are walking or cycling, gravity, the Sun making the conditions on Earth suitable for life, no asteroids hitting the Earth and wiping out all human life – and countless other things. Everything is, therefore, contingent in that it may or may not have existed and everything is dependent on many other things for its continued existence.

God, however, is not like this:

- *God does not depend on anything else for God's existence.*

- *God does not come into existence.*

- *God does not go out of existence.*

Sometimes children will ask "What caused God?" and it is a sensible question as everything they experience comes into existence and goes out of existence. It is hard to understand the answer, which is "nothing" – nothing caused God because God never came into existence and does not depend on anything else. This is expressed by saying that **GOD NECESSARILY EXISTS**. God cannot not-exist. God is not contingent.

SIMPLICITY

This view of God is brought together in the idea that **GOD IS WHOLLY SIMPLE** and to say this means bringing together everything said above. God is wholly simple as:

- *God is not made up of parts.*

- *God does not have a body.*

- *God is not in space or time.*

- *God is immutable.*

- *God has no potential.*

- *God is necessary.*

This idea was most clearly formulated by probably the greatest Christian theologian and philosopher who ever lived – St. Thomas Aquinas. Aquinas worked at the University of Paris from 1265–1274 and used the philosophy of Aristotle to make sense of Christian claims

St. Thomas Aquinas

and to explain them to Christians and to non-Christians. It was he who most clearly formulated the idea of the Christian God as wholly simple and who worked out the view explained in this chapter. However he was actually only developing more precisely the ideas that the early Fathers of the Church had developed in the first five hundred years of Christian history and also the Jewish and Islamic understandings. Aquinas, however, was able to give the understanding of God a philosophic precision that it had not previously had because he had access to the

Simple does not mean simple!

To say that God is simple, does not mean the same as saying that, say, "Peter is simple" (perhaps he is not very intelligent) or "That exam was simple" (meaning the exam was easy).

To say that God is wholly simple has a quite specific meaning which will not be found in normal language and which this chapter has outlined.

work of Plato and Aristotle. It is a mark of his genius that his analysis has stood the test of time. The Catholic Church formally and officially confirmed that Aquinas' analysis and understanding was correct and ever since then, the understanding of God as wholly simple has been normative in the Catholic tradition. THE GOD OF THE PHILOSOPHERS is therefore the accepted model of God amongst most (but by no means all) Catholic theologians today.

The Protestant reformers were to reject the 'scholastic theology' (basically the philosophical system based on St. Thomas Aquinas) and to call for a return to an understanding of God which has as its starting point the Hebrew and Christian scriptures. This provides a very different understanding of God.

QUESTIONS FOR CONSIDERATION

1) Why were the early Church Fathers so concerned that God should not be presented as a Being in space and time?

2) Why did Aristotle and Plato provide a way of understanding God for Christian and Muslim theologians?

3) What potentialities does a seagull have?

4) Why is everything in the Universe held to be contingent?

5) What does it mean to say that 'God necessarily exists'?

CHAPTER 3

THE GOD OF SACRED SCRIPTURE

All of the world's monotheistic religions have a tradition of exploring the nature of God by using the tools of philosophy but the God of the Philosophers is only one way of conceiving of God. In each of the great monotheistic traditions there is an equally strong and popular concept of God informed not by philosophy but by sacred scripture. As the last chapter made clear, the development of the idea of God in philosophical terms came from the primacy given to Greek philosophy – in the Christian tradition particularly this came through the scholastic philosophy of St. Thomas Aquinas whose primary influence was Aristotle. The God of Philosophy is not always understood by believers and even if this model of God is understood it may be regarded as a rather distant and impersonal concept and not at all like the God with whom believers feel that they have a relationship. Within all the monotheistic religions, therefore, there is another model of God which is often a more popular picture and it is from the inspiration of sacred texts that this model of God comes. Within the Christian tradition the wealth of ideas about God in sacred scripture were denied to regular believers for many centuries, as the translation of the Bible into any language other than Latin was forbidden. This meant that ideas and beliefs about God were dominated by the picture of God derived from the Church. However the more popular idea of God was still present and, in Christianity, was most clearly expressed in the philosophy and theology of the Franciscan tradition.

Aquinas and Bonaventure

Between 1260 and 1275 C.E. there were two great theologians at the University of Paris (which was the greatest University in the world at the time). These two belonged to two different religious orders. St. Thomas Aquinas was a Dominican and St. Bonaventure was a Franciscan. St. Thomas Aquinas used the philosophy of Aristotle to provide a picture of God that was philosophically satisfying and would provide a defense of Christianity to non-Christians. His view also explained and developed Christian theology and the moral understanding of the Christian life.

St. Bonaventure, working at the same time as Aquinas, adopted a very different approach. St. Bonaventure was master of the Franciscan order and was the academic equal of Aquinas. However, his starting point was not the philosophy of Aristotle but the inspiration of St. Francis himself. The whole of the Franciscan approach to theology and the whole of the Franciscan understanding of God is based on a relatively straightforward reading of the Bible and on the teachings of Jesus of Nazareth. Bonaventure maintained that the Christian doctrine of the Trinity was to be taken very seriously – Father, Son, and Holy Spirit are joined together in a dynamic love relationship and this love overflows and causes creation to come into being. The love which is at the heart of God is the love which brings the Universe and humankind into being. Bonaventure and the Franciscan tradition were not afraid of picturing God as a lover who lures human beings to love God and to love each other. The presence of beauty in the world was seen as a central part of this message – just as beauty is present everywhere so God is present throughout God's creation and God uses beauty as a way to open the minds of human beings to God. The God of the Franciscan tradition, portrayed through philosophers like Duns Scotus and William of Ockham, was a temporal God – a God in time.

Both the approach of Bonaventure and of Aquinas were initially treated with great suspicion by the Church and both risked being condemned by the Inquisition. Finally, however, the Church at the Council of Trent (held between 1545 and 1563) decided in favour of Aquinas, Aristotle, and the Dominicans. There were various reasons for this – not least because the Protestant church was providing an increasing threat to Catholicism and Aquinas provided a tight, well argued system of intellectual thought which could provide a sound defense against the Reformation. More than this, Aristotle had been widely accepted for hundreds of years as his approach to science was universally accepted.

The Franciscan tradition

Francis, unlike Aquinas, was not an academic. He was a simple man who insisted his followers should take their vows of poverty very seriously. He found good in everyone – no matter who they were. He accepted and worked with all people. On one occasion he crossed over in the middle of a war between Christians and Muslims to visit the Sultan – who treated him with courtesy and consideration as a man of God. He was gentle and many Christians see him as the closest that any person has ever come to living as Jesus himself lived. He called the Church back to the simplicity and love that was at the center of Jesus' own message.

If the Catholic Church had not ignored the Franciscan understanding of theology and the role of the Church, the Reformation might well not have happened as the Church might well have been a much simpler affair with a much greater emphasis on the Bible and the message of Jesus. However, the decision of the Church to adopt the position of Aristotle and Aquinas meant that, within the Catholic tradition, the Franciscan approach to theology was sidelined.

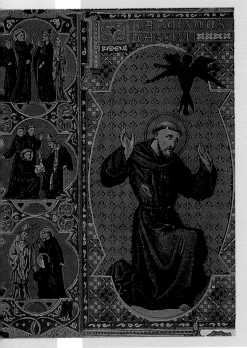

Francis was born into a wealthy household in Assisi. He was well educated and trained to be a soldier and, when he came to adulthood, he went off to fight for his city. He was injured and returned to his home and began to read the Bible and to think seriously about Christianity and this began to make a deep impact on him. He went off to fight once more but felt increasingly uncomfortable about the life he was living and much to the disgust of his friends he decided to leave and return to his city. He started to live a very simple life seeking to follow the commands of Jesus. He gave everything away and even rejected his parents. Whilst praying in a derelict church Francis had a vision in which he was told to "rebuild my Church." He took this literally and began to rebuild the church in which he was praying. Later he came to see this vision as a call to rebuild the whole church.

There is a sense then that the picture of God in time, the God of the Bible who can be spoken of in human terms, was a picture of God that was very familiar within mainstream Roman Catholic theology. Ultimately however this biblical picture of God was put aside to make way for the more philosophically satisfying God of Aquinas. The key difference between the Franciscan model of God and the Aquinas model of God is that the starting point for the Franciscans was revelation and for Aquinas the starting point was Greek philosophy.

THE REFORMATION

One of the major contributory factors to the Reformation and the division in the Western Church into Roman Catholic and Protestant was disagreement about the picture of God taught by the Church. The Protestant reformers argued that the picture of God in sacred scripture was at odds with it. A movement began to translate the Bible into local languages, so that ordinary people could read for themselves. This was illegal and the penalty was death. The Protestant reformers included figures such as:

John Wycliff (1320–1384) who was responsible for the first translation of the Bible into English and was Master of Balliol College, Oxford from 1360. Wycliff was a fierce critic of the established Church of his time and also of the papacy – he launched strong attacks on the Pope at a time when people speaking in this way were in real danger of torture and death from the Inquisition which had been established to suppress heresy. Wycliff rejected transubstantiation – the Church doctrine that Jesus was literally present in the bread and wine of the Eucharist. Wycliff held that Jesus was present but in a spiritual sense only. Wycliff also condemned the worship of saints and considered that every person had direct access to God and that there was no need for priests. Most important, Wycliff argued that the Bible should have priority over Church teaching. Wycliff claimed that every ordinary person had the right to read the Bible in their own language – this was a challenging idea which was rejected by the Church who held that only priests should read the Bible and it had to be read in Latin.

John Huss (1370–1415) was a student of John Wycliff. He also believed that Scripture took precedence over the dogmas and teaching of the Church and he actually claimed that the office of the Pope was the Anti-Christ foretold in Scripture. He was burned alive at the stake in 1415 for heresy and rebellion against the teaching of the Catholic Church.

Martin Luther (1483–1546) joined the Augustinian Friars in Erfut in Germany. His aim, he said, was "to find God." He became a member of the most strictly observant part of his Order of monks. In 1505, then Professor of Biblical Studies, he found through his study of the Bible a solution to why, however strictly he tried to live as a monk, this did not satisfy him. Luther came to challenge the traditions of the Roman Catholic Church and coined the phrase "Sola Scriptura," meaning that the Bible alone should be relied on for salvation and that faith and not reliance on good works or the Church should be central to the Christian life. The authority he claimed for this significant challenge to the Church was Scripture. He claimed that this was true to the origins of Christianity and that the Church had gone astray. What he had read in the letters of St. Paul showed him that there was no way to God other than through faith in Jesus. In 1517 Luther posted his 95 theses on the door of the church in Wittenburg, challenging the authority of the Papacy and in particular the sale of 'Indulgences.' Indulgences, which were authorized by the church, were sold to people as a way of buying salvation. Martin Luther declared the papacy to be "nothing else than the kingdom of Babylon and very Anti-Christ." Luther translated the Bible into German, so that the German people could read Scripture for themselves, in their own language. He was condemned as a heretic but was protected in Germany where the Catholic Church's power was limited.

John Calvin (1509–1564) was heavily influenced by Luther and grew up in a world where Luther's ideas were having a great influence. However, Calvin went further than Luther and was a more rigorous and uncompromising opponent of Catholicism. The most significant parts of his theology included a belief in the primacy of the Scripture as an authority for doctrinal decisions, a belief that God predestines everyone for either heaven or hell, a belief in salvation wholly accomplished by grace with no influence from works – so in other words it is not possible for a person to earn their way to heaven by being good – and a rejection of Church structures which included the Pope and Bishops.

Richard Hooker (1554–1600) was one of the most influential of all Anglican thinkers. He combined Aristotle's philosophy with the best of Reformation thought and he sought to enable Anglicanism to be a middle way embracing the best of Catholicism and Protestantism. Christianity, he held, should be a tolerant religion and he avoided the condemnation of Catholics by Protestants and Protestants by Catholics. God, he said, is on the side of human beings: "God is not… eager to trip us up whenever we say amiss, but a courteous tutor, ready to amend what, in our weakness or our ignorance, we say ill, and to make the most of what we say aright." Anglicanism today has been strongly influenced by Hooker.

The positions of the reformers on worship, on the authority of the Bible and on the authority of the Church was ultimately incompatible with the traditions of the Church, which held that the Church had ultimate authority on Earth and that the Pope, as the successor of St. Peter, in essence held the keys to heaven. The challenge to the authority of the church was only possible because the reformers claimed a higher authority – the authority of sacred Scripture. The translation of the Bible from Latin to languages of the people of Europe and the recent invention of the printing press helped the Reformation. Ordinary men and women could begin to have access to the Bible and to read it for themselves. Once ordinary people had access to the Bible text they too could begin to question the teachings and ideas of the Church and compare these to the words of Jesus himself as recorded in the Gospels.

Some of the consequences of the Reformation:

1. *The worship of God became much simpler. The position of the clergy as mediators between the people and God changed. The New Testament records that the only way to God is through Jesus.*

2. *The idea of paying for indulgences was rejected. The sale of indulgences was legitimized by the Catholic Church's claim to be the heirs of St. Peter who was given authority to admit people to heaven or to send them to hell (the papal coat of arms shows these keys). The Church taught that after death, human beings went either to heaven, to hell, or to purgatory. Purgatory was a place that most went to and was a place where sins were paid for and the soul cleansed. Those in purgatory would eventually achieve the beatific vision of God but only perhaps after hundreds or thousands of years of cleansing. The pains of purgatory were said to exceed any pain that could be imagined or experienced on Earth. Naturally, therefore, people were concerned to cut down their time in purgatory and the Church promised that, in return for the payment of large sums of money, "indulgences" could*

Cuthbert Gospel

A leaf from the Cuthbert Gospel which is part of the library of Heythrop College, University of London. The excerpt is taken from St. John's Gospel, and is written in a very clear hand, with almost none of the contractions used in manuscripts of the time. Cuthbert died in 687, and his body was originally buried in Lindisfarne. It was moved to Durham in 995, where it now rests behind the high altar. The Bible forms the basis for most Protestant Christian belief about God.

be granted which would reduce the number of years spent in purgatory. The Church became rich by old people paying huge amounts to reduce the time they spent in this place of cleansing. The reformers rejected the claim that the Church had authority to do this. There is some biblical authority to suggest that the disciples were given authority to forgive sins but the reformers claimed that salvation or otherwise could not be bought with money paid to the Church. The New Testament proclaims salvation by faith in Jesus, and not salvation by buying indulgences from the church.

3. Marriage came to be seen much more positively. The Catholic Church taught that celibate life was the better route to salvation as it facilitated a higher commitment to the spiritual life. Priests had to be committed to the celibate life. Marriage whilst not condemned was regarded as not as good as celibacy. Protestants saw no difference between celibate or married life in terms of being close to God and, when Protestant Churches formed, priests were allowed to marry. They argued that there is no demand in the New Testament to live a celibate life, although St. Paul does in fact recommend it for those who are suited to it.

4. The philosophical picture of God was subordinated to the biblical picture of God. The Bible became central and philosophy was largely disregarded.

5. "The word of God," as recorded in the Bible, became of central importance. Luther said that he would only accept judgment of his ideas by the "plain word of scripture." The Bible became, for Protestants, the ultimate test of truth and any church teaching that went against this teaching was challenged and rejected.

The Catholic Church's reaction to this was to totally condemn the Protestants. St. Ignatius of Loyola, the founder of the Catholic religious order known as the Society of Jesus (the Jesuits) has a statue over his tomb of the Virgin Mary driving Martin Luther and Calvin out of heaven and into hell. Mary holds a cross in one hand and a dagger in the other and Luther and Calvin are portrayed as recoiling before the cross. At the bottom of the sculpture is an angel tearing pages out of a book – representing their writings which the Church condemned – most important of these was the idea that the individual should be able to appeal to the Bible to challenge the teaching of the Church.

The Virgin Mary driving Luther and Calvin to hell

The Protestant challenge to Catholic Christianity was wide reaching. The authority of the Church was widely accepted and so to challenge this went to the very heart of Christian teaching. Equally the very concept of God, as wholly simple, timeless, and spaceless was challenged as the picture of God in the Bible is very different to that of the wholly simple God. The biblical God is essentially personal and enters into relationships with people and nations – the God of the Bible can be talked to as "Abba" (Father) in a very personal way. If God can enter into relationships then God fulfills his potential to do this and this challenges the idea of his immutability. There is equally a clear tension between the wholly simple God and fundamental Christian belief in Jesus. If Jesus was both fully human and fully divine then God dwelt among us in time and space. This clearly challenges what was seen in the Church as the philosophical necessity of God being outside of space and time.

The God of the Bible

1. In Genesis, God is held to have walked in the Garden of Eden with Adam. The wholly simple God cannot walk in any garden as God is bodiless and changeless.

2. Jacob is held to have wrestled God all night. Only a God who is in time could have a body and thus be able to wrestle.

3. God was held to dwell in the tabernacle which traveled with the people of Israel and then to have dwelt in the Temple in Jerusalem (although the Jews were also clear that heaven itself could not contain God – they never saw God as a local God). The idea of God dwelling in one place only seemed possible for a God who could be in a particular place and this meant a God in time and space as the wholly simple God was not in space at all.

4. Christians hold that Jesus is God, yet Jesus had a body and was clearly in time and space. This, therefore, seems to provide clear evidence that God must be in time and space since the best picture of God was given by Jesus.

5. The Christian God is a trinity of three persons who are nevertheless one – Father, Son, and Holy Spirit. If God the Father was wholly simple and timeless and God the Son was in time then this would have broken up the Trinity. As it was very clear that Jesus was in time, so it was held that the whole Trinity must be temporal.

6. Jesus died on the cross and rose again. His resurrection body was clearly a physical body – the disciples could see the marks of the crucifixion nails and where a soldier thrust a spear into his side.

7. Jesus talked to his disciples about heaven and hell as temporal places. Heaven was a place where he would reign as king and where his disciples would be on thrones judging the tribes of Israel. It was a place where the lion and lamb would lie down together and a little child would lead them.

Jesus with the disciples

Effectively the decision to opt for the God of Aquinas and to sideline the Franciscan tradition, was one that caused a massive backlash.

NATURAL AND REVEALED THEOLOGY

- *Within the Roman Catholic tradition the revelations of God in Scripture had been given second place to subsequent revelations which had been made to the Church and had also been given second place to natural theology. St. Thomas Aquinas and the Catholic tradition has always maintained that, using reason, it is possible to prove that God exists and that these proofs point to a God outside time and space. The use of philosophy to prove God's existence by reason is called NATURAL THEOLOGY and the Church claimed that natural theology would never contradict revealed theology. In other words, whatever could be deduced by reason about God would never contradict what is revealed about God in Scripture. It was also held that revelation includes truths that reason has not discovered. Aquinas did not think that the creation of the world could be proved by reason but could be known by the revelation in the Book of Genesis.*

Natural and revealed theology

Imagine two train tracks running parallel with each other. Natural and revealed theology are held to be like this. One does not contradict the other. Natural theology (the use of philosophy and reason) can take human beings to basic knowledge that God exists and what God is like, but revelation goes further and reveals doctrines that human reason could not discover without divine aid (such as the doctrine of the Trinity or the Incarnation).

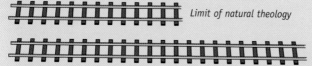

Limit of natural theology

Revealed theology – going further than natural theology but not contradicting anything within natural theology

This is the traditional Catholic position which holds that natural and revealed theology are handmaids – the one does not contradict the other. This is why philosophy and theology have always been closely related in Catholic theology and in the training of priests – both are required in order to understand something of the nature of God and of God's relationship with human beings.

Any approach to theology is clearly going to have to decide whether revealed theology or natural theology has ascendancy. Furthermore a decision is required on which revelations will be regarded as authoritative. The Reformation argued that revelations in Scripture were authoritative over natural theology and that any revelation to the Church which contradicted Scripture was invalid. Many Protestant thinkers have rejected the central importance given to philosophy by the Roman Catholic Church. Karl Barth, probably the greatest Protestant theologian of the 20th century, said that of all the reasons for rejecting Catholicism, natural theology was the greatest. This was because natural theology was seen to place philosophy and reason above or equal to revelation whereas most Protestants see revelation as being central and reject the idea that philosophy and reason can bring anyone to knowledge of God. Philosophy, if it has any role for Protestants, has to operate within faith and cannot underpin or justify faith. If, therefore, the Bible appeared to place God in time, then to Protestant Christians, the intellectual difficulties with the position were less important than that faithfulness to revelation was maintained. However, the intellectual difficulties of God being temporal are worthy of further exploration:

The key problems with a temporal model of God

If God is in time then God is everlasting – without beginning and without end. To such a God, "A thousand ages in God's sight would be like an evening gone," BUT time would still pass. However, time would not dominate God as it does the short lives of human beings. God would have created the Universe by deciding to actualize the Universe and will one day bring the Universe to an end, but God will never end. The intellectual difficulties of God in time are, however, considerable.

- *If God is in time, this may well mean that God is in space and this would mean that God would be in one place rather than another. God would then become another object in the spatio-temporal Universe and would be part of the Universe rather than the creator and sustainer of the Universe. Some have held, in reply to this, that God is everywhere and in everything in the Universe but Christians, Jews, and Muslims have always rejected the claim that God and the Universe are one and the same.[1]*

- *If God is in time, then the future is future to God and therefore God would be unable to know what happens in the future, although God might be able to predict the future with great accuracy (this issue is dealt with in more detail in Chapter 7).*

- *If God is in time, then God would be subject to time. What is more, it would appear that there was something that God did not create, namely time itself.*

In spite of these difficulties, many Protestant theologians have seen advantages in the idea of God being temporal as this opens up the possibility of God being able to change. If God can change, and realize his potential to act, it is philosophically plausible to argue that God can respond to prayer and to events in the created Universe. A God outside of time and space with no potential cannot logically do these things.[2] This is a major advantage to this model of God as it honors the experiences of believers. Secondly, if God is in time then God can suffer whereas the wholly simple God cannot suffer. This is a crucial difference between the two models of God. Traditional Catholic theologians must totally dismiss the idea of a suffering God as this requires a process of change and in the Aquinas model God is wholly simple and immutable. Aquinas certainly rejected the idea that God could suffer as suffering implies limitation and God, if God is wholly simple, cannot have any limitations. Many Protestant theologians, by contrast, see the suffering of Jesus as mirroring the suffering of God and see suffering as being right at the heart of the nature of God.

The suffering God

Jurgan Moltmann attempts a theological response to the problem of evil through the figure of Jesus. He, as a Protestant, rejects natural theology as traditionally practiced and maintains that the only way past the protest of atheism is through a Theology of the Cross – the suffering God who, on the cross, can cry out "My God, my God, why have you forsaken me?" For Moltmann, Jesus is fully God and fully man and in Jesus suffering on the cross, God also suffers. God therefore creates a world in which human beings can develop into a love relationship with God, but freedom is a necessary part of this process. Through human sin, evil comes into the world and God suffers with his creation as a result of this evil.

This is an almost human picture of a God who suffers just as a human being suffers. Critics would accuse this idea of God as being very anthropomorphic, but this view is close to the God portrayed in the Bible and Moltmann, as a Lutheran, sees the Bible as the finest example of God's revelation.

The idea of a suffering God is an extraordinary one. Normally the word God is associated with power – with the ability to create the Universe from nothing. The Greek gods could do anything and people lived in fear of them and sought to placate them. These gods were unpredictable and constant offerings were needed to ward off their anger. The Christian idea of God revealed in Jesus was radically different as Jesus revealed a God whose power was shown in weakness. The culmination of Jesus' ministry was the cross – nothing could be seen as more clearly showing the power of weakness, the power of love, at the heart of God as the idea of God, the creator of the Universe, dying on the cross as a common criminal. This was, naturally enough, a scandal and foolishness to most rational people. St. Paul put it well when he said:

"Has not God made the wisdom of the world foolish? For since in the wisdom of God the world did not come to know God through wisdom, it was the will of God through the foolishness of the proclamation to save those who have faith. For Jews demand signs and Greeks look for wisdom, but we proclaim Christ crucified, a stumbling block to Jews and foolishness to Gentiles, but to those who are called, Jews and Greeks alike, Christ the power of God and the wisdom of God. For the foolishness of God is wiser than human wisdom, and the weakness of God is stronger than human strength." (1 Cor. 1.20–25)

The suffering of Jesus

Protestant scholars point to passages from the Gospels showing how Jesus grieved. When he is told of the death of his friend, Lazarus, the Gospels record the shortest verse in the New Testament: "Jesus wept." (Jn. 11.35). In Matthew's Gospel, the writer records Jesus grieving over Jerusalem:

"Jerusalem, Jerusalem, you who kill the prophets and stone those sent to you, how many times I yearned to gather your children together, as a hen gathers her young under her wings, but you were unwilling!" (Matt. 23.27).

These passages indicate real regret that the people of Jerusalem refused to listen to the message of Jesus and his prophecy of the destruction of the City. Indeed, many would see the real suffering of Jesus as lying not in his suffering on the cross but in his inability to make himself understood by those to whom he spoke. In the book of Isaiah (53.3-8) some Christians see Jesus portrayed as the suffering servant. **Just as Jesus suffered so, it is held, God suffers over the sin of the world and over the refusal of people to listen to God's message.**

Michaelangelo's 'Pieta' is, perhaps, the most moving statue portraying the suffering of Jesus as his dead body is held by his mother, Mary.

THE GOD OF LIBERATION THEOLOGY

In more recent times the God of Scripture has also been hailed as the true picture of God, ignored by the church.

Liberation Theology arose in the late 1960s and early 1970s in South America where most people were (and are) Christian and yet the vast majority of the population lived in abject poverty whilst a small number of incredibly wealthy families lived lives of great opulence and wealth. The Church in the 1960s seemed to identify much more with the "haves" than with the "have nots". Following the Second Vatican Council of the Catholic Church in 1965, there was a reappraisal by many South American theologians of the traditional understanding of God and of God's role which, they saw, came from European universities and from the perspective of those who were powerful and successful. The theologians challenged this model saying that the biblical picture of God, in the person of Jesus, revealed that God had a preference for the poor. The God revealed in Scripture they said was on the side of the poor and the oppressed, the enslaved and weak, and all those whom human institutions ignored or maltreated. Liberation Theology was influenced by the philosophy of Karl Marx and his call for political revolution – to change the way society is conducted and to overturn the institutions which keep in power those with wealth, money, and influence and ignore the needs of the poor and weak. Marxism and the communist ideas to which it gave rise was put together with a picture of Jesus as a radical figure who was on the side of the weak in a struggle against the strong and those with money and power (Marx and his influence on 20th century Christianity is dealt with on p.214).

God, according to liberation theologians, is not the God of the strong and successful, of the saints and those who are always good. Instead God is the God of the failures, of those who are oppressed, of the mentally retarded and

> **Example**
>
> The story is told (by Michael Kirwan SJ) of a South American Bishop who, after a Church service, saw a mother with a baby who was screaming with hunger. He asked the woman why she did not feed her baby and she uncovered her breast to show her nipples covered with blood. She had no milk as she herself was starving and was feeding her baby with her own blood. The Bishop vowed to ensure that he fed at least one hungry person every day. Another Bishop asked why, when he fed people, he was called a saint but when he asked why people were starving he was called a dangerous revolutionary. Both these men were liberation theologians – seeing God on the side of the weak in a struggle against the strong and wealthy who oppressed them.

those who are not particularly intelligent. God is the God of the outcast, the God of those who suffer from malnutrition, plague or famine, earthquake or flood far more than the God of the successful and wealthy. The God of Liberation Theology is, above all, a suffering God – a God who suffers with God's people and who is on the side of justice in a struggle against injustice. This means that the Church needs to side with the oppressed and those who have nothing, against the powerful. Liberation Theology is also a call for the Church to get involved in politics. Indeed Archbishop Desmond Tutu said:

"For the church in any country to retreat from politics is nothing short of heresy. Christianity is political or it is not Christianity."

Origins

The term 'Liberation Theology' was used first by a Peruvian Catholic priest **Gustavo Gutierrez**. He argued that Liberation Theology involves bringing people to social and political liberation; being on the side of the weak, the poor, and the oppressed and liberating individuals from selfishness and sin, which are the root of evil.

Gutierrez considers that these should force the Church and all Christians to make a **"preferential option for the poor."**

Liberation Theology places emphasis on passages in the Bible which involve God's commitment to the weak. The story of how God brought God's chosen people out of slavery to freedom is particularly important as are passages such as Isaiah 6.1–2, Matthew 25. 31–46 and Luke 4.16–20. These passages speak of the need for Christians to "to set at liberty those who are oppressed" (Luke 4.18). God does not, in fact, desire those who are oppressed always to be poor and disenfranchised but rather God wants poor people to come to self-respect knowing that they are made in the image of God. This means that Christians have to be committed to political and social action in order to secure salvation from poverty in this life rather than simply relying on a life to come.

SUMMARY

In all monotheistic traditions there are two models of God that stand alongside each other and there are clear tensions between them. In simple terms this means the God of the Philosophers and the God of Sacred Scriptures: A wholly simple, timeless, and spaceless God or a God who is in time and who can respond to events in the world. These two models of God are radically different. It is possible for two people to believe in God but to mean totally different things by that claim. It is, therefore, important when talking of God to first be clear what is meant by "God."

QUESTIONS FOR CONSIDERATION

1) What were the two most important factors that led to the Protestant Reformation?

2) If the Franciscan approach to understanding God had been taken and not that of St. Thomas Aquinas and Aristotle, why might the Reformation not have happened?

3) Do the advantages of placing God in time outweigh the disadvantages?

4) If God is in time, does this mean God has to be in space as well and, if so, does this mean that God is in one place rather than another?

5) Why does Liberation Theology tend to put God in time?

6) What are the advantages and disadvantages of claiming that God can suffer?

Notes

[1] *This was a view held by, amongst others, the Jewish philosopher Spinoza who argued that to talk of God was to talk of the spiritual side of the Universe but God and the Universe were actually one and the same.*

[2] *Fr. Gerard Hughes SJ is one of a number of theologians who reject the idea that, if God is wholly simple, God can respond to prayer.*

CHAPTER 4

RELIGIOUS LANGUAGE

Everyday language usually concerns those things that can be seen, touched, felt, smelt, or otherwise experienced. Human beings talk about:

1. Trees, plants, and animals.

2. Stones, rocks, and mountains.

3. Fish, whales, and plankton.

4. Amoeba, viruses, disease, and health.

5. Other people.

6. Houses, cars, and jobs.

7. The Sun, Moon, and stars.

All these, and innumerable other things, are spatio-temporal objects or experiences within the Universe and ordinary human language can easily be used to talk of them. Other things, such as human emotions – anger, love, or jealousy – are also spoken of with relative ease as these are common experiences, although nobody has ever seen anger or love but they are felt so strongly that nobody doubts their existence and there is a rich language resource to express these emotions. Human language also incorporates talk about conceptual ideas. These demand a greater level of engagement to be understood and at one level a person either understands the concept or they don't. Talk of number, quantum mechanics, or gravity is talk about conceptual ideas. Many conceptual ideas cannot be proved or demonstrated as being there at all. The effects of what we call the force of gravity explains the way that objects are attracted to each other – we can see the effects of gravity but ultimately, unlike a tree, it cannot be seen. Nor can it be proven to exist – there may be another explanation to explain the fact that objects are attracted to each other. Whilst it is possible that there might be another explanation the impact of what we call gravity is so obvious that nobody seriously doubts its existence. Quantum theory is more complex. Science increasingly claims that quantum theory explains the way the Universe is, but few people understand the concepts behind quantum physics. The forces and/or particles involved cannot be seen, they function as both a wave and a particle and a single wave/particle may even exist in two places at once. The language of paradox and contradiction abounds in talk about the quantum level. Language is stretched to its limits in trying to express these concepts and many people are willing to accept that quantum theory involves concepts that they cannot understand.

> ### Language about God
>
> "To whom can you liken God? With what equal can you confront him?.... Do you not know or have you not heard? The LORD is the eternal God, creator of the ends of the Earth.... He does not faint nor grow weary, and his knowledge is beyond scrutiny. He gives strength to the fainting; for the weak he makes vigor abound. Though young men faint and grow weary, and youths stagger and fall, They that hope in the LORD will renew their strength, they will soar as with eagles' wings; They will run and not grow weary, walk and not grow faint."
> (extracts from Isaiah 40.18–31)

When it comes to language about the nature of God or other religious truth claims, it is important to note that there is equal difficulty. Religious language is used to express both personal experiences and concepts that are largely indescribable in human language. For very many people there is a primary experience of there being something out there – a sense of what might loosely be called a spiritual dimension, whether it is called God or not. This is a reasonably common experience[1] although those who have these experiences very often do not talk about them, and if they do, they experience great difficulty because they do not have the words to capture the experience and fear being misunderstood. It is not surprising that, when faced with such difficulties, religious language includes the language of paradox and contradiction as ordinary language is stretched to the limits. In spite of these difficulties, people do talk about God as well as religious concepts and experiences but philosophically the problem is what this language means.

If, as explored in chapter 2, God is outside time and outside space, then it is problematic to talk of God from our position within time and space. Human language is limited by the human experience of being in space and time[2] which means that talk of God is the equivalent of a goldfish talking about the world of dry land. What language could a fish have to describe the concept of dryness? There would be no immediately obvious language – 'not wet' might be a starting point, and that is precisely the place that the great Jewish theologian Maimonides started in his efforts to talk about God.

This chapter will trace the history of thinking regarding religious language and the claims made by religious people that in spite of the difficulties this language does have meaning.

THE VIA NEGATIVA

The great Jewish theologian, Moses Maimonides (1136–1204), was influenced by Islamic philosophy and also by the works of Aristotle. Much of the work of the great Greek philosophers had been lost to the West in the 'dark ages' which followed the fall of the Roman Empire and the burning of the library in Alexandria. However, some of the works were preserved in the great Islamic centers of learning in the ancient cities of Baghdad and Cairo and these had a great impact on Islamic thinking long before their influence was felt in Christianity or Judaism. Maimonides had access to the thinking of Aristotle through the work of Islamic philosophers. Maimonides accepted much of Aristotle's analysis of the idea of God and accepted the Aristotelian conclusion that God was outside space and time. He also affirmed the single most important Jewish claim about God: that God is one. He reasoned that if this is the case, then God is unique. God is not many-in-one, God is in a category of God's own. God must, therefore, be absolutely simple[3] and this means that God cannot have a body as a body can grow and be divided – this, not surprisingly concurs precisely with the philosophers', idea of God as wholly simple described in chapter 2.

Maimonides concluded from these reflections that if at any point the Hebrew scriptures pictured God anthropomorphically or as having a body then those passages were not to be treated literally. Wherever, therefore, in the Hebrew scriptures (the Christian Old Testament) God is described as if he is a person or a super-human then these texts were to be understood metaphorically.

In the picture opposite, Moses is shown as being given the tablets of the Ten Commandments by God – God is portrayed as a human being within the fire of the burning bush. Maimonides would have rejected all language and all attempts at understanding what happened which portrayed God in any anthropomorphic sense at all. Even the giving of the tablets, if this was seen to be similar to the physical giving of something by one human being to another, should not be interpreted literally like this. This resistance to portraying God in any sense like a human being was shared by both Jewish and Muslim thinkers and, in Islam, there is a refusal to portray God in any way in art.

Moses with the burning bush and receiving the Ten Commandments

In his book 'The Guide to the Perplexed', Maimonides considered the issue of how language can be used to apply to the wholly simple God and he came to the conclusion that human language is so rooted in temporality that it cannot be used to apply to God. As he says "The Torah speaks in the language of the sons of man" (The Torah is the first five books of the Hebrew scriptures – Genesis, Exodus, Leviticus, Numbers, Deuteronomy – which are regarded as the most important texts and are given a status within Judaism that far outweighs that of any other texts) and human language cannot, therefore, be used to apply to a wholly simple God.

Maimonides came to a radical conclusion – namely that God could not be spoken about at all and the proper response was silence. He quotes from Psalm 65.2 "Silence is praise to Thee" and this led him to argue for negative theology since any positive statements about God would limit God. He says:

"There is nothing both literal and positive that we can say about God on the basis of any reasoning not prompted by Divine revelation in the Scriptures. And even then.... most of what we can say informatively is metaphorical, allegorical, and untranslatable into literal positive truths."

This was the VIA NEGATIVA – the negative way. This amounted to a refusal to use any positive language about God at all and this had a significant influence on later Christian and Islamic thought. There have always been deeply religious people who have maintained that philosophy and talk about God are misleading and instead of bringing human beings closer to an understanding of God, language may have the opposite effect. These people will tend to emphasize the importance of mysticism, spirituality, and prayer as paths to a deeper understanding of God rather than mere words.

St. Thomas Aquinas

St. Thomas Aquinas (1206–1280), whilst agreeing with Maimonides about the absolute simplicity of God, came to a different view about how language can be applied to God. Aquinas' starting point is very similar to Maimonides:

"Now it can be shown how God is not, by denying whatever is opposed to him, viz composition, motion, and the like. Therefore we discuss his simplicity, whereby we deny composition in him."
Aquinas S.T. 1, 3 Introduction

Aquinas first establishes that God exists and that God explains the Universe. He next argues that God is wholly simple, timeless, and spaceless quoting St. Augustine who says that God has:

"The complete possession of eternal life all at once."

And Boethius who says God has:

"The whole, simultaneous, and permanent possession of eternal life."

So far, then, he agreed with Maimonides but whereas Maimonides refused to use language about God, Aquinas insists that language can be used – albeit in a very particular manner.

FIRSTLY, Aquinas rejects **univocal language** – this means that language as used in the spatio-temporal world cannot be applied in the same sense to God. Aquinas therefore says that one cannot say that:

- *My parents and friends love me but God loves me more than this.*
- *John is good, but God is much more good than John.*
- *Marie is forgiving, but God forgives even more than Marie.*

Any of these types of statements place God in broadly the same category as humans and this cannot be done. God is so very different from human beings that this univocal language must be rejected. Maimonides would have agreed with this.

SECONDLY, Aquinas claims that **equivocal language** must be rejected. Words are equivocal when they have completely different meanings in two different situations. For instance:

- *The nut on the tree and the nut on my bicycle wheel.*
- *The baseball bat and the bat which lives in my attic.*

In both these cases the word nut and bat are used in completely unrelated ways. If language about God was like this, then there would be no connection at all between the way language is used in the world and language about God and language about God would be effectively meaningless.

Having rejected both univocal and equivocal language, Aquinas introduces a novel way in which God can be meaningfully talked about. This is analogy; however analogy does not mean what that word is taken to mean today. There are two types of analogy used by Aquinas and these are very precisely defined.

a) Analogy of attribution

This begins from Aquinas' claims that God exists as the creator of the Universe. This being the case there is a causal link between God and the Universe because God created the Universe. God is wholly simple and wholly other, but there is a connection between God and the Universe. Because of

Analogy of attribution

An example given by St. Thomas Aquinas is as follows. In the Middle Ages, doctors were not allowed to cut open human bodies so one of the few ways to examine what happened inside a human body was to examine the person's urine and feces (this was seen in the film *The Madness of King George* where the King's doctors spent much time examining these). The same, of course, applies today when tests for pregnancy, drugs, diabetes, and other conditions are carried out by testing urine. Doctors knew what healthy urine was by its color, smell, and taste – they were experts at recognizing healthy urine. It is therefore possible to say:

• The bull is healthy.

• The bull's urine is healthy.

The health of the urine has to do with its color, taste, and smell, the health of the bull is completely different from this but nevertheless the two are linked because the bull produces the urine. Similarly God produces everything in the Universe, so one can say:

• God is good, wise, and loving.

• Charlotte is good, wise, and loving.

We know what it is for a human being to be good, wise, and loving but this does NOT mean that God's goodness is a magnified version of human goodness. Rather, God is causally responsible for goodness, wisdom, and love in Charlotte (and, of course, for the goodness of oak trees, snakes, amoeba, and dandelions) however this does not mean that God's goodness can be understood as being a greater version of the goodness of Charlotte, oak trees, snakes, amoeba, or dandelions. To say that God is good means that God has the qualities necessary to produce goodness in the world around us – NOT that God is a moral agent like Charlotte.

this link, Aquinas says that religious language can be shown to be meaningful. Aquinas gives the example of the bull and urine in the box. Bull and urine are both healthy but what it means for these to be healthy are very different. Just as the bull and the urine are linked, so God and Charlotte are linked. God created Charlotte as the bull created the urine and so there is a connection. When Charlotte is good that is because God made her with the capacity for human goodness. God has whatever is needed to bring about the capacity for goodness in Charlotte, as the bull has the capacity to bring about the health of the urine. The goodness of God is connected to the goodness of Charlotte but is not identical to it. God's goodness is NOT a magnified version of Charlotte's goodness. It is different. We can say that the goodness of God facilitates human goodness – that is meaningful, but we cannot define God's goodness in human terms. Analogy of attribution only enables us, therefore, to say that God is good, wise, and loving but what this means is that God has the qualities necessary to bring about these qualities in humans. It is saying very little about the CONTENT of these claims with reference to God. But whilst content is very limited, such claims are not without meaning.

Why is this so significant? For various reasons:

- *It prevents people talking of God like a super-human being and thereby degrading God to another object in the world.*

- *It means that Maimonides is mistaken and that it IS possible to speak about God and that silence is not the only way forward.*

Both these are important points and once understood prevent a naïve anthropomorphic understanding of God. God has the attributes needed to create the Universe and all things in it. God also has the attributes needed to create moral goodness in human persons. This is not to say that God is morally good like a human person or in any way like a thing in the Universe. Analogy of attribution offers a way of saying positive things about God; we may not know what attributes are necessary for one who would create the Universe, but we can say that whatever those attributes are – God has them.

b) Analogy of proportion

Analogy of proportion was, for Aquinas, a second way of saying something about God. He claimed that all things, in that they are created, have the potential to fulfill their nature, to be 100% good. All things have this potential as all things are created by God. For a thing to be 100% good means, for Aquinas, for that thing to perfectly fulfill its nature, so:

- *A perfectly good mouse is 100% what it is to fulfill the nature of a mouse.*

- *A perfectly good seagull is 100% what it is to fulfill the nature of a seagull.*

- *A perfectly good bald eagle is 100% what it is to fulfill the nature of a bald eagle.*

- *A perfectly good wombat is 100% what it is to fulfill the nature of a wombat (the wombat in the picture is a perfectly good wombat as it is everything that a wombat should be – it fulfills the wombat nature perfectly).*

- *A good human being is 100% what it is to fulfill human nature.*

A wombat

BUT mice, seagulls, eagles, and humans can all fall short of perfect goodness by being physically defective. If they fall short because of any type of physical imperfection they are no longer perfectly fulfilling their nature. The level of defectiveness defines the proportionality of the imperfection. For example a seagull without a wing might be described as defective in proportion to its potential perfection by, say, 15%. It is 15% less than a perfectly good seagull should be. The perfect nature of seagull is that nature as intended by God the creator and can be ascertained by observing seagulls at large. Humans can fall short physically of their perfect physical nature (for instance by having defective eye sight or hearing or more serious defects such as Downs Syndrome or Cystic Fibrosis[5]), but in addition they can also fall short morally, as part of a perfect human nature is to be morally perfect as well as physically perfect. Each person and each thing in the created Universe is proportionately good according to how far they fulfill their nature.

Aquinas contrasts God with things in the created Universe. Using the philosophy of Aristotle he claims that God is pure actuality – he has no potential. He is wholly simple, timeless, and spaceless and therefore God cannot, as a matter of logic, change. This means that God cannot be other than what God is. It is therefore possible, using analogy of proportion, to say that whatever God is, he is 100% whatever it is to be God. God perfectly fulfills his nature and is perfectly whatever it is to be God. He cannot change and cannot be anything else. Interestingly Aquinas quoted biblical support for this view – in Exodus 3 God reveals his name to Moses "I AM THAT I AM," which Aquinas took to mean that God is everything that it is to be God. This again allows us to say something about God – it allows us to say that God is perfectly 'good' but what this means is that God perfectly fulfills his own nature. God is perfectly good because God perfectly fulfills the nature of God and God could not be anything other than this since, being timeless, spaceless, and lacking no perfection, God cannot be other than God is.

Aquinas argues, therefore, that we can use language about God – we can say that God is good BUT what that means is that God is perfectly whatever it is to be God. He is 100% whatever it is to be God. BUT WE DO NOT KNOW WHAT IT IS TO BE GOD. For Aquinas then, human language can be used to say some positive things about God, but the content is quite limited.

METAPHOR

Aquinas, therefore, effectively rejects the conclusion of Moses Maimonides, and allows talk of God as good, loving, and wise but draws the conclusion that the content of these words when applied to God is very limited indeed.

Using human language to talk about the wholly simple God appears at first sight therefore to be very limited. There is, however, a third way of talking about the wholly simple God and that is through the use of metaphor. When a child tries to describe something and they do not have the words they resort to metaphor – "it was like a…"; "it was as if a…" Not surprisingly for those who have experiences of God and find that they do not have the words metaphor is found to be the only way forward. The Hebrew and Christian Scriptures and the Qu'ran are full of metaphors and these are rich in content. For instance:

- God as a father.
- Jesus is the vine and we are the branches.
- God as a strong shield and a mighty warrior.
- God as a rock.
- Jesus is the good shepherd.
- Jesus as the light of the world.

The Light of the World *by Holman Hunt*

Metaphor is different to analogy. In an analogy a comparison is made in which there is a clear relationship – for example in the claim explored above, "**Charlotte is good**" and "**God is good**" the word "good" is analogous as there is a relationship between Charlotte's goodness and God's goodness. The goodness of God is related to human goodness. There is a sense in which God really is good. We can use the word 'good' of God and it means something. In a metaphor two completely unrelated ideas are combined and there is no claim that there is a direct relationship between the two. If someone say "**God is my rock**," no one is

Flags are an example of symbolic representation

going to be so foolish as to say "Limestone or granite?" There is no sense in which there is any link between the rock and God. There is no sense in which God is literally to be understood as a rock. Yet there are characteristics of rocks which can be used to describe aspects of God's nature. "God is my rock" might be used to describe the strength and reliability of God, or the feeling that God is always there and can be leant on, or the idea that God never changes and is wholly dependable and reliable. Paul Ricoeur has pointed out that it is the absurdity of the literal meaning which draws attention to the new meaning which the words of a metaphor convey. It is absurd to think of God literally as a rock. Monroe Beardsley points out that often in a metaphor we need to ignore the immediate ideas that come to mind. So, when we think of a rock we may think of something hard, "impenetrable", unresponsive, and cold to the touch but in the metaphor "God is my rock" it is the other associations that need to be brought to mind.

The tremendous advantage that metaphor has over most other types of religious language is that metaphors are less likely to mislead than any alternatives. Metaphor acknowledges God's otherness – there is no direct or literal comparison being made. It also allows the character of God to be meaningfully compared to things in the world in which we live. It is not intended to be taken literally but allows meaningful interaction to be made without risk of misinterpretation. Metaphor embraces much symbolism which is very powerful for the believer – just as the national flag is a powerful symbol for a country and points beyond the literal reality of a colored piece of material on a stick to a sense of unity, belonging, and pride so religious symbols point beyond themselves and express the power of that which is symbolized. Believers would want to be able to say some things about God that are not metaphorical but literal – "God is good, God exists" and such things require analogy, as discussed above, and analogy is limited in content and meaning.

Metaphor opens up a much wider field of language for God and contributes to the richness of language found in sacred texts from around the world with regard to God. Just as science turns to metaphor when expressing concepts for which there is no adequate literal paraphrase,[6] so religion turns to metaphor to express theological truths for which there is no literal equivalent. The problem of metaphor is that if religious language is seen to be purely metaphorical it may be thought that it lacks substance.

Logical positivism and the verification principle

Great philosophers such as A.J. Ayer and Bertrand Russell demanded that the meaning of all language, and especially religious language, be given greater clarity before it could be established that it does in fact have any meaning. Out of this demand for clarity came the work of what became known as the 'Vienna Circle' of philosophers and, in particular, the "Verification Principle."[7] This said that in order to be meaningful a statement had to be capable of being verified by sense experience. This principle gave rise to a rule by which to judge whether language was meaningful – exclude any language which cannot be verified by sense experience and what is left is meaningful. Language had to have a literal meaning or it was to be cast aside as meaningless. The verificationists did not say that statements which did not meet this criteria were false – instead they was regarded as meaningless. All statements about God were put into this category as, it was held, statements such as "God exists" or "God loves me" cannot be verified by sense experience and are therefore meaningless. The verificationists therefore ruled as meaningless most religious statements and also poetry and much ethical language as well.

The problem with this principle is obvious, not much language is left! In particular the language of ethics and religious language are excluded from any meaningful status as they are not concerned with things that can be empirically verifiable. One challenge to the verification principle is that on its own criteria, it is meaningless. In other words the statement "any statement that is not capable of being verified by sense experience is meaningless" is itself meaningless as it cannot be verified by sense experience. Nevertheless this principle has posed a powerful challenge to religious belief. Even though this principle has been rejected in most philosophical circles, many people today are CLOSET VERIFICATIONISTS – in other words they are effectively verificationists even though they may not recognize this. They insist that to be meaningful a statement must be able to be verified and they therefore reject much religious belief because it fails to pass this test.

Ian Ramsey

Ian Ramsey[8] introduced significant replies to the demand from the Logical Positivists for some kind of empirical basis for religious language.

1. He argues that the religious life involves a commitment and religious language should therefore be seen in the context of this commitment. Religious commitment is "a total commitment to the whole Universe; something in relation to which argument has only a very odd function." In other words the debate about language and the meaningfulness of religious language in relation to God is a footnote when compared to the commitment to God that is central in the life of the believer. However he argues that in other situations where a person demonstrates a similar level of commitment language is used to effectively communicate the commitment, and that the language of apparent tautology and contradiction are understood perfectly well. If a person was asked why they rose at four they might say that they chose to because they wanted to go fishing. The listener understands from this that fishing has a claim on the person such that they freely chose to get up at 4.00. The listener understands the obligation that the person feels for fishing and no longer wonders at the strangeness of rising so early. The listener may not share the love of fishing and may even consider it very odd BUT when our fisherman or woman says: "Fishing is fishing" we do not reply that this is a meaningless, insignificant tautology but instead we discern that fishing is part of the person's life and part of what defines them as a person. Language about commitment and loyalty and relationship often involve tautologies that are significant and are understood as meaningful, and one should therefore expect the same type of irregularities in religious language, because it is language that has been formed from the perspective of a commitment which means that the ordinary rules of language must bend in order for any communication to be effective.

2. Ramsey argues that there are some concepts that language from the world of observation can never fully capture. He gives the example of "I". The "I" of each person is part of the empirical world and can be observed shopping and driving a car or reading a book by others and the "I" can be described in physical terms and the character of the "I" can be described by those who know the person well. Watching a person and recording accurately their every move will never be sufficient to describe the "I" of the individual. **The '"I" "can never be exhausted by such language."** There is a

*something more to the "I" than language from the world of pure
observation can capture. The same will be true of God. Language will always
leave room for a deeper perception.*

3. *Ramsey claims that whilst the literal meaning of religious language may be
understood, the concept may not be. For the concept to be understood
requires a moment of discernment, when the "penny drops." An example he
gives of this is a child learning to read. The child may know the letter "C"
and may know the letter "A" and may know the letter "T". The child has
learned the alphabet and can accurately say the sound of each letter and
recognize them. The child cannot yet put letters together to make words. The
child can read C-A-T but not "cat" – the child does not yet know that the
letters it has learned can be put together to make the words that he/she
already knows. When this moment comes there is a "situation
characteristically different" from before. The penny has dropped. The child is
now at a stage where it can begin to learn to read. With language about
God there are similar moments of discernment, when the words are
understood at the conceptual level.*

4. *Language about concepts and perception is based on objects in the
empirical world but when language is used to talk about such things words
and phrases are given special qualifications. Language for such things needs
to somehow be qualified – observational language is used to talk of God but
qualifiers are needed to indicate that the language is pointing to something
more than the literal level of what may be observed. Where meaning is too
deep and mysterious special qualifiers are used to point the reader or listener
beyond the literal level. An example of this is the qualifier "infinite." For
example "loving" with respect to God is used with the qualifier "infinitely."
God is not just loving – God is "infinitely loving." This points to the
experience of God as being not just "more loving than humans" and not just
"as loving as the most loving person you can imagine" but the qualifier
"infinite" takes the language of "loving" outside of the limits of human
love. Human language can only capture something of the essence of the love
of God by pointing beyond it. Examples of human goodness may well be
used to explore what the love of God is like but as with learning to read and
as with many other conceptual ideas such as quantum theory, there comes a
point where the concept of infinite love is understood to be beyond the
realms of human love. There is a moment of perception – the penny drops,
the person understands the concept where once they did not. God is*

infinitely wise, infinitely good, infinitely powerful, infinite in knowledge;
all are meaningful, but they are concepts which require a moment of
discernment and are easily misunderstood if the way language is employed
is not understood.

In summary, Ramsey is unpacking the ideas of metaphor in detail in an attempt to demonstrate that religious language can never be understood literally and in this respect religious language shares the qualities of other types of language such as the language of commitment and the language used of other complex concepts. There is a real sense that for the language to be meaningful a person must be within the community of believers and share their "language game."

Wittgenstein's later philosophy has been used by some to argue that religious language is just a self-enclosed language game – although this is a false reading of Wittgenstein's own intention. However, his work has been used to say that religious language only has meaning within the form of life of the believing community.[9] Those who hold this view claim that, outside the community of believers, religious language has no meaning but within the form of life it is meaningful. This opens up the debate about realism and anti-realism discussed in chapter 5. The challenge that this poses for religious language is whether this language refers to anything outside of itself. There is no problem using language to talk about religious beliefs, religious practice, and rituals. Describing what religious people do and say in certain situations which may be described as religious is non-problematic and this is what the study of the sociology of religion attempts. The real problems arise when religious people claim that their language points beyond itself and can be used to talk meaningfully about a reality beyond the world and this issue is dealt with in chapter 5.

Just as metaphor is claimed to be able to refer to God without describing God, so literature and great art can create meanings which refer to reality without describing it literally. As an example, the painting by Holman Hunt of 'The Hireling Shepherd' looks, at first glance, as though it is simply a painting of a pleasant pastoral scene – but it is far more than this. Holman Hunt is here seeking to convey an essential truth from the Christian tradition, namely that Jesus is the shepherd of the Christian flock who cares for each and every individual. Indeed Jesus is quoted by the Gospels as saying that there is more joy in heaven over one sheep who is lost and which returns to the fold than over ninety nine sheep who never get lost at all. The faithful shepherd cares for

The Hireling Shepherd *by Holman Hunt*

every individual in the flock and, in the final analysis, is willing to give his life for his sheep. This, of course, is precisely what Jesus is said by Christianity to have done when he died on the cross, he died in order that his followers might have eternal life. In the picture, the shepherd is simply a hireling, that is he is paid for his services. Such a person does not really care deeply for the flock, thus the shepherd has his back to the flock and is far more interested in the young girl, the picnic, and other delights she has to offer than in the fate of the flock. The result is that one sheep is seen as straying from the flock and in the distance a dog is attacking the flock. The picture is making the point that a real shepherd, Jesus, would not do this. Great art, therefore, can act like a metaphor and can convey truth, but people have to learn the symbolism and to understand the depth of the story that is being communicated before they can engage with such art. The same applies to great literature.

Conclusion

This, then, is the history of the debate concerning religious language so far: Moses Maimonides argued that God could not be talked about literally and that the best way to talk of God was in negative terms – indeed, for

Maimonides, silence was the best praise of God. Aquinas argued against this maintaining that positive statements could be made about God by means of analogy, but the content of these statements was very limited. Metaphor, according to Aquinas, may be a richer way of talking about God. Ian Ramsey has further explored the complexity of using language drawn from the world about God and he showed that understanding requires a moment of discernment.

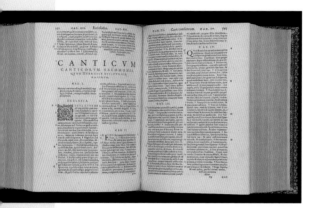

A Latin Bible – understanding the Bible has always required interpretation

What is clear is that a great deal of care is needed with talk about God and the same kind of care will clearly be needed with the language of sacred texts too. Here the written word communicates spiritual truth often through a record of historical events. Understanding the symbolism and the deeper level at which the language is working will be vital for a full appreciation. It is worth noting that religious language is not the sole means of communicating religious truths and its primary function is not to offer the philosopher or the atheist a way of understanding religion at a rational level. It is primarily there to give expression to the religious experiences and the religious life of the believing community. The meaningfulness of religious claims specifically does not, therefore, depend on language working at a literal level.

All of the world's great religions acknowledge the limits of language when talking about God and know that any attempt to define God will be limited and offer only a partial truth. Hence all world religions have other ways of communicating spiritual truths which do not involve human language at all. The value of silence for example is recognized by all as an active form of communication as is music and the repetition of set forms of worship, prayers, chants, or mantras. Ritual and liturgy are also forms of communication which evoke a profound sense of truth which religious language can only gesture towards.

QUESTIONS FOR CONSIDERATION

1) Why did Moses Maimonides reject any literal talk about God?

2) What are the strengths and weaknesses of understanding religious language analogically?

3) Why is the goodness of a mouse, a wombat, and an oak tree and a human being different? What significance might this have?

4) What are the main advantages of using metaphor to talk about God?

5) Why might many people today be described as 'closet verificationists'?

6) Select any one painting not featured in this book and suggest how it conveys a metaphorical understanding of God's relation to the world.

Notes

[1] *See David Hay,* Exploring Inner Space.

[2] *Immanuel Kant maintained that human beings have to experience the world in spatio-temporal terms and all we can know is the phenomenal world – the world as it is experienced in space/time terms. However what the world is really like independent of our experience (the noumenal world) is in principle unknowable. The same, he considered, applied to God and this is one reason that he rejected all attempts to prove the existence of God as he considered that it is not possible to reason from the world of experience to God who lies beyond all experience.*

[3] *The simplicity of God is explained further in chapter 2.*

[4] *Cf James Ross p. 108 in Brian Davies,* Philosophy of Religion: A guide to the subject *OUP 1998.*

[5] *This raises important contemporary issues related to the possible use of genetic engineering to correct physical defects. These are discussed in* Being Human *by Peter Vardy published by Darton, Longman and Todd 2003.*

[6] *Metaphor and Theory Change: 'What is 'metaphor' a metaphor for?' in Andrew Ortoney (ed.)* Metaphor and Thought, *Cambridge University Press: Cambridge, 1979.*

[7] *Possibly most clearly stated in A.J. Ayer,* Language, Truth and Logic.

[8] Religious Language, *Ian Ramsey, Xpress Reprints SCM Bookroom 1993.*

[9] *Anti-realism arose from the mistaken use of Wittgenstein's philosophy. This is dealt with in chapter 5.*

THE CHALLENGE OF ANTI-REALISM

Most theologians do not recognize the challenge of anti-realism. It is, arguably, the greatest challenge to the existence of God that has ever been produced but most religious people are not even aware of it and most theologians dismiss it – often without engaging with the challenge it represents. Atheism has always been a position taken by some people. They have, in good conscience, rejected belief in the existence of God.[1] Most religious believers have considered the atheistic position at times during their lives and, whilst they may have accepted that there is a possibility that atheism could be right, they have rejected this.

However, the challenge of anti-realism is different as anti-realists believe in God – but what they mean by this is radically different from what most ordinary believers mean. In order to understand this it is necessary to examine different theories of truth and what it means to be a realist and an anti-realist.

Realism and anti-realism are theories of truth. They both claim that certain statements are true. Christian realists and anti-realists will both agree that:

- *God exists.*

- *Jesus is the son of God.*

- *Jesus died on the cross and rose again on the third day.*

- *Mary was a virgin.*

Muslim realists and anti-realists will both agree that:

- *Allah exists.*
- *Muhammed is the final prophet sent by God.*
- *The Holy Qu'ran was dictated to the Prophet by the Archangel Gabriel.*

However, what realists and anti-realists mean by these statements will be radically different.

REALISM

Realism is the theory of truth which is held by realists. Realists claim that a statement is true if it corresponds to the state of affairs that it attempts to describe. Thus "the cat sat on the mat" is true if there is a cat and it is sitting on the mat. What makes the statement true is the state of affairs that is described.

Realism truth claims are held to be **verification transcendent** – this means that the truth or falsity of the claims does not depend on whether or not they are verified. Take the following statement:

"There are green, three-eyed worms on a planet circling the star Alpha Centurae."

This statement will be true, realists maintain, if and only if (this is usually written 'iff') there are green, three-eyed worms on the planet described. To say that truth is verification transcendent is to say that the truth of this statement does not depend on

Tolstoy's *Confessions*

Tolstoy was an incredibly wealthy Russian nobleman who came to a crisis in his early fifties when all life seemed meaningless and he contemplated suicide. His *Confessions* record his conversion to taking Christianity really seriously and this passage occurs at the beginning of these *Confessions*.

"I was baptized and brought up in the Orthodox Christian faith. I was taught it in childhood and throughout my boyhood and youth. But when I abandoned the second course of the university at the age of eighteen I no longer believed any of the things I had been taught.

Judging by certain memories, I never seriously believed them, but had merely relied on what I was taught and on what was professed by the grown-up people around me, and that reliance was very unstable.

I remember that before I was eleven a grammar school pupil, Vladimir Milyutin (long since dead), visited us one Sunday and announced as the latest novelty a discovery made at his school. This discovery was that there is no God and that all we are taught about Him is a mere invention (this was in 1838). I remember how interested my elder brothers were in this information. They called me to their council and we all, I remember, became very animated, and accepted it as something very interesting and quite possible."

Atheism has always been fashionable in some circles!

Realism

The statement: **"The picture is of penguins"** is true, on a realist view, if the picture is of penguins. If the picture is actually of a model or if it is men dressed up in penguin suits, then the statement is false. Even if the truth of this statement cannot be proved, the statement is either true or false depending on whether there are penguins in the picture.

us knowing whether or not it is true. It is either true or false based on the state of affairs being described. To be true is one thing, to know something is true is another. The truth of the existence of the green, three-eyed worms depends, for the realist, on whether or not they are there. It is a separate issue for us to claim that we either know or do not know this to be the case.

Realists also maintain **bivalence** – this means that a statement is either true or it is false, even though we may not know whether it is true or false. It is either true or false that there are green, three-eyed worms on a planet circling the star Alpha Centurae. There is no way that we can know whether or not this is true, but that is the point – it is either true or it is false.

The final principle that realists adhere to is called the **Principle of Non-Contradiction**. This means that a statement cannot both be true and be false at the same time. Either it is true or it is false, it cannot be both.

Most people are realists about most things. We consider that it is true that there is coffee in the coffee mug because there actually IS coffee in the mug. If it is tea, then the claim that there is coffee in the mug is false. We consider it is true that there is an oak tree in our garden because there actually IS an oak tree in our garden – if we discover that it is a maple tree then the statement that it is an oak tree would be false. We consider it is true that our boy or girl friend or wife or husband is faithful to us if he or she is faithful – if this is not the case, then our claim is false.

These however, are relatively straightforward cases and once one enters the area of religion, aesthetics, or morality the situation is more complex.

Take the statement: "A man can only have one wife." In most of the western world this would be considered to be true. But what would make the statement true? To what would the statement correspond that would guarantee its truth? This is not easy to answer. One approach would be to say that there is an absolute moral order and that what makes this statement true is that it corresponds to what is laid down in the absolute moral order. However, many dispute the existence of such an absolute moral order and instead consider that morality is relative to different societies – in Islam, for instance, a man may have four wives.

An alternative theory of truth is, therefore, supported by many philosophers and this is the basis for anti-realism.

ANTI-REALISM

Anti-realists work with a coherence theory of truth – they maintain that statements are true because they cohere or fit in with other true statements within a specific "form of life." A "form of life" is an expression derived from the philosopher Ludwig Wittgenstein and is not easy to define. It is closely linked to culture or to particular groups. Thus Islam might be a particular form of life and so might being Irish. Forms of life can overlap with each other – so a person may belong to the Irish form of life and also to the Islamic form of life. What makes statements true, according to the coherence theory of truth, is that these statements fit in with other statements that are accepted as true. It is rather like a jigsaw – a piece of a jigsaw will correctly fit into one jigsaw but not into another.

Anti-realists say that truth is **verification dependent** – in other words to claim something as true means being able to verify that it is true. A statement that cannot be verified is neither true nor is it false. Anti-realists **reject bivalence** and say that a statement may be true within one form of life and false in another. The best way of illustrating anti-realism is by means of statements drawn from aesthetics, morality, and religion. Take the following examples:

1. *This woman is beautiful.*

2. *Sex before marriage is wrong.*

3. *The Holy Qu'ran was dictated to the Prophet Muhammed by the archangel Gabriel who was sent by Allah.*

4. *Mary, the mother of Jesus, remained a virgin until she died.*

Anti-realists will argue that within certain forms of life these statements are true and what makes them true is that they cohere or fit in with other statements made within that form of life. There is nothing to which they correspond – rather because they are accepted as true within a particular form of life, this makes them true within this form of life. Within some Western societies thin women are generally considered to be more beautiful and, therefore, within these societies the statement "this woman is beautiful" made about a thin woman would be true. In many African societies, however, it would be false as unless a woman "casts a big shadow" she would be considered unattractive. Similarly in much of traditional Hindu society, the statement "sex before marriage is wrong" would be accepted as true, whereas in much of modern western society it would be false.

Perhaps, however, the difference between realism and anti-realism comes out most clearly in the last two statements on the previous page. Anti-realists will claim that the statement that the Holy Qu'ran was dictated by the Archangel is true in Islam because this is accepted by all Muslims and is at the heart of the Muslim faith. It would, however, be false to non-Muslims. The truth and falsity of the statement within different forms of life do not contradict each other as truth depends on coherence within a form of life. It follows that what may be true within one society may be false in another and there is no contradiction involved. Anti-realists, therefore, **reject the principle of non-contradiction** as they say that the same statement can be both true and false at the same time within different forms of life.

The same would apply with the statement "Mary, the mother of Jesus, remained a virgin until she died." This would be accepted as true by both Muslims[2] and most Christians but rejected by almost all non-Muslims and non-Christians. Anti-realists hold that there is no contradiction between these statements.

Realists will reply to this by saying that it is nonsense. Truth, they will claim, depends on correspondence:

- *Either God sent plagues on the Egyptians to force Pharaoh to let the Israelites go, or he did not.*
- *Either Mary was a virgin or she was not.*
- *Either Jesus rose from the dead or he did not.*

- *Either the Holy Qu'ran was dictated to Muhammed by Allah or not.*

- *Either the prophet Muhammed was taken on a night journey to Jerusalem and then up to heaven to meet Jesus, Moses, and God, or he was not.*

The truth of these statements, realists will claim, does not depend on what is agreed but on whether or not the events described happened. Whether Mary was a virgin depends on the state of her body when she died. Whether Muhammed was taken on his night journey depends on whether this actually happened (the medieval painting on the next page is a very unusual one in that it is one of the few that portray Muhammed – even though his face is blank. Normally Islamic art never portrays human figures. The Prophet is riding the fabulous horse, Al-Burak, which can cover huge distances in a single bound and which took the Prophet to Jerusalem and then on his journey to heaven where he met Moses, Jesus and finally saw the face of God). At first sight the realist claim that either this journey happened or it did not may seem to be obviously true and the anti-realist position may be absurd, but anti-realism is actually far more persuasive than that.

There is no evidence at all that the Holy Qu'ran was actually dictated to Muhammed other than what the Prophet himself said. In the case of Mary's virginity, there is again no evidence in the Christian Gospels. Anti-realists will, therefore, point out that since there is absolutely no evidence which would justify or refute either of these claims their truth depends on them being agreed by the communities of faith within which these claims are important and NOT on whether the events actually occurred.

THE EXISTENCE OF GOD

Realists and anti-realists may both be believers in God. Indeed realist and anti-realist believers will be able to recite the Creeds together and will able to maintain exactly the same claims to truth. It is therefore very difficult to tell the difference between a realist and an anti-realist unless one has done some philosophy or read a book such as this one. This can be a source for confusion as it is possible to listen to a priest or theologian talking about God and, unless one is trained in philosophy, most people will assume that the priest is a realist – however it may well be that the priest is a anti-realist.[3]

Where realists and anti-realists will differ is in what they consider makes religious claims true.

Muhammed riding Al-Burak

1. REALISTS will say that the claims are true because they correspond to the actual events or state of affairs described. Thus "God exists" is true because this statement corresponds to a God who actually exists – either the wholly simple God who exists beyond time and space (chapter 2) or the everlasting, suffering God who can change and react to the petitions of believers (chapter 3).

2. ANTI-REALISTS, by contrast, will say that the claims are true because these cohere with other claims held to be true within the form of life of believers. What makes these claims true is that they are accepted and form part of what is agreed to be true within the religious community of believers.

The Apostles' Creed

I believe in God, the Father almighty, creator of heaven and Earth.

I believe in Jesus Christ, God's only Son, our Lord, who was conceived by the Holy Spirit, born of the Virgin Mary, suffered under Pontius Pilate, was crucified, died, and was buried; he descended to the dead.

On the third day he rose again; he ascended into heaven, he is seated at the right hand of the Father, and he will come again to judge the living and the dead.

I believe in the Holy Spirit, the holy catholic church, the communion of saints, the forgiveness of sins, the resurrection of the body, and the life everlasting.

It is clear what it means for a realist to say that God exists – either this means that there is a wholly simple, timeless, and spaceless God or that there is an everlasting suffering God who created and sustains the world.[4] However, what does it mean for an anti-realist to believe in God? It is going to mean something very different from the realist as, of course, the anti-realist rejects the correspondence theory of truth. Anti-realist believers maintain that God exists – God really really, truly truly exists BUT GOD EXISTS AS AN IDEA WITHIN THE COMMUNITY OF BELIEVERS. Within the form of life of religious believers it is true that God exists, within the form of life of atheists it is not true.

On the face of it, this seems a strange idea. God is not a being or a substance. Indeed God is nothing. This seems even stranger but it is exactly what anti-realists maintain. The leading Dominican scholar, Fr. Gareth Moore OP[5] said exactly this.

"...there is nothing, exists nothing, that can be called God." (*Thinking about God*. T & T Clark p.40)

God, for the anti-realists, is nothing but God still exists. God exists as a concept within the form of life of the religious believer.

Anti-realists argue that if a realist approach is taken, then there is no way of establishing that God exists. There are two ways of seeking to establish the existence of God.

- *NATURAL THEOLOGY – this seeks to use argument and reason to prove the existence of God. Some of these arguments are dealt with in chapters 6 and 13. Anti-realists hold that the arguments for the existence of God are not convincing to the non-believer and cannot establish anything,*

- *REFORMED EPISTEMOLOGY – this rejects the use of reason and instead insists that reliance should be placed on revelation (see box). However, anti-realists hold that there is no way of choosing between the competing revelations of different faith communities.*

There is, anti-realists argue, no way of establishing correspondence between the statement "God exists" and either the wholly simple or the everlasting God and the answer lies in abandoning correspondence and instead holding on to a coherence theory of truth. God, anti-realists claim, exists and is real but only within the language of the community of believers. There is no being or substance called God – instead 'God' is an idea within the religious form of life.

This position is held to have considerable advantages. As the Dominican Gareth Moore puts it:

"What value is there in this approach, in seeing God as nothing, not a thing, not a part of the Universe? To begin with it avoids all the difficulties and obscurities of the traditional 'arguments for the existence of God', and it avoids putting Christianity on such shaky foundations as might be established by these arguments" (p.41)

Because anti-realism rejects arguments for the existence of God and any appeal to revelation, it is held to be on firm ground:

"The question whether God exists is not a factual question, a question about

what we might find. It is a question whether to adopt the concept 'God' (the word and its use) into the language, or to retain it. For me, the question of the existence of God is the question whether I can find a use for the word 'God' in my talk..." (p.39)

Reformed epistemology

Reformed epistemology comes from the Reformed Christian tradition in the United States. It rejects the use of reason to arrive at the existence of God saying that this is an act of arrogance and pride by sinful human beings. It also takes literally the story of the Fall (based on the temptation story at the beginning of Genesis). Human reason is fallen and cannot attempt to judge God. Instead reformed epistemology argues that it is right to rely on God's revelation given in Jesus Christ. God, it is held, reveals himself to human beings through the Christian Bible and the Christian does not require any justification for his or her belief. Christians, it is held, have a "properly ordered noetic structure." They see the world correctly and those who do not agree with them have their minds distorted by sin and pride.

Reformed epistemologists consider that God's presence is so clearly obvious to them when they pray or when they read their Bibles that the idea of asking for justification is as ridiculous as a man standing in the presence of his wife asking for proof that it actually is his wife.

Reformed epistemologists say that they rely on the grace of God to ensure that they see the world correctly. They will, therefore, pray for those who do not see the truth as they do, but they will not use reason to argue with them as to do so would mean accepting that reason can be used to judge God (see also chapter 11).

The main problem with this view of course, is that in a multi-faith world it is difficult to decide which revelation should be accepted. A devout Muslim or Jew could put forward exactly the same argument as the Christian reformed epistemologist and the atheist could simply dismiss the rejection of reason as a refusal by believers to engage in rational debate (see also p.200).

Flight to Egypt

This painting shows the Holy Family's flight to Egypt. This story is recorded only in Matthew's Gospel and some modern commentators maintain that Matthew, writing to a Jewish audience, wanted to portray Jesus as the new Moses and the story of going to Egypt was inserted by Matthew to enable him to record Jesus coming out of Egypt. These commentators would, therefore, say that this story was not literally true although they would acknowledge that seeing Jesus as the new Moses might well provide insights into his significance. Anti-realists, by contrast, would say that the story was true because it was accepted by the Christian faith community. Working with a coherence theory of truth, the story is held to be true as it coheres with other elements of the Christian story.

Anti-realists maintain that religious people are educated into a "form of life." This process starts with early childhood when the child is taken to church and taught to pray. The child then goes to school and often this is a religious school where he or she is again educated into "the truth" of the religion in question. Anti-realists point out that where one is born and brought up will often determine one's religion. If people are born in much of India, they will be Hindus, if in Tibet (at least before the Chinese invasion) they would have been Buddhists, if in Iraq they would be Muslim. In Africa, Anglicanism is strong in the former British colonies whereas Catholicism dominates in countries colonized by the Portugese or French (since these were Catholic countries). Truth, for the anti-realist, depends on the form of life or culture within which a person lives and truth is not decided by intellectual inquiry but by what is agreed by the leaders of the religious community. Fr. Gareth Moore puts this clearly when he says:

"... in all fields a large importance is given to AUTHORITY... In religion, what is said and done is not to be in conformity with what is established by impartial enquiry, by going and looking at how things are, by experimenting. Rather is it to be conformable to what is AUTHORITATIVELY SAID." (p. 28)

In other words those in authority decide what is true and this then needs to be accepted by the faithful. For instance, anti-realists argue, the early Christian Councils decided what was true rather than false by taking a vote at great Councils of the Church (see chapter 10). The majority vote decided what was orthodoxy and what, therefore, had to be accepted by devout Christians and those who disagreed and lost the vote were the heretics. In many cases heretics were burnt at the stake or killed in warfare.[6] Deciding on what is true, according to the anti-realists, has nothing to do with a correspondence theory of truth and everything to do with what is accepted within the community of faith. Gareth Moore puts this as follows:

"...it is a feature of religion that people CORRECT each other in religious matters, or at least try to. Those people with a more authoritative voice, the leaders, correct the followers.. " "Now he has a wrong opinion. He has to be corrected, not in the sense of having his mistake pointed out to him... but in the sense of being persuaded to orthodoxy, won from his error. He has to be taught what is the right thing to say." .... "In the end the argument of the orthodox may have to come down to saying, 'This just is what the Christian faith is. This is what is believed and is to be believed. Believe this, not that.' It is not that no other position is reasonably tenable, but that no other opinion IS TO BE HELD." (p.32)

Anti-realists therefore maintain that within each form of life what is true is determined by what is agreed to be true (coherence theory of truth) and what is true is decided by those in authority within the community. The existence of God is unquestioned within forms of life that accept the existence of God. God exists as a concept within these communities but God is nothing, there is no reality to God outside this community.

"Part of the way that Christians are taught to see and live their lives is that they are disposed to be grateful even when there is nobody to be grateful to." (Gareth Moore, p.146)

God is nothing, there is nothing that is God and this has radical consequences for a traditional understanding of prayer and miracles (see chapter 8). God does not exist as an independent reality but is rather a construct within the community. Fr. Gareth Moore makes this clear in the final sentence of his book when he says:

"People do not discover religious truths, they make them." (p.287)

Religious truths are, therefore, created by religious communities. Within Islam it is true that there is one God who is Allah, Muhammed is the final prophet and the Holy Qu'ran was dictated by Allah and represents the final and complete revelation of Allah to all human beings. Within Christianity it is true that God is a Trinity of three persons, Jesus is the Son of God, died on the cross, and rose again after three days. Within Buddhism it is true that the Buddha represents the perfect attempt to become fully human, following the teachings of the Buddha enables the individual to pierce through the veil of illusion represented by this world and to achieve enlightenment. Within atheism there is no God and no life after death and religion is an illusion which needs to be recognized as such.

Truth, then, is dependent on the community or form of life a person inhabits and this makes truth relative to community.

FAIRIES, FATHER CHRISTMAS, AND GOD

Michael Leunig, one of the most famous Australian cartoonists, has a cartoon of a sad looking man sitting in a graveyard surrounded by gravestones reading:

- *R.I.P.[7] Father Christmas*
- *R.I.P. the Tooth Fairy*
- *R.I.P. the Easter Bunny*
- *R.I.P. God*

Is God rather like fairies? To many young children, fairies are real and they exist but children grow out of belief in fairies. Fairies only exist in stories and anti-realists argue that God only exists within the stories told by religious believers.

Most religious believers are realists and, when they have understood what anti-realism involves, their first reaction will be to reject it. However, it is important to recognize the considerable strengths of this position. The problem that the realists have is that they claim that the truth of religious statements depends on correspondence and there seems no way of establishing which religious claims correspond to the state of affairs they claim to be true.

Soren Kierkegaard

Ludwig Wittgenstein described the Danish philosopher and theologian, Soren Kierkegaard, as the greatest philosopher of the nineteenth century – and a saint. Kierkegaard has had a profound influence on subsequent philosophy although he is often misunderstood. His approach to philosophy gave rise to a movement called existentialism which focussed on philosophy needing to engage with existence and to relate to life. He was reacting particularly against the philosophy of Hegel which, in many ways, provided the seeds of modern anti-realism. Hegel had rejected the principle of bivalence and saw truth as emerging through history by what is known as the dialectical process. Statements could be both true and false at the same time, in fact Hegel's philosophic nickname was BOTH/AND as he held that a statement could be both true and false.

Kierkegaard completely rejected this. He was a philosophic realist and maintained that statements were either true or false (not surprisingly, his philosophic nickname became EITHER/OR). He accepted that there was no proof for the existence of God nor for the Christian claim that Jesus was both God and man but he argued that, in spite of the lack of evidence, these claims were EITHER true OR they were false. Christianity means an individual staking their life on truth claims that they cannot prove. This is a vulnerable position as it means a person staking their whole life on a claim that could be mistaken. This, perhaps, portrays the vulnerability of religious faith and it is this vulnerability which anti-realism denies. Anti-realism argues that once a religious community has decided on what is true, then this IS true. What makes it true is that the community of faith has accepted it. Kierkegaard rejects this and considers that it is possible for a religious person to stake their lives on claims that are false. He says that this is like living one's life:

"Suspended over 70000 fathoms."

This extreme vulnerability precisely rests on a realist theory of truth – it means that a religious life involves staking the whole of one's life on claims that could be mistaken. Socrates said:

"I cannot prove the immortality of the soul but am ready to stake my whole life on this 'if'."

This is exactly the realist position which Soren Kierkegaard argues for. Either the soul is immortal or it is not. Socrates cannot know for certain which is the case but his whole life is based on the claim that it is true. He accepts that he could be mistaken but he stakes his life on the claim. St. Paul recognized the same position when he said:

"If Christ be not raised, we are of all men the most to be pitied."

This is precisely the nature of a realist truth claim and it is on this that traditional Christianity, Islam, and Judaism have always depended.

QUESTIONS FOR CONSIDERATION

1) Do you consider that claims to truth in morality are based on a correspondence or coherence theory of truth?

2) What does Fr. Gareth Moore mean by the claim that "people do not discover religious truths, they make them"?

3) Why do anti-realists reject bivalence?

4) Anti-realists accept different truth claims in different religions and this is a tolerant position. What do you think are its main weaknesses?

5) Does it make sense to stake one's life on something that cannot be proved?

Notes

[1] *The arguments of David Hume, A.J. Ayer and Bertrand Russell for disbelief in God were set out in* The Thinker's Guide to Evil *by Peter Vardy and Julie Arliss, John Hunt Publishing, 2003.*

[2] *Muslims hold that Mary was, indeed, a virgin when she conceived Jesus and that she remained a virgin. Mary is revered in Islam – a fact many Christians do not always realize.*

[3] *In Britain, New Zealand, and Australia the 'Sea of Faith' movement has become influential – this consists of priests, teachers, and others but, because the anti-realist position is not always accepted, the records of membership are kept confidential to prevent, for instance, certain parishes being aware that their priest may be an anti-realist.*

[4] *There are other possibilities including that held by the Jewish philosopher, Spinoza, who maintained that God and the Universe are one and to talk of 'God' is to talk of a different aspect of the Universe. However, few people today hold this pantheist view.*

[5] *The Dominicans are one of the leading and most intellectual order of Catholic priests. Fr. Gareth Moore died in 2002.*

[6] *For instance tens of thousands of Cathars were killed by warfare organized by the then Pope and the institutional Church in order to suppress what was seen as the heresy of Catharism.*

[7] *Rest In Peace.*

CHAPTER 6

ARGUMENTS FOR THE EXISTENCE OF GOD

Anti-realists reject reference – they maintain that talk of God does not correspond to the being or substance called God who creates and sustains the Universe and "God" is, instead, an idea which is real and exists within the form of life of religious belief. One way to undermine this claim is to show that there does, indeed, exist a Being or Spirit rightly named God – and this has always been claimed to be possible, in the Catholic Christian tradition, using **NATURAL THEOLOGY**.

Some argue that there is a significant shortage of evidence for the existence of God – whether the wholly simple, timeless and spaceless God (chapter 2) or the everlasting suffering God (chapter 3). Unless there is any evidence of God what does it matter how religious language is used? One might equally postulate the existence of the Great Zudulu in the sky with a whole array of other-worldly attributes, that no one fully understands, but unless there is a REASON to believe that the Great Zudulu in the sky exists at all, why listen? Atheists claim that the very concept of God is a colorful invention by religious believers which religious believers need, as some sort of emotional or psychological prop. Talk about God, without any evidence to support the existence of God, can be seen as an internal exercise of interest only as a spectator sport unless one is prepared to believe it. The non-religious person will claim that they have no need of such a mythical support system.

All world religions have faced these and similar challenges for many centuries. Within monotheistic world religions there is a long history predating the

Greek philosopher, Aristotle, of offering so called 'proofs' for the existence of God. These are offered both for the benefit of the atheist and for the benefit of those within a faith who would like a rational basis for their belief in God. The proofs use philosophical arguments in an attempt to demonstrate that the existence of God is more probable than not. There are five main types of argument:

1. *COSMOLOGICAL ARGUMENTS argue from some feature of the world to God. The two main types of cosmological arguments are:*

- *THE KALAM ARGUMENT argues that the Universe had a beginning and therefore something must have brought it into being. This it is claimed is God.*

- *THE DEPENDENCY ARGUMENT argues that the Universe needs something to sustain its existence now and that this something is God.*

2. *ONTOLOGICAL ARGUMENTS argue from the concept of God to the existence of God.*

3. *MORAL ARGUMENTS argue from the idea of an absolute moral order in the Universe to God as the source of this order.*

4. *DESIGN ARGUMENTS argue that the world shows signs of design and that God is the great designer.*

5. *RELIGIOUS EXPERIENCE ARGUMENTS argue that reports of religious experience make it more likely than not that God exists.*

Natural theology and reavealed theology

NATURAL THEOLOGY is the attempt to use reason to establish the existence of God. Any attempt which uses philosophic argument to seek to prove God's existence is a part of natural theology. In the Catholic tradition it is held that it is possible to arrive at the existence of God using human reason alone. However **REVEALED THEOLOGY** goes further than this and provides additional truths which are not accessible to reason – such as the incarnation, Trinity, and the doctrine of creation. In the Catholic tradition, nothing in revealed theology contradicts reason.

Protestants, by contrast, reject natural theology and maintain that faith is based on revelation alone. Reason operates within faith but cannot provide a basis for faith.

In the pages that follow most of these arguments will be set out (the Moral Argument which seeks to argue from the claimed existence of absolute moral values is dealt with in *The Thinker's Guide to Ethics* and the Design Argument is dealt with in chapter 13 of this book) together with the criticisms of the arguments. Much depends on the presuppositions on which the arguments rest. It must be accepted that few people come to belief in God based on arguments – one does not get an atheist saying "I thought that God might not exist but now I have read about a new argument for God's existence so I am going to become a believer"! It simply does not work that way. Perhaps, however, there are ways to judge the success or otherwise of the arguments:

1. *Do they enable believers to see that their existing beliefs can be supported intellectually, and*

2. *Do they challenge those who do not believe in the existence of God to accept that belief is not wholly irrational?*

The Kalam cosmological argument

The Holy Qu'ran calls Muslims to reasoning and to seek learning. In the first two centuries after the death of the Prophet Muhammed, this led to philosophy being taken seriously by Islamic scholars. Ancient Greek philosophic texts were translated and were available in Arabic. In fact it was due to Islamic philosophers that many of the works of Aristotle were preserved when they had been lost in the West. Wealthy and influential rulers and their patronage led to the establishment of centers of learning in Cairo and Baghdad and these still remain the centres of Islamic scholarship down to the present day. The Kalam argument originated in the Islamic Kalam school of philosophy but has been updated recently by the American philosopher, William Lane Craig. Like all arguments for the existence of God apart from the Ontological argument, it is an *a posteriori* argument – this means that it takes experience in the world as a starting point. The Kalam argument has three steps:

1. Everything that begins to exist has a cause of its existence.

2. The Universe began to exist.

3. Therefore, the Universe has a cause for its existence.

It is difficult to prove (1), although one may feel that it is intuitively probable. Craig says: "...it is so intuitively obvious that I think scarcely anyone could sincerely believe it to be false" yet some hold that at the micro-particle level there are uncaused events and if even ONE beginning could be shown not to have a cause, then premise (1) is false and the argument collapses. Paul Davies, *Superforce* (Simon and Schuster New York,

1984 p. 200) has argued that this assumption is false as it appears that electrons can pass out of existence at one point and re-appear somewhere else. Craig has replied to this saying that this does not affect the Kalam argument, as in modern physics a vacuum is not nothing, but rather a state of minimal energy. The electron fluctuations, he holds, are due to vacuum fluctuations and the vacuum needs to exist for electrons to exist so electrons are not coming into existence from nothing as his critics maintain.

(2) Is difficult to prove but if the Universe did originate in a 'Big Bang' then this would support this premise. At the Big Bang, the initial singularity exploded at a rate faster than the speed of light. Nuclear explosions took place which caused concentrations of hydrogen and helium and some of the lithium found in inter-stellar space. Time and space also came into existence with the initial explosion and the background radiation in the Universe is a residue from this original "Big Bang". However, there are other theories for the origin of the Universe including the idea of matter continuously coming into existence and the issue is by no means yet decided.

If (1) and (2) are accepted, then (3) follows from it. Even if this is accepted, however, there is an implicit fourth premise in the argument namely:

4) The cause of the existence of the Universe is God.

This is sometimes thought to be obvious but it may be that there could be other causes. For instance if the Universe expands and contracts, expands and contracts and goes on doing this indefinitely, then the singularity which is the Big Bang may have resulted from a previous Universe collapsing in on itself and this Universe being formed by a new explosion.

One problem with the Kalam argument is that it can be argued that whatever caused the Universe to begin to exist may no longer itself be in existence. However, the argument maintains that the cause of the Universe, being outside space and time (which came into existence with the Universe) must be unchanging and necessarily existent. If this cause cannot change, then it cannot go out of existence.

The dependency cosmological argument

St. Thomas Aquinas put forward his "Five Ways"' of proving the existence of God in the 13th century although most of these were based on arguments found in Aristotle – four of these arguments were versions of the Cosmological argument. These argued from features of the Universe and all attempted to arrive at God who could not not-exist. It was, however, Leibniz (1646–1716) who put forward possibly the best known argument which he summarized as follows:

"Suppose the book of the elements of geometry to have been eternal, one copy always having been written down from an earlier one. It is evident that even though a reason can be given for the present book out of a past one, we should never come to a full reason. What is true of the books is also true of the states of the world. If you suppose the world eternal you will suppose nothing but a succession of states and will not find in any of them a sufficient reason."

Leibniz often uses the word 'reason' but it is clear that this effectively means 'cause' – for instance he quotes the example of Archimedes' balance which is held in equal balance unless there is a reason (i.e. cause) why one side should be weighed down. He argues for the existence of "the ultimate reason for things" which he takes to mean the ultimate cause of things. Effectively he wishes to maintain that everything (including the Universe itself) must have a reason or cause for its existence and this must mean there is an ultimate, uncaused cause – which he takes to be God. The world depends on God now rather than God just creating the world.

Leibniz considered that there must be a complete or sufficient explanation, and therefore the geometry book (in the example above), like the world, must have had a first cause. Leibniz's argument can be summarized as follows:

1. The Universe is changing.

2. Whatever is changing does not have within itself the reason for its own existence.

3. There must be a sufficient reason for everything either within itself or outside itself.

4. Since there is no reason within the Universe for its existence, there must be a reason beyond the Universe.

5. Either this reason is itself caused or it is a complete and sufficient reason on its own.

6. There cannot be an infinite regress of causes because this will never provide a sufficient reason.

7. Therefore there must be a First Cause of the Universe which has no reason beyond itself but is its own sufficient reason.

8. This first cause is God.

The key to this argument is the PRINCIPLE OF SUFFICIENT REASON, which Leibniz thought to be self-evidently true. This means that there must be a complete reason for everything that happens. In practice, people are normally content with proximate reasons – reasons that satisfy. Thus the reason this book is written is to make philosophic issues clearer. One might ask further questions such as why we bother since few people read books about God, whether this is the best way of helping people to think about these issues, or even why anyone should be interested in these issues at all. The principle of sufficient reason says that there must be a complete and total explanation for everything. In practice, however, most people would not consider that there has to be an ultimate explanation of my action in order for the explanation to make sense. It is the assertion of an ultimate explanation that the Principle of Sufficient Reason maintains.

The Principle of Sufficient Reason assumes that there cannot be an infinite regress. An infinite number of numbers may be possible, but there cannot be an infinite series of causes – there must be a first cause which is God. Kai Neilsen says that "If a series were literally infinite, there would be no need for there to be a first cause to get the causal order started, for there would always be a causal order since an infinite series can have no first member." However, even if a series existed eternally, then it could still be argued that God is needed to sustain the series – which brings the discussion back to whether the whole causal series is simply a brute fact or requires God to explain it.

This argument, and the 'Five Ways' of St. Thomas Aquinas which also seek to show that there is a necessary God on which the Universe depends, can be challenged in three ways:

1. Why should one accept that there has to be a total explanation? Maybe there is just an infinite regress of explanation which continues without end.

2. The argument ends up with God who necessarily exists and who cannot not-exist but it is debatable whether this makes sense. Anything that exists might not exist and perhaps a necessarily existent being is nonsense. This was the position take by Hume and Immanuel Kant who rejected the very idea of God as necessarily existent. They maintained that the only things necessary were statements such as "triangles have three angles" and the idea of God as necessarily existent is a contradiction in terms. Anything that exists may exist or may not exist and the same, Kant maintained, applied to God.

3. Even if there is a God who is necessary, timeless, and spaceless, would this be the personal God of religious belief?

The ontological argument

The ontological argument for the existence of God is completely different from all the other arguments in that it is an *a priori* argument. This means that it does not depend on experience as a starting point. Instead it seeks to argue from the concept of God to the existence of God. The best known formulation of the argument is by St. Anselm who was a monk and put this argument forward as part of a prayer to God:

1. The concept of God is agreed on by both believer and unbeliever alike – *God is that than which no greater can be conceived.*

2. It is greater for a thing to exist both in the mind and in reality than for it to exist only in the mind. A chocolate bar in the mind may be absolutely the most sublimely delicious thought or concept but if it exists in reality as well then it is greater than if it only exists in the mind.

3. If God is that than which no greater can be conceived, God cannot exist only as a concept. If God exists only as a concept then there is something greater – namely God who exists *both* as a concept in the mind and in reality.

4. The believer and the unbeliever accept the concept of God as that than which no greater can be thought. The unbeliever is a fool however because the unbeliever does not fully understand that the concept of "that than which is no greater can be conceived" must logically include existence.

Another monk, Gaunilo, rejected this argument and said that it was absurd. He asked Anselm to imagine the most perfect possible island that had all perfections. If it has all perfections then this must include existence and therefore the island must exist. St. Anselm, however, replied to Gaunilo that Gaunilo had failed to understand him. Only God had all perfections and only God, therefore, had to exist necessarily. Only God could not not-exist.

St Anselm's book

St. Thomas Aquinas also rejected Anselm's argument as he rejected premise (1) – he did not think that everyone agreed with Anselm's definition. Some people even thought that God had a body (which Aquinas considered to be absurd) so it was false to argue that everyone agreed on the concept as Anselm wanted them to. What is more, Aquinas held that it was not possible to argue from a concept to the existence of something. This is why all Aquinas' arguments were *a posteriori* – they all started from experience, from features of the world.

The influence of Aristotle and Plato is evident in these two positions. Anselm was effectively a Platonist who starts with a concept and moves to the reality beyond this world that the concept represents. Aquinas by contrast is effectively an Aristotelian, arguing from experience – from the facts of the world.

Rene Descartes' version of the argument is in some way clearer than that of Anselm. Descartes holds that just as we cannot conceive of a triangle without it having three angles; just as we cannot think of a mountain without a valley; so we cannot think of God without conceiving of him as existing. Descartes' clearest formulation of the argument is as follows:

1. Whatever is of the essence of something must be affirmed of it.

2. It is of the essence of God that he exists for by definition his essence is to exist, therefore

3. Existence must be affirmed of God.

Descartes did qualify his argument in order to guard against the sort of attack that Gaunilo developed against Anselm. He says that:

1. The argument applies only to an absolutely perfect and necessary being (it cannot, therefore, be applied to something like a lost island).

2. Not everyone has to think of God, but if they do think of God then God cannot be thought not to exist.

3. God alone is the being whose essence entails God's existence. There cannot be two or more such beings.

Aquinas rejects precisely the point that Descartes wants to affirm. Descartes says we can know God's essence and therefore we can say that God must exist. Aquinas does not think that God's essence is knowable to us.

David Hume and Kant also rejected the ontological argument.

They both rejected the idea that anything could necessarily exist. Any statement about the existence of something could be doubted or rejected. Whatever is claimed to exist may or may not do so and the only way to determine whether this is the case is to have empirical evidence. The very idea of a necessarily existent being was a contradiction.

It was Kant who called this the "ontological argument" – the reason for the name is that he thought that the argument made an illegitimate jump from the idea of God to the claimed reality ("ontos") of God. For more than two hundred years the argument was, therefore, thought to be irrelevant. Today, however, it has a new influence in the way explained in the next panel.

The ontological argument and anti-realism

Norman Malcolm was a close friend of Ludwig Wittgenstein. Malcolm became a major philosopher in his own right but the influence of Wittgenstein on everything he did was considerable. Malcolm considered that the first of Anselm's arguments fails. He re-states the first argument as follows:

1. By definition, God is an absolutely perfect being possessing all perfections.

2. Existence is a perfection.

3. Therefore God must possess existence [from (1) and (2)].

Malcolm, along with Hume and Kant, rejects the second premise by holding that existence is not a perfection. However he goes on to develop Anselm's second argument.

ANSELM'S SECOND ARGUMENT – NORMAN MALCOLM'S VERSION

Anselm has two arguments. The one above occurs in *Proslogion 2*, but the more interesting one may be in *Proslogion 3*. Malcolm begins by stating that if God does not already exist, God cannot come into existence since this would require a cause and would make God a limited being which, by definition, God is not. Similarly, if God already exists, God cannot cease to exist.

Once this is accepted, then EITHER GOD'S EXISTENCE IS IMPOSSIBLE OR NECESSARY. Malcolm then argues that God's existence could only be impossible if it were logically absurd or contradictory and, as it is neither, then God's existence MUST be necessary. The statement "God necessarily exists," therefore, can be held to be true. This argument is sophisticated and not many understand what Malcolm is actually doing or its significance. Malcolm's argument can be stated in the following steps:

1. Given the statement "God necessarily exists" there are only three possibilities about this statement. Either it is: (a) impossible, (b) possibly true, or (c) necessarily true.

2. There is no way of showing that the statement "God necessarily exists" is impossible. It would only be impossible if the statement contained a contradiction and it does not. Therefore (a) can be ruled out.

3. The statement "God necessarily exists" cannot be possibly true. It is either true or it is false. Since God is defined as a necessarily existent being, then God cannot just possibly exist. A possibly existent being is one which may or may not exist and this cannot apply to God as God is necessary. So (b) can be ruled out.

4. Therefore (c) must be true – "God necessarily exists" must be a true statement.

John Hick rejects this when he maintains that the most that can be said is that if God exists, God exists necessarily. This is problem free BUT there is no way of getting rid of the 'if'. This is rather similar to Descartes' comments on a triangle or a valley – namely

1. If there is a triangle, it must have three angles.

2. If there is a mountain, it must have a valley.

3. Similarly if there is God, then God must necessarily exist.

However Hick (as most other philosophers) misunderstand Malcolm – mainly because they do not understand anti-realism. For the anti-realist (see chapter 5) God is real and God exists. However, God is not a being or a substance, God is neither wholly simple and timeless nor everlasting. Instead "God" is an idea, a concept within the language game or story shared by certain religious believers. For those within the religious form of life, those who take part in the liturgy, sacraments, worship, and religious rituals, God is indeed real and God indeed exists but "God" is only an idea within the community of belief.

On this basis, "God necessarily exists" is true for religious believers, for those who inhabit the world of religious belief. For these people, God's reality is unquestioned and undoubted. God is the center of their world. God is that in which they live and move and have their being – but God is merely an idea or

concept which lies at the center of the world which they have created and which gives meaning to their life. God has no independent existence outside this form of life.

To those, therefore, within the religious form of life, "God necessarily exists" is a true statement, but to those who are atheists or agnostics, the statement is false.

Some people say there is a God and others say there is not. This seems to involve a dispute about a kind of object, a 'something'. However, this may well be an error. Anselm wrote his argument as part of a prayer to God. He says:

"...the fool hath said in his heart 'There is no God,' but at any rate this very fool, when he hears of this Being of which I speak – a being than which no greater can be conceived – understands what he hears, and what he understands is in his understanding; although he does not understand it to exist."

To those who believe, God's reality is unquestioned –
"God necessarily exists" is true for them.

Believers understand that, for them, "God necessarily exists" is true. Believers do not go round saying "God exists" – rather they take part in worship, they pray, go to Church, sing hymns, and read their Bibles. All these activities PRESUME the existence of God. They do not first set out to prove the existence of God and only then go to church. They are either brought up in a group of people who go to church or they come to see the value of belonging to a religious community and, for those within this community, God's existence is necessary.

To such people, therefore, "God necessarily exists" is true and the ontological argument shows the self-evident truth of this statement.

What, however, this does NOT show is that the God of traditional Christianity (whether wholly simple or everlasting) exists. To show this it would be necessary to argue from experience, from some feature of the world – and it is this that Kant and Hume rightly recognized.

THE ARGUMENT FROM RELIGIOUS EXPERIENCE

Through recorded history human beings have recorded experiences of the Divine. Great mystics and prophets of all the world religions as well as countless numbers of ordinary people have claimed to be aware of God or, at the least, of a transcendent Power. The question is whether these reports of religious experience can make the existence of God more probable or not. The problem is whether it is possible to move from saying:

1. *It appeared to me that I experienced God last night*, to

2. *I experienced God last night.*

The first statement records the way something appeared, the second the way something actually is and the problem is that these are not the same. The Sun appears to go round the Earth, a stick in water appears to be bent, there can appear to be an oasis in the desert, but all these appearances are deceptive. Skeptics will, therefore, maintain that the fact that someone thinks they have experienced God, does not mean that they have done so.

William James was an American psychologist and his book, *The Varieties of Religious Experience* is possibly the best analysis of religious experience ever produced. James defined religious experience as

---

"...the feelings, acts and experiences of individual men in their solitude, so far as they apprehend themselves to stand in relation to whatever they may consider the divine."

James focussed particularly on individual, mystical experiences and he analyzed four distinct features of these experiences:

Winnie the Pooh

Winnie the Pooh is an empiricist – he was convinced that the only way to test if there really was honey down to the bottom of the honey pot was to see for himself (and to eat all the honey in the process).

Sometimes, of course, even empiricists can misread the evidence. When walking round the tree with Piglet and seeing all the footsteps in the snow, Pooh and Piglet became frightened, convinced that they were following a threatening creature, but they misread the evidence, they were only following their own footprints.

Arguments for the existence of God are all (except for the ontological argument) *a posteriori* – they seek to move from experiences in the world to the existence of God. The Religious Experience argument is a classic *a posteriori* argument which seeks to establish, from looking at claimed experience of the Divine or the Other, that God or some transcendent reality does, indeed, exist.

1. **Ineffability.** *(Religious experience, like love, needs to be directly experienced in order to be understood. No adequate report on its content can be given in words – it must be immediately experienced and no real sense of its content can be communicated. Mystical states are more akin to feelings than intellectual states.)*

2. **Noetic quality.** *(Mystics speak of revelations and illuminations which are held to provide knowledge and transcend rational categories. "They are states of insight into depths of truth unplumbed by the discursive intellect. They are illuminations, revelations, full of significance and importance and, as a rule, they carry with them a curious sense of authority.")*

3. **Transiency.** *(Mystical experiences last for a short time. "Except in rare instances, half an hour, or at most an hour or two, seems to be the limit beyond which they fade into the light of common day." They cannot even be accurately remembered but they can be recognized again when they re-occur.)*

4. **Passivity.** *(The experience is beyond the individual's control and cannot be obtained by effort; it is a gift. "The mystic feels as though his own will is in abeyance, and indeed sometimes as if he were grasped and held by a superior power.")*

James considers that religious experiences lie at the heart of all religion and that creeds and dogmas are overlaid on top of these experiences. James argues that:

1. *Mystical states, when well developed, usually are, and have the right to be, absolutely authoritative over the individuals to whom they come. In other words for the person having the experience they are so real that they cannot be denied.*

2. *No authority emanates from them which should make it a duty for those who stand outside of these experience to accept their revelations uncritically.*

3. *They break down the authority of the non-mystical or rationalistic consciousness, based upon the understanding and the senses alone. They show it to be only one kind of consciousness and that there is something beyond everyday awareness of physical objects.*

Religious experiences

The Acts of the Apostles provides three different accounts of possibly the most famous Christian account of a religious experience – namely the conversion of St. Paul on the road to Damascus. Even though the accounts differ, it is clear from the reports that something extraordinary happened to turn St. Paul from a passionate opponent of Christianity to perhaps its most powerful advocate.

ACTS 9.3-8:

As he neared Damascus on his journey, suddenly a light from heaven flashed around him. He fell to the ground and heard a voice say to him, "Saul, Saul, why do you persecute me?"

"Who are you, Lord?" Saul asked. "I am Jesus, whom you are persecuting," he replied. "Now get up and go into the city, and you will be told what you must do." The men traveling with Saul stood there speechless; they heard the sound but did not see anyone.

Saul got up from the ground, but when he opened his eyes he could see nothing. So they led him by the hand into Damascus.

ACTS 22.6-11:

"About noon as I came near Damascus, suddenly a bright light from heaven flashed around me. I fell to the ground and heard a voice say to me, `Saul! Saul! Why do you persecute me?' `Who are you, Lord?' I asked. `I am Jesus of Nazareth, whom you are persecuting,' he replied. My companions saw the light, but they did not understand the voice of him who was speaking to me. `What shall I do, Lord?' I asked. `Get up,' the Lord said, `and go into Damascus. There you will be told all that you have been assigned to do.' My companions led me by the hand into Damascus, because the brilliance of the light had blinded me."

ACTS 26.13-19:

"About noon, O king, as I was on the road, I saw a light from heaven, brighter than the Sun, blazing around me and my companions. We all fell to the ground, and I heard a voice saying to me in Aramaic, `Saul, Saul, why do you persecute me? It is hard for you to kick against the goad.' Then I asked, `Who are you, Lord?' `I am Jesus, whom you are persecuting,' the Lord replied. `Now get up and stand on your feet. I have appeared to you to appoint you as a servant and as a witness of what you have seen of me and what I will show you. I will rescue you from your own people and from the Gentiles. I am sending you to them to open their eyes and turn them from darkness to light, and from the power of Satan to God, so that they may receive forgiveness of sins and a place among those who are sanctified by faith in me.'

So then, King Agrippa, I was not disobedient to the vision from heaven..."

Religious experience is sometimes accompanied by a bright light

In recent years, there has been an unprecedented increase in research on reports of religious experience and the work of the 'Oxford Religious Experience Research Unit' has been particularly important. The Unit has among its patrons some of the most influential religious figures in the world including the Dalai Lama, the Chief Rabbi, and the Archbishop of Canterbury and it has been involved in carefully listening to and analyzing reports of religious experience. There have been innumerable reports of these experiences (many of which are shown on the Unit's web site). The Unit has also conducted opinion polls through Britain asking people from all walks of life the following question: *"Have you ever had a spiritual or religious experience, or felt a presence or power, whether you called it God or not, which is different from your everyday life?"* The results were extraordinary as 25-45% of those interviewed, irrespective of age, background, socio-economic group, or religious belief answered "Yes" to this question.

What is, perhaps, more remarkable is the number of people who had never before spoken of their experiences to even their closest friends as they felt that there was too much danger of being misunderstood. Almost always the individuals involved did not seek the experience – as William James said, the individuals were passive and the experience happened to them in a totally unexpected way. The following is one example of a report of such an experience:

"I decided to write after keeping my experience to myself for forty years. I was 16 and had always enjoyed solitary walks around my village home. One evening I set out, by myself, as usual, to walk up a lane towards the wood. I was not feeling particularly happy or particularly sad, just ordinary. I was certainly not 'looking' for anything, just going for a walk to be peaceful. It must have been August, because the corn was ripe and I only had a summer dress and sandals on. I was almost to the wood when I paused, turned to look at the cornfield, took two or three steps forward so I was able to touch the ears of corn and watched them swaying in the faint breeze. I looked to the end of the field – it had a hedge then – and beyond that to some tall trees towards the village. The Sun was over to my left; it was not in my eyes.

"Then ... there must be a blank. I will never know for how long, because I was only in my normal conscious mind with normal faculties and I came out of it. Everywhere surrounding me was this white, bright, sparkling light, like Sun on frosty snow, like a million diamonds, and there was no cornfield, no trees, no sky, this light was everywhere; my ordinary eyes were open, but I was not seeing with them. It can only have lasted a moment I think or I would have fallen over.

"The feeling was indescribable, but I have never experienced anything in the years that followed that can compare with that glorious moment; it was blissful, uplifting, I felt open-mouthed wonder.

"Then the tops of the trees became visible once again, then a piece of sky and gradually the light was no more, and the cornfield was spread before me. I stood there for a long time, trying in vain for it to come back and have tried many times since, but I only saw it once; but I know in my heart it is still there – and here – and everywhere around us. I know Heaven is within us and around us. I have had this wonderful experience which brought happiness beyond compare.

"We see God in the miracle of life, in trees, flowers and birds – I smile when I hear talk of God as a man, wrathful or otherwise – I know I have seen and felt and am humbly grateful for the inner rock to which I cling.

"I wrote it down, but I never told anybody."
[Record number 4405]

This experience, like so many others, fits all the features analyzed by William James.

The bar of iron analogy

William James likened a person's religious experience to a bar of iron feeling attraction and being unable to explain this:

"It is as if a bar of iron, without touch or sight, with no representative faculty whatever, might nevertheless be strongly endowed with an inner capacity for magnetic feeling; and as if, through the various arousals of its magnetism by magnets coming and going in its neighborhood, it might be consciously determined to different attitudes and tendencies. Such a bar of iron could never give you an outward description of the agencies that had the power of stirring it so strongly; yet of their presence, and of their significance for its life, it would be intensely aware through every fibre of its being." *Varieties of Religious Experience* p.4.

Human beings, claims James, experience the Divine and cannot doubt that this is the case once they have had such an experience even though they cannot explain it in rational terms.

It obviously had a very great impact on the person who had the experience but they did not want to share this or talk about it with others. There is a real sense in which these experience are so deep and so profound that analyzing them philosophically seems irrelevant given the overwhelming reality of the experience – this is why many people who have had these experiences prefer not to talk about them because they do not want friends providing a rational analysis of something that is so profound and so important to them.

It is not only William James in the Western tradition who is aware of such religious experiences. D.T. Suzuki is a Buddhist writer on aspects of religious experience and his analysis is remarkably similar to that of William James. He considers the following to be common to all these experiences:

1. *There is a sense of "something" beyond and much greater than oneself.*

2. *This "something" feeds and is the source of who you are.*

3. *The individuals feels exalted and at one with the Universe.*

4. *The experience is not simply a personal event.*

5. *The individual feels free and sees the essence of things; he or she sees things for what they truly are.*

6. *The individual accepts things for what they are.*

7. *The experience cannot be expressed in words.*

8. *The individual is absolutely certain of this experience: NO ONE can refute it.*

Again, therefore, these experiences are seen to be individual and to point to a much wider realm of reality than the everyday world. Again the experience cannot be doubted by the person who has it.

Immanuel Kant

Kant rejected all claims to religious experiences. He did so because God is not an object in space and time and, since human beings have only got five senses which are used to record experiences of spatio-temporal objects, then it is impossible for God to be experienced at all. Kant drew a distinction between the world as it is experienced by human beings, the PHENOMENAL WORLD, and the world as it really is in itself, the NOUMENAL WORLD. Human beings all share five senses and they have no alternative but to experience the world through the senses. Kant certainly did not reject the existence of God, he simply rejected the possibility of human beings experiencing God.

This painting by Millais (1856) called 'The Blind Girl' expresses Kant's position well. The woman can experience her daughter's hair as she can touch it and she can experience the music from the accordion as she can hear it but she cannot experience the rainbow as she cannot see. Similarly, for Kant, human beings cannot experience God as human senses only enable objects in space and time to be experienced.

A modern American philosopher of religion, William Alston, has replied to this suggesting that human beings have more than five senses. Just as dogs and cats have senses of which human beings are not aware, so Alston argues human beings may have faculties of which we are only dimly aware and which would enable us to experience God. Alston argues for a perceptual model for experiencing God: *"... perceiving X simply consists in X's appearing to one, or being presented to one, as so-and-so. That's all there is to it..."* God is experienced, only if God exists to be experienced.

Alston accepts that religious believers do make use of their prior beliefs when they have religious experiences, but he does not consider that this undermines the veracity of these experiences. Humans do this, he maintains, with normal experience. If he sees his house from 5000ft, he certainly sees his house and he may learn something new but it would basically be as he expected his house to look. Similarly when experiencing God, God is experienced as believers expect God to be experienced – there is no difference between ordinary experiences and religious ones. This does not, however, solve the challenge to religious experience which says that the likelihood of religious experience pointing to God is undermined by the fact that most people claim to see what their prior framework leads them to expect. Thus Catholics see the Virgin Mary, not the Hindu god Kali and this points, critics claim, to prior beliefs creating the experiences. However, it can be replied to this that if there is a transcendent 'Other' which some call God, it may be reasonable that different cultures will experience this through their own understandings but this does not mean that God does not exist. The famous poem about the blind men of Hindustan (on the next page) puts this well – the fact that so many religious people may have different views of the reality of God does not mean that God does not exist.

The psychological and physiological challenges

Perhaps the most powerful challenge against the idea that religious experience points beyond itself to God or a transcendent reality comes from some psychologists and physiologists who, whilst they may acknowledge that people do have the experiences they claim, nevertheless say that these can be explained entirely in psychological terms. As one example, in Ireland epilepsy was known as "Saint Paul's disease." The name points to the centuries-old assumption that the apostle suffered from epilepsy. Psychologists might, therefore, agree that St. Paul had the sort of experience he described but instead of attributing this to God they would explain it in physiological terms.

The Blind Men of Indostan
– John Godfrey Saxe 1816–1887

It was six men of Indostan to learning much inclined

Who went to see the elephant though all of them were blind,

That each by observation might satisfy his mind.

The First approached the elephant, and happening to fall

Against his broad and sturdy side, at once began to bawl;

'God bless me! But the elephant is very like a wall!'

The Second, feeling of the tusk, cried, 'Ho! What have we here

So very round and smooth and sharp? To me 'tis mighty clear

This wonder of an elephant is very like a spear!'

The Third approached the animal, and happening to take

The squirming trunk within his hands, thus boldly up and spake:

'I see', quoth he, 'the Elephant is very like a snake!'

The Fourth reached out an eager hand, and felt about the knee

'What most this wondrous beast is like is mighty plain' quoth he;

' 'Tis clear enough the Elephant is very like a tree!'

The Fifth, who chanced to touch the ear, said: 'E'en the blindest man

Can tell what this resembles most; deny the fact who can

This marvel of an elephant is very like a fan!'

The Sixth no sooner had begun about the beast to grope,

Than, seizing on the swinging tail that fell within his scope,

'I see', quoth he, 'the Elephant is very like a rope!'

And so these men of Indostan disputed loud and long,

Each in his own opinion exceeding stiff and strong,

Though each was partly in the right, and all were in the wrong!

Moral: So oft in theologic wars, the disputants, I ween,

Rail on in utter ignorance of what each other mean,

And prate about an elephant; not one of them has seen!

To support this view, people usually point to Saint Paul's experience on the road to Damascus, quoted in full on page 91, in which Paul, or Saul as he was known before his conversion to Christianity, is reported to have a fit similar to an epileptic seizure: "...suddenly a light from the sky flashed around him. He fell to the ground and heard a voice saying to him: 'Saul, Saul! Why do you persecute me?'... Saul got up from the ground and opened his eyes, but he could not see a thing... For three days he was not able to see, and during that time he did not eat or drink anything." Some argue that this account could well be of an epileptic seizure, not of a religious experience.

In his letters St. Paul occasionally gives discreet hints about his "physical ailment," by which he perhaps means a chronic illness. In the second letter to the Corinthians, for instance, he states: "But to keep me from being puffed up with pride... I was given a painful physical ailment, which acts as Satan's messenger to beat me and keep me from being proud." (2 Corinthians 12.7). In his letter to the Galatians, Paul again describes his physical weakness: "You remember why I preached the gospel to you the first time; it was because I was ill. But even though my physical condition was a great trial to you, you did not despise or reject me." (Galatians 4.13-14). In ancient times people used to spit at "epileptics," either out of disgust or in order to ward off what they thought to be the "contagious matter" (epilepsy as *morbus insputatus*: the illness at which one spits).

It is possible to argue that St. Paul suffered from epilepsy but it is not possible to reduce all religious experience to types of mental illness:

1. *Although it may be possible that SOME religious experiences can be explained in psychological terms, this does not mean that ALL religious experiences can be so explained.*

2. *The degree to which those who claim religious experiences are often intelligent, well balanced and able to be self-critical counts against religious experience being simply explained as a psychological delusion.*

3. *One of the marks of a genuine religious experience is that it changes the person concerned and remains of enduring importance throughout their life. A psychological aberration is much less likely to have this effect than a profound experience of the divine which places the whole of life in a completely different context.*

4. *Even if many religious experiences were to be explained in psychological terms, this in no way rules out God being responsible for these experiences. After all, if God exists, how else would God communicate except through the human psyche?*

5. *God is not another object in space and time (see chapters 2-3) and, therefore, the fact that most religious experiences cannot be communicated in normal language which deals with spatio-temporal objects does not undermine their credibility but rather makes them more probably true.*

6. *The evidence of the Oxford Religious Experience Research Unit about the very wide scale of religious experiences and that these experiences often occur only once and come to many individuals who are not 'religious' or tied in to a particular faith community undermines the idea that such experiences are merely a psychological effect.*

These arguments do not, of course, prove that religious experiences are true, but they do, perhaps, undermine the attempt to simply write off religious experience on psychological grounds. Carl Jung was one of the greatest psychologists who has ever lived and he considered that, in all his patients in later life, coming to a proper understanding of their position as spiritual beings was vital in coming to psychological wholeness. Jung maintained that all individuals have within their shared, collective unconscious the archetype of God the father and, for Jung, the central question psychology needed to answer was whether this archetype represented an 'imprint' of the God who existed beyond the psyche. He did not believe that he could ever prove this to be true, but he was in no doubt at all that the archetype of God WAS an imprint of the God who existed within. When asked on a BBC radio program whether he believed in God, Jung paused and then said "I do not believe... I know." Many who have had religious experiences feel exactly the same way. They are in no doubt that they will survive death, that life has meaning and purpose and they feel surrounded by love but they also accept that this is not something which they can prove.

CONCLUSION

Whichever model of God one is working with, the "proofs" for the existence of God attempt to demonstrate that belief in God is not the same as belief in fairies at the bottom of the garden or Santa Claus. Religious people argue that there is good reason to believe in God and that it is not an irrational view of the world. Whilst Aquinas' Five Ways do not offer what would strictly speaking be called philosophical proof it can be argued that, cumulatively, they point to a way of making sense of the Universe and the continued existence of a world which exists as a perfectly balanced harmonious system. Whilst there are other explanations for the existence of this world, and these may be held to be equally plausible – the world may just be here by chance and there may be no creator and no ultimate purpose to life – the religious believer will argue that their beliefs about the world are just as probable as any other and perhaps more probable (this is dealt with in more detail in chapter 13). They might argue that it is up to the atheist to demonstrate that belief in God is irrational or to demonstrate that there is no God. Richard Swinburne argues that the claims of those who have had religious experiences tip the balance of probability in favor of God. He appeals to two principles:

- *The Principle of Credulity – which says that things are normally what they seem to be and if it appears to a person that they are experiencing God, then – in the absence of factors like the person being unreliable, habitual liars, on drugs, etc – it is reasonable for them to believe that what they think they are experiencing they actually are experiencing, and*

- *The Principle of Testimony – which says that it is reasonable to believe reports of what people tell us.*

Swinburne's aim is to shift the burden of proof onto the skeptic to show why religious experiences should not be taken as true unless evidence is presented to the contrary. The weakness of Swinburne's argument, however, is that it depends on first establishing that there is a reasonable probability that God may exist before relying on religious experience, and assessment of probability depends very much on the individual and is exceptionally hard to justify to someone else. In the final analysis, James' argument that these experiences are authoritative for those who have them is probably decisive – for such people they will not be able to deny the reality of this experience.

St. Thomas Aquinas was in this position. After devoting his life to philosophy and theology and producing a great volume of writings, he had a mystical experience late in life and he said that, after this experience, everything he had written seemed like straw – it seemed superficial and inadequate after the depth of the experience. This is just as true today and, for those who have had religious experiences, philosophic speculation about God may have little appeal.

QUESTIONS FOR CONSIDERATION

1) If the Universe began to exist with the Big Bang, did this need a cause and, if so, what do you think it might be?

2) Is Leibniz's "Principle of Sufficient reason" plausible?

3) Could the Universe be infinite having no beginning and no end?

4) "God necessarily exists." What might this mean for an anti-realist?

5) If a very close friend of yours who you trusted completely told you that they had had a religious experience would you believe them and how would you react?

6) Do you consider that the fact that different people from different religious traditions give different descriptions of religious experience undermines the likelihood that their claims about the experiences are true?

7) Are reports of religious experience a good pointer to the existence of God?

CHAPTER 7

THE ATTRIBUTES OF GOD

Within the great monotheistic traditions of the world there are many examples of religious language at work. The God of monotheistic religious belief is a spiritual being who is supernatural, omnipotent, omniscient, and omnibenevolent. In other words God has the qualities of power, knowledge, and love to the fullest extent possible. At the same time, this God is immutable (unchanging), impassible (unable to suffer), perfect, and a judge. This picture was hand drawn in 1500[1] and shows God on his throne with Mary kneeling before him about to receive a crown. The power of God, like a great king on his throne, is clearly symbolized. The question is how God's power and God's other attributes are to be understood. These attributes are each examples of religious language and therefore are to be approached with the caution recommended in chapter 4. This chapter will explore the two key attributes of the omnipotence and omniscience of God and also what it means to talk of God as judge. It will consider the philosophical debate, that is still on-going, about how these ideas are to be understood, to what extent they are compatible and whether, philosophically, it is rationally possible to maintain this concept of God.

Dnuerte nos deus salutaris nost
et auerte iram tuam a nobis

OMNIPOTENCE

God is omnipotent. God is all powerful in the monotheistic tradition because it is claimed that God created the world out of nothing – *ex nihilo*. This means that God created the matter out of which the Universe was made and was the animating force of the whole of creation. If God creates all things, out of nothing, then it is a contradiction to say that there are things that God cannot do. There can be no limit to God's power. The Norse gods and the gods of the Greeks and the Romans were powerful, but their individual power was limited. These gods were often fighting amongst each other and no one god could hold all power. In monotheism, by contrast, there is a single god, and this God is all powerful or **omnipotent**. It is a necessary attribute of God because, unless God is all powerful, God cannot be relied on to ensure that goodness and truth triumph over evil and lies. Equally, if God is not all powerful he cannot keep his promises. There is a hope within monotheism that after this earthly life people have resurrection – only the promise of God can offer confidence that there will be an afterlife, and if God is not all powerful this promise might fail. There is also the promise of salvation and again if God is not all powerful there could be no hope that this promise would be fulfilled. If it could be shown that God is not all powerful this would be a significant challenge to monotheistic religions.

In the Hebrew scriptures, God is seen as being radically different from the idols worshiped by surrounding tribes:

- God is not more powerful than other gods, God is all powerful.
- God does not know more than other gods, God is all knowing.
- God is not wiser than other gods, God is all wise.
- God does not demand more devotion than other gods, God demands total devotion.
- God is not the most important among other gods, God is the only god.

Which model of God?

Before addressing the question of omnipotence, there is a prior issue to address which often causes confusion – which model of God are we talking about when we make claims about God's nature? As discussed in chapters 2 and 3, there are two models of God – one who is wholly simple and one who is everlasting. The everlasting God can act in time, and so to claim that the everlasting God is omnipotent does not pose any immediately obvious problems concerning his ability to do things.

However, the wholly simple God of Aquinas and of philosophy is a God who it would appear cannot act. This is because the wholly simple God cannot do

The Archbishop of Canterbury's millennium message

In 2000, the Archbishop George Carey said: **"The religious knowledge of many churchgoers is 'rather shaky'."**

Many believers have an over-simplistic understanding of God and nowhere is this more the case than in their understanding of the attributes of God.

anything. God is complete actuality with no potential and therefore he cannot act as to act means changing from having the potential to act to actually doing so and this requires time. Aquinas, having adopted the wholly simple model of God from Aristotle was aware of this problem and solved it by claiming that God acts timelessly with a single timeless act. This single timeless act of God produces temporal effects. The mistake many people make is to assume that because there is a temporal effect – for example a miracle happens and a mountain suddenly comes into existence – that God has acted in time and in space to bring about the existence of the mountain. This clearly contradicts the model of the wholly simple God who cannot act. Aquinas' response would be to claim that God did act to bring the mountain into existence but it was a part of the single timeless act of God that brought the mountain into existence. It was a timeless action with an effect in time and space. So, the wholly simple God can act and can be regarded as omnipotent, but his actions are all accomplished in one single timeless action.

OMNIPOTENT or ALMIGHTY

Both models of God can be spoken of as 'omnipotent' or all powerful but what exactly does that mean? The philosopher is going to ask for greater clarity on this. English has two words 'almighty' and 'omnipotent' and each has differ-ent connotations. 'Almighty' is a familiar word that appears in the creeds of the Church and is spoken in many prayers whilst 'omnipotent' is rather more formal and appears in theological discussions. Almighty comes from the Latin 'omnipotens' and is a Latinization of the Greek word *pantokrator*. Omnipotence comes directly from the Greek *pantokrator*. These two words, omnipotent and almighty, are linguistically clearly related but in English they are distinct. There are two words because they suggest different things and this is crucial when it comes to saying what is meant by God is "all powerful." Does it mean that God has power over all things, or does it mean that God can DO anything? Almighty is a word that suggests God has power over all things whilst omnipotence is usually understood by philosophers of religion to suggest an ability to do anything.

CAN GOD DO ANYTHING?

The claim that God can do anything gives rise to many of the questions posed by young people at school, such as: "If God is all powerful, can God make a square circle?" or "can God make a stone too heavy for God to lift?" It is not, however, only young people who raise these questions – they are still actively debated in learned journals by great philosophers. The point can be simply put:

1. *If God is all powerful then God should be able to do anything, yet*

2. *There are some things that simply do not make sense for God to be able to do.*

The difficulty with this way of formulating the problem lies in statement (1). St. Thomas Aquinas was one of many theologians who recognized this difficulty. He denies that God can do anything – there are some tasks that look as though they are tasks but actually they are 'pseudo-tasks'. These are forms of words which look as though they represent a task but in fact they are simply nonsense. Examples include:

- *A square circle (this is nonsense – a square cannot be a circle and a circle cannot be a square).*

- *A married batchelor (this is nonsense – a batchelor is an unmarried man and it is nonsense to say that an unmarried man can be a married man).*

- *A male spinster (this is nonsense – a spinster is necessarily a female and cannot be a male).*

- *A rock too heavy for an omnipotent God to lift (this is nonsense – by definition if God is omnipotent, God can do anything and there cannot be a rock that such a God cannot lift).*

It is important to recognize that Aquinas is not saying that these are tasks that God cannot do. Instead they are not even tasks at all – they are forms of words that have no content, they are nonsense and meaningless. They look as though they represent tasks but are actually empty forms of words.

Aquinas said that God can do anything, absolutely. However, what is absolutely possible means anything that does not involve a contradiction. He therefore said:

1. *God can do anything absolutely possible.*

2. *This means that God can do anything that is logically possible, anything that does not involve a contradiction.*

There are two ways in which a possible task can contradict the nature of God:

I. *If the task itself is contradictory. The first three of the above examples are logically contradictory tasks.*

II. *If the task contradicts the nature of God. The last of the above examples falls into this category.*

The second of these requires explanation. It basically means that any task cannot contradict who or what God is. For instance:

- *God could not create a being more powerful than God as this would contradict the nature of God as all powerful.*

- *If God is all powerful, God cannot make himself not powerful as then the nature of God would be contradicted (this does not, of course, prevent God choosing not to use God's power).*

This, therefore, is the definition of God adopted by most Christian theologians – God is all powerful but this means God can only do whatever is logically possible for him to do. God for Aquinas is bound by the rules of logic and cannot do things that contravene his divine nature.

Rene Descartes attempted to defend the doctrine of absolute omnipotence by maintaining that since God created the Universe, God created the laws of logic. It is a mistake, therefore, to say that God is limited by logic since if logic is created by God, God could do things which go against logic as we understand it. Many people misinterpret Descartes here. He is NOT saying that God can do the logically impossible. What he is saying is that human beings simply do not know what is and is not possible for God and that God is certainly not limited by the laws of logic that he created. For all we human beings know, God MAY be able to do things which we would regard as impossible. Descartes is therefore saying that God is so transcendent, so different from human beings that we cannot use logic to set limits on what God can do. We simply do not know what is and what is not possible for God. In many ways this is to retreat behind a claim to mystery. Descartes does not address the question of whether it would be possible for God to commit suicide, although Aquinas would say that this was a **logical** impossibility as God, being wholly simple, cannot change and to cease to exist would be a change in God. If there is anything which God could not do, such as commit suicide, then Descartes has not successfully defended the attribute of absolute omnipotence as there are still things that God cannot do. However, Descartes could reply to this by saying that all he is doing is to maintain that, given the nature of God, human knowledge is not adequate to set any limits to God's power.

RENATVS DESCARTES
GALLVS PERRONI DOMINVS, SVMMVS MATHEMATICVS ET PHILOSOP
IAGS, TVRONVM PRIDIE CALENDAS APRILES 1596, DENATVS HOLI
CALENDIS FEBRVARIIS 1650.

Scholars such as McTaggart and Hobbes would agree that God is omnipotent and that this means that God can do everything but argue that "God is omnipotent" is not to be regarded as a philosophical proposition. To try to prove that God can do everything and to understand God's omnipotence as literal and to fail to appreciate it as a piece of religious language leads to a great many tangles which the believer has no need to be ensnared by. However, this leaves the question unanswered as to what meaning can be given to 'omnipotence'.

GOD AS ALMIGHTY

If instead of thinking as philosophers do that God's omnipotence means "can do anything" we instead understand it to mean "God has power over all things" then this is far less problematic. Firstly it is recognizable as a piece of "religious language," as discussed in chapter 4, and this means that it must be seen in the context of the situation in which it is meaningful, which is a situation that is characteristically religious. It also means that within the Ian Ramsey framework it can be seen as a model with a qualifier – "mighty' is the model and 'all' is the qualifier. Once we recognize this it is clearly an example of human language and human concepts being applied in such a way that may be helpful in understanding the attributes of God, but is not literal – it is an analogy. There is a connection between human might and power and God's might and power, but to understand human might and power is only a part of the journey to understanding God's almighty nature. The proposition "God cannot do x" is true – but this does not imply a limit to God's almighty nature. What God cannot do is that which in his perfection he cannot will to do – and in God there can be no logical wedge between what he is able to do and what he wills to do since God's will and God's power are really identical. Monotheists must believe that God is almighty but that does not mean that they must believe that what this means is that he can do everything. It is not possible for God to break his own word – which is logically possible, it is not possible for God to lie, it is not possible for God to commit suicide, it is not possible for God to create something that is too heavy for himself to lift, God cannot change. There are things that God cannot do. In fact P.T. Geach[2] argues that when Aquinas defends God's omnipotence it is clear that, as we have seen above, he does not understand omnipotence to mean that "God can do anything." Rather omnipotence for Aquinas means that God can do anything that is not excluded by logic or his nature. This means that Aquinas is not defending God's absolute omnipotence, instead he is defending God as almighty.

God as 'all-mighty' is a meaningful analogy and a concept that arguably requires a certain level of perception to understand – God is not just more powerful than any creature; no creature can compete with God in terms of power, for God as creator is the source of all power. All creatures come from God and all creatures are maintained for only the span God wills. In heaven and on Earth God does whatever he wills. God is almighty means that God as creator has power over all things, as creator. It is a statement which is made from within a faith commitment and does not involve the philosophical problems of 'omnipotent' which if understood literally – as it is within Philosophy of Religion – can be taken to mean "able to do anything," which as Aquinas has demonstrated, is not meaningful.

OMNIPOTENCE/ALMIGHTY GOD AND THE PROBLEM OF THE INCARNATION

It has been argued that whether God is regarded as wholly simple and almighty or omnipotent there are things that God cannot do. God cannot, for example, be subject to any power as he created all power, nor can God as the creator and sustainer of all life die. Logically this means that God cannot have a body as he would then be limited by the flesh, he cannot feel tired, get angry, feel pain, or die. Where does this leave the Christian doctrine of the

Incarnation? According to Christian belief God did take a body "And the Word became flesh" (John 1.14), and as a human being God did feel tired, did feel anger and compassion, did feel pain, and did die. This objection says that there are things within the Christian tradition that God has already done that if he is wholly simple are against his nature. When God became flesh he became subject to the powers of time, space, the powers of logic, the powers of other human beings, the limits of life, and ultimately he died. All these things contradict his all mighty, all powerful nature. Since the Christian tradition maintains that God did these things it is incoherent at the same time to claim that God is omnipotent.

Aquinas would have replied that God did become man, so God can become man and have a body: but God AS God cannot be man or have a body. The logic of this is problematic but it is not uncommon to find this sort of language in use today. We might say that Fred gets a salary as a teacher and an expense account as town mayor. He is always a teacher and always the mayor but signs some checks as Fred the teacher and some checks as Fred the major. Fred is the same person but can be talked of as having two roles. Hence we can talk of Christ as man and Christ as God. Christ as God cannot have a body and cannot be subject to the flesh and cannot die, but Christ as man was able to do these things.

OMNISCIENCE

Freedom

If God knows that you will get married or remarried in 8 years' time and knows when the marriage will take place are you free to choose not to do this? This is complicated by two different ideas of what is meant by "human freedom."

Either:

A. *Human beings are totally determined by genetics, social conditioning, and other factors and although they may think they are free, in actual fact they have no real freedom at all. This is called LIBERTY OF SPONTANEITY and is discussed in more detail in chapter 11 of* The Thinker's Guide to Evil,[3] *or*

B. *Human beings, although influenced by their genetics, social conditioning, and other factors, have a measure of non-determined freedom. This is called "LIBERTY OF INDIFFERENCE."*

Randomness seems to lie at the heart of the Universe

If human beings only have liberty of spontaneity then, although they think that they are free, in fact this is due to their ignorance and they are actually completely determined. Many psychologists maintain this view and see freedom as an illusion. However, this is based on a Newtonian idea of a "clockwork" Universe and we now know that the Universe is not like this. Chaos and randomness operate at the fundamental particle level and the idea of human beings actually being rather like program robots is highly unlikely as well, of course, as running directly counter to ideas of morality which assume non-determined freedom. However, if humans are genuinely free, then the whole issue of whether God can know what human beings will do in their future arises.

The claim that "God is omniscient" means that God knows everything. God is all knowing and all wise and knows all that is true. God knows the truths of mathematics and of logic, God knows all empirical truths such as how many leaves on each tree and how many fleas on a particular dog as well as the heart and mind of every person. The attribute of being all knowing is essential for monotheistic religions as God's justice depends on it. God cannot be just if God does not know everything. To be just, God needs to know all things – the true motives in a person's heart and his or her secret desires, as well as the individual's potential and the limits that every person works within. Omniscience means that nothing can be kept secret from God. This is vital as unless God knows everything his judgment may be unjust. Even if in this life the righteous suffer, the attribute of omniscience guarantees the believer that in the afterlife there will be justice.

The philosophical problem with the claim that God is omniscient arises from the question of whether this means that God can know things that have not yet happened. Can God know the future? If God can then, it is argued, human beings have no freedom and can never choose to take one path over another because the path they take is already known by God. They cannot choose to do other than that which is known by God. If people have no freewill and cannot choose between good and evil then no person may be held responsible for their behavior, because their choices were determined. If God is omniscient, the evil and suffering done by one human being to another becomes the direct fault of God. Within the great monotheistic religions of the world the claim that God is omnipotent and that humans have freewill to choose between good or evil are foundational claims. Philosophical reflection on the claim that God is omniscient results in an apparent contradiction that threatens some of the basic claims of monotheism.

This needs further examination with respect to two of the models of God with which we have been dealing and secondly by a consideration of what is meant by human freedom. The two models of God are:

1. *God as wholly simple, outside time and space (see chapter 2), and*

2. *God as everlasting and therefore in time (see chapter 3).*

The wholly simple God and omniscience

If God is wholly simple, outside time and space, then God knows all that has happened, all that is happening, and all that will happen. St. Augustine explains this with the following illustration in which the road is a metaphor for time:

"... he who goes along the road does not see those who come after him; whereas he who sees the whole road from a height sees at once all those travelling on it."

In other words to us on the road of time things appear to happen one after another and we cannot see the things that come after us – in other words we cannot see into the future because we are limited by our perspective of time. But God, for St. Augustine, is outside of time and is therefore like the person looking down on the road. God can see everyone on the road, both those who have gone before us and those who come after us. To a person on the road, some people will be in front of them and some people behind them but for God it is not like this. God, being outside time, can see all moments in time – the whole history of the Universe – at once. To human beings who are within time, some things are in the past and some things are in the future – your parents and grandparents are in the past and your children and grand children are in the future. God, however, sees all events at once and so the future is known to God, but it is not known to God as the 'future', that is a human perspective on time from our place in time. What is the future to us is known to God as one eternal now. For Aquinas,

"The present glance of God extends over all time."[4]
"Things reduced to actuality in time are known by us successively in time, but by God they are known in eternity, which is above time."

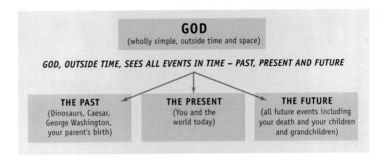

On this basis, the wholly simple God can know everything and is omniscient but this leaves the issue of human freewill with a problem: if God KNOWS what you will do in the future, are you free? There are two alternatives here. Either:

1. God KNOWING what will happen in your future causes the events to happen. It is not because the events will happen that causes God to foreknow them – **it is God's knowledge that causes them to happen.** This was how Aquinas understood the knowledge of God:

"For the knowledge of God is to all creatures what the knowledge of the maker is to things made by his art… the form in the intellect must be the principle of action."[5]

In other words Aquinas maintains that just as an artist or sculptor needs to have the knowledge of his creation before the image or sculpture is made, so God's knowledge as creator of all things is the source of all things. God's knowledge is therefore the cause of all things. Our knowledge of things depends on the world around us providing us with the stimulus for understanding, but God's knowledge is not like this. God is the creator of all things in the natural world and it was his knowledge that brought it into existence in the first place. It cannot be that things in the natural world therefore are the source of God's knowledge, since God's knowledge is the cause of all things. This is rather like saying that when Giovanni made Pinnochio his knowledge of the puppet was needed for the puppet to come into being. Without Giovanni's knowledge there would have been no Pinnochio. So far, there is no problem. However, Aquinas takes the analogy farther and is effectively saying that once the puppet was made, Giovanni as his maker remained the cause of all Pinnochio's actions. Nothing Pinnochio did informed Giovanni of Pinnochio's actions – Giovanni knew already and it was Giovanni's knowledge of the events that caused Pinnochio to do them. This is a further step in the argument which demonstrates the philosophical problem with the attribute of omniscience. IF Giovanni's knowledge had been the cause of all Pinnochio's actions then we would have to say that Pinnochio was not free – and not a real boy because of this. It is surely because Pinnochio was able to act freely and able to rebel against his maker that he was a real boy. The fact that Giovanni could do nothing to control Pinnochio's choices guarantees Pinnochio's freewill and underpins the claim that he is a "real boy" and not a puppet. IF he is only a puppet then he is neither free nor responsible for his behavior. Equally IF God's knowledge causes things to happen then human beings are not free. The attribute of omniscience then leads, logically to PREDESTINATION – the idea that God determines everything. In Islam this idea is strong – everything is held to happen by the will of Allah. Some Christians (for instance Calvinists) hold this position and consider that God predestines some people for heaven and some people for hell. John Calvin wrote:

"When we attribute foreknowledge to God, we mean that all things have ever been and perpetually remain before his eyes so that to his knowledge nothing is future or past but all things are present.... he holds and sees them as if actually placed before him."[6]

Calvin is claiming that God knew the outcome of every single human action from the beginning of time. In saying this he is in line with the major traditions of the Church. In the *City of God* Augustine writes:

"For to confess God exists and at the same time to deny that He has foreknowledge of future things is the most manifest folly... One who is not prescient of all future things is not God."[7]

However, the problem with this view is that, if it is accepted, human beings are not free. For nearly 1700 years theologians and philosophers have wrestled with this problem and, although various solutions have been proposed, none really works. Augustine argues that if you have a friend who is known very well to you, you may know that he is about to sin. Your knowledge does not cause him to sin. "Similarly God compels no man to sin though he sees beforehand those who are going to sin by their own will."[8] God's foreknowledge and the foreknowledge of the friend are however qualitatively different. Human foreknowledge can be wrong – that is part of being human. However, God's foreknowledge cannot be wrong, as he is perfect in his omniscience unlike a human person. Since the sinful actions of the friend are voluntary it might be argued that the 'knowledge' that he/she will sin is nothing more than an intuition, whereas God's knowledge is not.

2. The second alternative is that put forward by a major, modern Jesuit theologian, Gerard Hughes[9] who accepts that Aquinas' solution fails and that it leads to determinism. Hughes therefore proposes the alternative that human actions CAUSE God to know what happens. In this case freedom is guaranteed. It is your free choices that cause God to know. God still knows the past, present, and future but God knows because God timelessly sees all that is happening – God timelessly sees the whole of time but he knows what happens because it happens.

The alternatives of Aquinas and Hughes can be put as follows:

1. *Aquinas effectively says: "If God knows that X happens, then X happens because God knows it."*

Whereas:

2. *Hughes effectively says: "Whatever happens, God knows that it happens because it happens."*

Hughes' alternative seems the only way forward but Peter Vardy in *The Puzzle of God* (HarperCollins) has argued, in agreement with Aquinas, that this position is inconsistent with God's simplicity as it means that God depends on human beings for God's knowledge. God can no longer be regarded as a unity if God's knowledge is not identical to God's other attributes, which is essential in the wholly simple model of God, adopted by Aquinas. This sounds more complicated than it is. If God's knowledge is dependent on human beings then God's knowledge is not fixed in eternity but subject to events in TIME. If God's knowledge is dependent on the free choices of human beings God's knowledge depends on God timelessly seeing what happens. This means that God's knowledge is dependent on a decision made in space and time. God's knowledge is still immutable since God sees the whole of time in one timeless act of awareness. This, as we have seen, preserves freedom but at the expense (if Peter Vardy's argument is right) of compromising this model of God to such a degree that it becomes incoherent.

The everlasting God and omniscience

The second model of God therefore needs to be considered. If God is everlasting and therefore in time, then time passes for God just as time passes for human beings. God knows all events in the past and everything that is happening in the present. God also knows all factors which will determine the future. There is a famous hymn which says:

"A thousand ages in his sights are but an evening gone..."

On this basis the future is future to God, but time does not dominate God in the way time dominates the short lives of human beings. Nevertheless events that are in the future to us are also in the future for God. If this is the case, then we are free and God sees our free actions. However, God cannot know the future – the future is genuinely open both to us and to God. It is we human beings who must decide how to act and we human beings who must decide what sort of people we wish to become. God, of course, knows everything we do and everything we decide, but God respects our freedom.[10] However, the major problem is that God does not know the future. Of course, God knows each individual exceptionally well and can predict what will happen in the future, but this is not the same as knowledge. This is the solution proposed by Richard Swinburne when he claims that God's omniscience means that God knows all that it is logically possible to know – and he goes on to say that this does not include the future. It is logically impossible, given human freedom, for God to know the future.

This pictures fits in well with the idea of chaos and randomness at the fundamental particle level in the Universe. The future is genuinely open but within limits set by God's creation and it is within this open Universe that human beings have evolved to be creatures who can choose to respond to God or not, who can choose to develop into people of compassion, love, and gentleness or who can choose to reject this path. God values and cherishes this human freedom because only in freedom can true love be possible.

GOD AS JUDGE

The traditional view of God is that God is not only a loving father, omnipotent and omniscient but also that God is a Judge who will review the lives of all those who live on Earth and, after death, will consign some to heaven and some to hell. The idea of God as a wrathful and angry God has, at times, been strong in Christianity, Islam, and Judaism. This idea is particularly strong in the Hebrew scriptures where God punishes disobedience through many generations. King Saul died and lost his kingdom because of his disobedience to God, the disobedience of the people of Israel was held to have resulted in God causing the Babylonians to destroy their King, their city (Jerusalem), the Temple of God in Jerusalem, and to take off into captivity many of the leaders of the southern kingdom.[11]

In Van Eyck's picture of the Last Judgment, God sits on his throne surrounded by angels and the elect who have been gathered into heaven whilst below him, guarded by a fierce warrior angel, is the realm of hell where pain and suffering take place without end. This picture, with God like a Judge on his throne, dominated much Christian thought in the Middle Ages and sermons threatened the dreadful judgment of God on everyone who was a sinner or disobeyed the commands of the Church.

The Franciscan tradition and Protestant thinkers, however, stressed much more strongly the centrality of the love of God. God, according to St. Bonaventure, is like a lover who lures people toward God by the beauty in the world. Protestant theologians saw God's free gift of grace enabling people to be saved. Everyone was a sinner – human beings were loved by God as they were and not because they were good or righteous. God simply wanted people to accept and acknowledge this love.

Today, the emphasis on God as judge by many theologians is much reduced and instead some hold that each individual has to judge him or herself. In life each person has constant choices to make and, in a real sense, has to "make themselves." Some choose lives of selfishness, self-centredness, greed, and

Judgment in the Gospels

"Stop judging, that you may not be judged." (Matt. 7.1)

"Stop condemning and you will not be condemned. Forgive and you will be forgiven." (Luke 6.37)

"And even if I should judge, my judgment is valid, because I am not alone, but it is I and the Father who sent me." (John 8.16)

"I do not seek my own glory; there is one who seeks it and he is the one who judges." (John 8.50)

"Whoever rejects me and does not accept my words has something to judge him: the word that I spoke, it will condemn him on the last day." (John 12.48)

Van Eyck's picture of the Last Judgment

Parable of the sheep and goats

"All the nations will be assembled before him. And he will separate them one from another, as a shepherd separates the sheep from the goats. He will place the sheep on his right and the goats on his left. Then the king will say to those on his right, 'Come, you who are blessed by my Father. Inherit the kingdom prepared for you from the foundation of the world. For I was hungry and you gave me food, I was thirsty and you gave me drink, a stranger and you welcomed me, naked and you clothed me, ill and you cared for me, in prison and you visited me.' Then the righteous will answer him and say, 'Lord, when did we see you hungry and feed you, or thirsty and give you drink? When did we see you a stranger and welcome you, or naked and clothe you? When did we see you ill or in prison, and visit you?' And the king will say to them in reply, 'I say to you, whatever you did for one of these least brothers of mine, you did for me.' Then he will say to those on his left, 'Depart from me, you accursed, into the eternal fire prepared for the devil and his angels. For I was hungry and you gave me no food, I was thirsty and you gave me no drink, a stranger and you gave me no welcome, naked and you gave me no clothing, ill and in prison, and you did not care for me.' Then they will answer and say, 'Lord, when did we see you hungry or thirsty or a stranger or naked or ill or in prison, and not minister to your needs?' He will answer them, 'I say to you, what you did not do for one of these least ones, you did not do for me.' And these will go off to eternal punishment, but the righteous to eternal life." (Matt. 25.32–46)

power as well as a denial of love, compassion, and gentleness and these people create themselves into beings who cannot stand being loved and, by their choices, exile themselves from God. They would simply not wish to be in a state where love dominates. Others, by contrast, choose the path of self-sacrifice, of love, compassion, and care for others even though this may mean putting their own interests and those of their families and friends into second place. There are passages in the Christian Gospels that support this approach – for instance John's Gospel records Jesus as saying: *"Whoever rejects me and does not accept my words has something to judge him: the word that I spoke, it will condemn him on the last day" (John 12.48)*. This implies that the individual will be confronted by Jesus' teaching and this will condemn him or her.

The theme of God as judge who will condem some to hell and reward others with entry to heaven is, however, strongly mitigated in the Christian tradition by the even more important theme of the forgiveness of God. God in the New Testament is portrayed as a loving father, always willing to forgive people and to forgive again, again, and yet again. This is, possibly, the central theme of the Gospels and it gives rise to a central idea in C.S. Lewis' Narnia stories.

Narnia, Aslan, and the White Witch

The Narnia stories feature four children (Peter, Susan, Lucy, and Edmund) who initially enter the magical word of Narnia through the back of a wardrobe in their uncle's house. In this kingdom is a great lion, Aslan, who represents the figure of Jesus. Aslan appears at key moments in the history of Narnia and all who are good, considerate, and motivated by concern for others are on Aslan's side. However, there is a White Witch who opposes Aslan. She persuades Edmund to become a traitor to his friends and to Aslan by giving him some magical Turkish Delight and he will do anything to get more of this. He lies and deceives – and is very human in that he wants his own ends and has made a choice to follow the White Witch.

The Deep Magic of Narnia, put into Narnia by the Emperor over the Seas (who in the story represents God), is that any traitor deserves to die and belongs to the White Witch. The White Witch accordingly orders Edmund's death. Edmund can do nothing. He is rightly condemned and has no power. Edmund has lived to suit himself. Edmund deserves to die and is rightly condemned to death and Aslan accepts this (he is in the role of a judge who carries out the sentence the law requires). Aslan, as judge, condemns Edmund but then offers to take his place and to die in Edmund's place. The White Witch is delighted as Aslan has always been her greatest enemy.

Before Aslan's death he talks to Edmund, and although the conversation is not recorded in the book it is clear that Edmund knows he has done wrong and bitterly regrets it. Aslan is killed and the White Witch is triumphant. All Narnia is plunged into despondency and hope seems extinguished. However, what the White Witch and Aslan's friends are unaware of is that there is a Deeper Magic, also put into Narnia by the Emperor over the Sea. This says that if an innocent person dies in place of a traitor, then the altar will crack and death will work backwards. By the Deep Magic, Aslan rises again because he is innocent and has given his life for a traitor.

In this story the picture of judgment is complex. Edmund stands judged because he became imprisoned by his own wishes. His life lived for himself represented being a traitor to Aslan. He had no power to save himself and according to the magic of Narnia was rightly condemned.

Within the monotheistic traditions of the world this is how judgment is seen. God has laid down "rules" by which a person must live their life and breaking these rules results in judgment.

C.S. Lewis however gives an illustration of the particular notion of judgment within the Christian tradition. In the story Aslan can take the place of Edmund, and because he is innocent will not himself die. The "sin of Edmund" is therefore paid for and justice is accomplished, but Aslan does not die, as hoped for by the White Witch, because he is innocent. In the Christian tradition Jesus, as an innocent man, is believed to have paid the price of all the wrongdoings of believers. Justice is accomplished but the believer does not have to face judgment because Jesus paid the price for their wrong acts.

The Jewish rabbinic tradition

The rabbinic tradition tells of God saying about forgiveness: "Open for me one gate of repentance as wide as a needle and I will open for you gates wide enough to drive carriages through."

Christianity portrays God as a judge but also as a father – as Judge, humans stand condemned but since the Judge is also Father he takes on himself the punishment which is why forgiveness is so important. This is why God is portrayed in Christianity as both a loving Father and also as a Judge – the two are in no way incompatible.

Notes

[1] *This picture is from Horae ad usum Parisiensem (The hours according to the usage of Paris). Paris: produced by Thielman Kerver for Guillaume Eustace, 20th June 1500. This forms part of the collection in Heythrop College, University of London.*

[2] *Peter Geach Omnipotence Ch1 Providence and Evil CUP 1977.*

[3] *By Peter Vardy and Julie Arliss. John Hunt Publishing 2003.*

[4] The knowledge of God. Summa Theologica.

[5] The knowledge of God. Summa Theologica *Part 1 Question 14 Aquinas.*

[6] *John Calvin* Institutes of the Christian Religion *Bk lll Ch xxi Philadelphia, 1813.*

[7] City of God *Book V Sec 9.*

[8] *De Libero Arbitrio.*

[9] *Master of Campion Hall, Oxford, previously Vice-Principal of Heythrop College, University of London. He explores these ideas in his book* The Nature of God *(Routledge) which is one of the finest modern books on the attributes of God but it not easy to follow for those who have not read a reasonable amount of philosophy.*

[10] *This fits in well with the Irenean approach to the problem of evil – see* The Thinker's Guide to Evil *by Peter Vardy and Julie Arliss, John Hunt Publishing 2003.*

[11] *After Solomon, the Kingdom of Israel split into two – a northern and a southern kingdom. The northern kingdom was conquered quite quickly but for hundreds of years the southern kingdom, with Jerusalem as its capital, survived until it was destroyed by the Babylonians. The Book of Jeremiah prophesies the destruction of Jerusalem by God because of the wickedness of its people.*

QUESTIONS FOR CONSIDERATION

1) Do you consider the definition of omnipotence given by St. Thomas Aquinas or Rene Descartes to be the more plausible?

2) What are the difficulties in maintaining that God is wholly simple and that human beings are free?

3) Is the approach of St. Thomas Aquinas or that of Gerard Hughes more plausible in explaining the relation between God's knowledge and human actions?

4) If God cannot know the future, would this significantly limit the concept of God? If so, would this matter?

5) What role does the idea of God as judge have in the understanding of most religious believers today? Is it possible to combine this idea with a God of love?

CHAPTER 8

LIFE AFTER DEATH

L ife after death is an ancient human belief. Humans have revered the dead, buried them in ceremonies and reflected on the hereafter for thousands of years. All of the world's major religions believe in life after death. How coherent are these claims philosophically? In the 21st century some argue that it is time to say goodbye to these primitive notions. This chapter will trace ideas about life after death in some of the most ancient civilizations before exploring the development of beliefs in some of the world's religions today. Finally a way forward will be suggested which takes seriously the criticism made of historical approaches.

PLATONIC DUALISM

PSYCHE was the Greek word for the principle of life and, in the opinion of the Greek philosopher Thales, it was PSYCHE that allowed a body to move itself rather than being simply inanimate matter. The PSYCHE is the breath or soul of life (in the Hebrew scriptures God breathes life into the first human person). In Latin, this is the ANIMUS or soul and is the place where the passions, desire, and will are located. These ideas may well have had an influence on perhaps the earliest view of what it is to be a person – namely that developed in Greek philosophy by Socrates and Plato.

Plato thought of a human person as being like a charioteer with two horses. The charioteer represents human reason and the two horses represent the emotions and the desires of a person. The only way to live a well balanced life is to control the passions and the emotions with reason. The rational mind is the part of a human person that is distinctive and for Plato it is this that

Death of Socrates

survives death. The rational principle is the 'real me' and survives the body at death. The soul inhabits a body but the soul itself is eternal. On death the soul departs from the body and contemplates the Forms (see ch. 1) before entering another body. This is known as SUBSTANCE DUALISM: the body and soul are separate but they interact. The soul is a "spiritual substance" – by which is meant that it can exist on its own (it is therefore a substance) but it is not a material substance. In an account of Socrates' death,[1] recorded by Plato, Socrates was about to drink the cup containing the poison hemlock when one of his friends, Crito asked him: "In what fashion are we to bury you?" but Socrates laughed and replied:

"He imagines that I am that dead body he will see in a little while.... But... when I drink the poison I shall no longer remain with you, but shall go off and depart for some happy state of the blessed..." (Phaedo)

It is not clear whether these are the words of Socrates or whether this is Plato placing here in the mouth of Socrates his own ideas about the immortality of the soul. If the body dies, which it clearly does, what is it that survives death? Whatever it is would need to be disembodied and not depend on the body. This Plato calls the soul. It is clear from the texts that not everyone, even in the time of Socrates and Plato, accepted these ideas. Plato records that Simmias, who was a friend of Socrates, argued with him about his ideas of the immortal soul. Simmias used the image of a lyre to show that the soul and the body could relate to each other as a lyre relates to its tuning. The tuning is invisible and non-physical but it does not outlast or exist apart from the lyre. Simmias' conclusion was that the idea of life after death was not necessary to explain human nature. This view, which today would be expressed by saying that mental states are a product of bodily states, was unacceptable for Plato who wished to maintain the soul's separate existence although in the text Socrates does not provide any convincing argument against Simmias' view.

ARISTOTLE

Aristotle talked of soul and body but what he meant by these was completely different to what Plato meant. The difference between Plato and Aristotle in their ideas about life after death is confusing because they use the same words but mean quite different things by them. Aristotle rejected dualism. The soul for Aristotle is the form or the pattern of a thing. The form is the blueprint of a thing that makes it what it is or what it will become once it realizes its potential. A tadpole has the potential to be a frog and the frog has the potential to move, communicate with other frogs, and to reproduce – talk of the soul of a tadpole is to talk of the potential it has to do these things. Talk of a soul, for Aristotle, is talk about what makes a thing what it is and about what potentialities it has. Everything is made up of soul or form, and matter. Matter is what makes a thing up, but soul or form is the specification that makes it what it is. Human beings are made up of matter, but the specification of what a human is, is the soul or form of a human being. For Aristotle, soul or form cannot be separated from matter. Anything needs matter to make it what it is but matter needs the soul, form, or specification to define what makes the thing what it is.

It is important to recognize that we do not have all Aristotle's original texts – some have been lost. There is a small fragment in Aristotle which appears to indicate that he did think that a human soul, unlike the soul of anything else, could separate on death. This is a disputed text and is not universally accepted as Aristotle's view.

IDEAS OF LIFE AFTER DEATH IN ANCIENT EGYPT

The idea of life after death has an ancient history pre-dating the world of Greek philosophy. Bronze Age human beings buried their dead with reverence and the rituals they performed give every indication that they believed in life after death. However, the Egyptian belief in life after death was, perhaps, the beginnings of a more systematic formulation of ideas of what post-mortem experience might be like. Egyptians initially began with the belief that the Pharaoh would survive death, but this developed into the belief that rich Lords would also rise from the dead and finally it came to be believed that everyone would live on after death. The Egyptians considered that human beings were made up of at least five elements of which one was the **Ka**. The Ka can be thought of as something like a shadow of a human being. It was a spiritual or astral double that accompanied the person through life but it could exist without the body. The Ka was not fully a complete person but it was the part of the person that survived death. The Ka required feeding after death and food was therefore left in the tombs but the Ka did not feed on the food itself but rather on the **Kwa** or "essence" of the food. The food, therefore, appeared to be untouched but this did not rule out the Ka feeding on its essence. The Ka could not survive if the physical body was destroyed, hence the Egyptian efforts to mummify and preserve the bodies of the dead.[2] Of the five elements of a person the Ka and the **Ba** were the most important and these were united on death. The Ba is represented as a human headed bird which leaves the person on death and the face of the bird is the face of the person who died. (The Papyrus of Ani pictures the Ka/Ba hovering over the mummified body of the dead person.) The most interesting part of this idea is that the Ka was a spiritual double – very different to the idea of a soul but this could be of interest in modern discussions of near-death experiences.

The Papyrus of Ani

BUDDHISM AND REINCARNATION

Christianity, Islam, and Judaism all teach that a human being is born once, lives a single life, and then dies and what happens after this single death is the result of what a person has done or failed to do in this single life – albeit with assistance from the grace of God. Buddhism, by contrast, teaches that most human beings have lived many previous lives and will live many more lives in the future. Everyone is on the great wheel of life with birth and death following each other in a continuous circular motion. Most people do not remember their past lives and the life a person is born into now is directly related, through the law of Karma, to the previous lives a person has lived.

Buddhism teaches that the first requirement is for each individual to become aware, for him or herself, of the inevitabilty of death and then to come to recognize the Great Wheel of Life and the inevitability of reincarnation.

Death is the temporary end of a temporary span on Earth – indeed central to Buddhism is the idea that everything is temporary, everything changes. Death is inevitable and it is essential to prepare for it throughout life.

A radio set can transmit a signal which can be picked up by a radio receiver next door, in a neighboring country, or on the other side of the world. So on death, the individual's "life principle" (in western terms this might be regarded as the soul) leaves a body on death and comes into another body. This can be instantaneous or there can be a gap of months, years, or even centuries between the death of one body and reincarnation in another.

The Buddha taught that, even in this life, most human minds are uncontrolled. They flit about between one thing and another and most people do not take the time and trouble to train their minds. We are not our minds – our minds can control our brains and our bodies but for our minds to be able to do this they need training. This training is long and hard and it is for this reason that meditation is so central in Buddhism – it is through meditation that Buddhists see human beings as able to control their minds rather than darting about after the latest distraction. If a mind has developed no control, then after death it will have no control either – it will easily be able to be absorbed by any body and can then begin a regress down the chain of being.

The Buddhist argues that it is essential to prepare for death. Instead of death being something that is never talked about, it should be freely and willingly accepted as an inevitable part of life. Once we accept death and prepare to greet it as part of life, then the power of death to produce fear will be undermined and destroyed. As Montaigne said:

"To practice death is to practice freedom. A man who has learned how to die has unlearned how to be a slave."

This fits in perfectly with the Buddhist claim – freedom from fear of death means that life can be embraced in a new and far more positive manner. The person who has prepared for death, who can actively "live through" their death and not be frightened by the experience will be sufficiently "recollected" to be able to control their identity after death and to make choices about the body into which they will be reincarnated next. As an example, the Dalai Lama has said that when he dies he will choose not to be reincarnated into a baby born in Tibet – because Tibet is under Chinese control and therefore he could not continue to practice as a Buddhist. However, this type of choice can only be exercised by someone with a high level of control and this may take many lives to develop.

Once we prepare for death then all those things that cause human beings so much concern and suffering in the world will be renounced. Material possessions or appearance will simply no longer matter. Instead there will develop a tremendous compassion for every other person since every other person is like us – destined for death. What matters more than anything else is to help them awake from their ignorance and to see their true state clearly and then to start on their own journey of meditation and controlling their minds ready for their own deaths. For the Buddhist, to learn how to die is to learn how to live and this is why some great Buddhist Masters will ask a visitor who comes to see them "do you believe in a life after death?" They do this because someone who does have this belief will live their life differently and see their life differently from those who believe that this life is all that there is.

Death, therefore, needs to become a friend – something which one is aware of every day and which one chooses to think about actively. Then, when death comes, it will not take the individual by surprise.

In response to the charge that no one can prove reincarnation, the Buddhist will point to the countless thousands of people who

Death

Everyone will die and death is something everyone has to face alone – even if friends or family may be close by. In death, possessions and appearance do not matter at all. Often death is painful and many people are frightened when death approaches as they have not thought about death or prepared for death. Death can come unexpectedly when a person is in perfect health through accident or an act of violence; it can also come in old age and after prolonged illness. We cannot know when it will come, but its coming is inevitable. Plato said that philosophers should "practice dying" and, in Christianity, Orthodox monks often keep their coffins in their rooms to remind them of death. Peter Vardy keeps his coffin in his office at the University of London.

can remember their past lives. Someone who is a closet verificationist and insists on physical evidence will be simply and gently dismissed by Buddhists – clearly the self that is reincarnated is not a physical thing. This, they might say, is like denying the reality of radio waves because one cannot see them inside a radio set.

DUALISM AND LIFE AFTER DEATH

The ideas about life after death traced above depend on certain ideas about what it is to be a human person. Platonic, and ancient Egyptian ideas about life after death depend on the view that humans are made of body and soul and that these are in some way distinct. The entity that survives death is the spiritual part of a human person. This is known as **dualism**. Aristotle's position, however, is different. He maintains that a person's soul and body are inseparable. This is known as **monism**.

Islam and Christianity both acknowledge the massive influence of Judaism on their own origins but each, equally, has been influenced by a range of other ideas.

Life after death in Judaism, Christianity, and Islam

The most ancient biblical accounts record that there was no specific belief in a life after death. The early Hebrews believed that they lived on only in their children – which was why lack of children was considered to be such a disaster. The development of a concept of life after death can be seen emerging in the book of Job, and it is clearly held by some by the time of the book of Daniel and 1 and 2 Maccabees. In these accounts life after death is viewed in terms of the person being given a new body after death which could feel pleasure or pain. The quality of life lived in the afterlife depended on the quality of life lived on Earth. This view influenced the development of Christian and Muslim thinking and these religions also maintain that there is a life after death in which the individual is judged and lives again in some kind of body that has the capacity to experience sensations.[3] There are still Jews today who reject belief in personal survival of death. In Christianity, however, the accounts of Jesus rising from the dead are central to Christian belief, and belief in life after death is accepted by almost all Christians. In Islam the claimed dictation of the Qu'ran to the prophet, Muhammed, includes teachings about life after death and this belief is, therefore, central for Muslims.

Philosophical questions concerning claims about life after death

What does it mean to say that a person rises from the dead? According to Christians, Jesus died on the cross and his dead body was placed in an empty tomb. After three days, this same dead body came to life once more and Jesus appeared to his disciples looking the same as before he died – indeed one of his disciples, Thomas, would not believe in the resurrection until he saw the mark of the spear in Jesus' side and the marks of the nails in his hands and his feet. Jesus rose from the dead and could be seen living, eating, and breathing in full bodily form. After quite a short time, the New Testament records that Jesus ascended into heaven – again in bodily form. Jesus is the only example in history

The Ascension *by Rembrandt*

of this.[4] The picture by Rembrandt of the ascension shows Jesus rising in bodily form to heaven – this is in accordance with a literal reading of the biblical text. However, few theologians today interpret the text in this way.

Some modern philosophers ask, even if Jesus did rise and ascend as described, what it would mean for other human beings to have "life after death" given that their bodies do not survive in the way Jesus' is claimed to have done. Human bodies after death either rot in the grave or are cremated. Unlike the case of Jesus, our bodies will cease to exist – so what sense can be given to the idea of resurrection? What is more, there seem to be real questions about where any resurrected life would be lived and what the identity criteria would be that made the person who died the same person as the one who was resurrected.

Rene Descartes, a leading French philosopher and a brilliant mathematician tried to address some of these problems. Writing nearly 2000 years after Plato and Socrates, in his *Meditation* 11 and V1, Descartes presents one of the best known arguments in support of the dualist position on life after death.

"My essence consists solely in the fact that I am a thinking thing. It is true that I may have (or, to anticipate, that I certainly have) a body that is very closely joined to me. But nevertheless, on the one hand I have a clear and distinct idea of myself, in so far as I am simply a non-extended thinking thing, and on the other hand I have a distinct idea of body, in so far as this is simply an extended non-thinking thing. And accordingly, it is certain that I am really distinct from my body and can exist without it." (Meditation 6, 54)

Descartes effectively argues that as he considers himself to be a thinking thing, then this is what he must be. Descartes considered that he could think of himself without a body but he could not deny that he was a thinking thing – as the body can be doubted and the soul cannot, it follows that the body and the soul cannot be one and the same. The flaw in this argument was effectively pointed out by Brian Davies OP who argues that the fact that I consider myself to be sober does not mean that I am sober. To put it more precisely, Norman Malcolm challenges Descartes' view as follows:

"If it were valid to argue 'I can doubt that my body exists but not that I exist, ergo I am not my body,' it would be equally valid to argue 'I can doubt that there exists a being whose essential nature is to think, but I cannot doubt that I exist, ergo I am not a being whose essential nature is to think.' Descartes is hoist with his own petard." ('Descartes' proof that his Essence is Thinking' in the book edited by W. Doney)

If there is no philosophical justification for claims to the existence of a thing called a "soul" is the concept of a soul coherent? **What sort of existence can a disembodied soul have?**

It is not clear what it would mean for a soul (if there is such a thing) to survive death. A soul which did not inhabit a body would have no means of movement, no brain with which to think, no sensory equipment with which to communicate or to relate to others. H.H. Price has attempted to address some of these issues. Price seeks to consider whether any meaning can be attached to the expression "discarnate human personality." He maintains that "it is easy enough to conceive that experiences might occur after one's death which are linked with experiences before death in such a way that personal identity is preserved." The problem is what sort of experiences these would be.

Price maintains that post-mortem perceptions might be broadly similar to 'experiences' in dreams. In sleep, our image producing powers provide us with a multitude of objects which can be the focus of our dreams and even our desires. A world, he maintains, formed out of such mental images which had been acquired during bodily life could include images of our own bodies and perceptions of the world we have experienced during life and which would be available after death through memory. The image world would be just as real as the world experienced in bodily life. Price sees no reason to suppose that images should not be tactile, auditory, and smell images within a 3-dimensional world. We would, effectively, have carried our world with us in our memory. We would 'exist', then, in a dream world of our creation – effectively we would be locked into a heaven or hell of our own making dependent on our experiences on Earth. The world inhabited would not be a physical world as we presently understand it, but then the post-mortem self would not be a physical self. Effectively, the post-mortem self would learn much about the world of his or her desires. As Price says:

"Each man's purgatory would just be the automatic consequences of his own desires."

The image world inhabited by the post-mortem self would not need to be completely private as Price maintains that it would be possible to communicate by telepathy. There could be groups of telepathically inter-connected minds which, together, could form their own worlds. His point is that, after death, our disembodied selves may create a world which is dependent on the power of 'our' ideas. Price's conjectures can, of course, be rejected by saying that the whole idea of a spiritual substance is incoherent and without a physical brain a soul cannot exist. However, Price replies that:

".... this proposition, however plausible, is after all just an empirical hypothesis, not a necessary truth. A discarnate mind could have its memories and desires and the power to construct out of them an image world to suit it. We cannot take our material possessions with us – nice homes, pleasant gardens – but we can create them for ourselves from our memories."

Effectively the image world could be a world in which we refine our ideas and images to make an acceptable image world in which to live. Those whose

Gilbert Ryle gives two examples to illustrate his argument that to talk of a soul as a separate substance is a category mistake:

1. Imagine showing a visitor round a University. You show him the staff offices, the libraries, the College buildings, and all other parts of the University. He then says "Yes, I have seen all this, but where is the University?" The mistake the visitor makes is to think that "The University" is another thing beyond all those things which he has seen.

2. Imagine showing a foreigner a game of cricket. You shown him the fielders: silly mid on, square leg, short leg, long leg, extra cover, mid-wicket, the wicket keeper, and the bowler. You show him the batsmen and explain their order of play. He then says "Yes, I have seen all this, but where is the team spirit?" The mistake the visitor makes is to think that "Team Spirit" is something other than what he has seen. If a team does not have team spirit, it is not something one can buy – it is a feature that describes how the players relate to each other.

images are violent or negative might find themselves confined to an image world of their own making, a true hell.

It should be emphasized that Price is not putting forward an argument for disembodied existence. Instead he is trying to show that the idea of disembodied existence can be given content.

A further challenge to dualistic ideas about life after death: Gilbert Ryle

Apart from the difficulties in explaining how the soul and body interact or what content can be given to talk of the soul in the light of increasing knowledge about the mind, dualism has been subject to sustained philosophic criticism not least from Gilbert Ryle. In *The Concept of Mind* Ryle described the dualist view as the "Doctrine of the ghost in the machine" and said that it rested on a "category mistake." Ryle argues that it is a mistake to regard the soul as a separate substance – to think of it in these terms means placing the word in a mistaken category.

The second of the two examples given by Ryle and included in the box is more sophisticated than the first as some teams may have team spirit and others do not. However, if a team lacks team spirit, it is not possible to go out and buy some in the way that one would buy another player. Instead team spirit will only be fostered by the ways the different players work together. Similarly, Ryle argues that "the soul" is not another thing – rather it is a feature of human beings that may or may not be present. Thus we might say of an individual "he/she has no soul." This does not mean he/she is missing a part (a parallel might be "he/she has no eye") but rather a comment on his/her personality. It might mean, for instance, that the individual lacked humanity and acted somewhat like a robot without any regard for other human beings as people in their own right. If this view is accepted, then it is a mistake to look on 'soul' as a substance which can exist after death at all – it is instead to talk about the feature of the life of a human being. Ryle is a monist and this position is dealt with later in this chapter.

MODIFIED DUALISM

The great Christian theologian, St. Thomas Aquinas, put forward an amended idea of dualism. Aquinas followed the philosophy of Aristotle whose views on life after death are complicated by problematic textual readings. In the majority of his works Aristotle whilst talking of soul and body, rejected dualism. As we have seen, to talk of a thing's soul was to talk of the potentialities of a thing – of the potential it has to become what its nature is intended to be. Soul, or form, is the specification which makes a thing what it is. Every animal and plant has a soul which makes it what it is, but this is not a separate substance that can be separated from the matter which makes the thing what it is. Human beings are made up of matter, but the specification of what a human is, is the soul or form of a human being.

St. Thomas Aquinas, using Aristotle's philosophy, maintained that the soul was the form of the body and that body and soul were inseparable. Aquinas, nevertheless, held that the soul separated from the body on death. Aquinas recognized that this gave rise to a problem:

1. *If whatever survived was my soul, then my soul would be me and this is a dualist position which Aquinas rejected.*

2. *If the soul was not me, then I would not survive death.*

Aquinas recognized this problem and said "Anima meo non est ego" – my soul is not I. This seems flawed as either I am my soul and survive death or I am not.

Aquinas held that, on death, three possible fates[5] await a human being:

- *Hell. This was a state of everlasting exclusion from God.*

- *Purgatory. This is the Catholic idea of a place of punishment or cleansing where individuals go to be purged of the sins they committed in this world.*

Transition

A caterpillar goes into a chrysalis which appears dead and inactive but out of this comes a butterfly. The chrysalis can do nothing – it has none of the features of a caterpillar and none of the features of a butterfly. Similarly the spirit or astral body may have none of the features of a human being and none of the features of the glorified body which Christians maintain will be received after death but it may be a necessary transition state from one form of existence to another.

However, eventually, after a long and painful period in purgatory, everyone in purgatory would be given a new, resurrected body and would then achieve 'the third state.'

- *The Beatific Vision. This is a timeless state in which the individual sees God and since Aquinas considered that humans were made for fellowship with God, this was the final state for the blessed. Before they reached this stage, however, the soul of the person received a new and glorified body.*

At the third stage, Aquinas sees the soul as being united with a new and glorified body[6] and thus returns to Aristotle's principle of soul and body being united.

Aquinas' position is far more significant than many modern commentators allow and, perhaps, is faithful to the position of Aristotle. Aristotle, whilst generally against the idea of survival of death, does in one disputed text hold that the rational faculty in human beings cannot be made up of matter and he, therefore, potentially holds out the possibility of a form of disembodied survival – even though this is not developed.[7]

Aquinas seems to be arguing along similar lines to the ancient Egyptians – that there is an intermediate stage, after death, when the soul survives independently of the body. But this 'soul' is a pale reflection of the fullness of what it is to be human and only when this spirit receives a new and glorified body from God does it become fully what it was intended to be.

The idea of the human being clothed with a heavenly body given by God is supported by some scriptural texts.

Heavenly bodies

St. Paul, one of the most significant Christian apostles who wrote many letters during his various missionary journeys in the first two decades after the death of Jesus, recognized that Jesus' resurrection was central to the faith of Christians. He said:

"But if Christ is preached as raised from the dead, how can some among you say there is no resurrection of the dead? If there is no resurrection of the dead, then neither has Christ been raised. And if Christ has not been raised, then empty too is our preaching; empty, too, your faith.... For if the dead are not raised, neither has Christ been raised, and if Christ has not been raised, your faith is vain.... If for this life only we have hoped in Christ, we are the most pitiable people of all." (1 Cor. 15.12-19)

St. Paul also wrestles with the idea of life after death. Aware of Jesus having risen in the body and also aware that the first Christians who died did not rise in full bodily form he offers his idea of what resurrection means for a Christian:

"But someone may say, 'How are the dead raised? With what kind of body will they come back?' You fool! What you sow is not brought to life unless it dies. And what you sow is not the body that is to be but a bare kernel of wheat, perhaps, or of some other kind; but God gives it a body as he chooses, and to each of the seeds its own body.... the brightness of the heavenly is one kind and that of the earthly another.... It is sown a natural body; it is raised a spiritual body. If there is a natural body, there is also a spiritual one.... Behold, I tell you a mystery. We shall not all fall asleep, but we will all be changed, in an instant, in the blink of an eye, at the last trumpet. For the trumpet will sound, the dead will be raised incorruptible, and we shall be changed. For that which is corruptible must clothe itself with incorruptibility, and that which is mortal must clothe itself with immortality. And when this which is corruptible clothes itself with incorruptibility and this which is mortal clothes itself with immortality, then the word that is written shall come about:
'Death is swallowed up in victory.
Where, O death, is your victory?
Where, O death, is your sting?'" (1 Cor. 15.35–55)

Paul argues here for a resurrection body of a completely different nature to the earthly body but it is clear that this is based on faith and that he does not even attempt to offer rational argument to support his claims. Paul himself recognizes that this is the case.[8] It may be that humans have both a physical body and a spiritual body – this seems, it must be acknowledged, unlikely to most of us for whom the physical is visible and verifiable. To the philosopher there appears to be no evidence and, as the concept of dualism is difficult to sustain rationally even by those who believe in the separate substance called 'soul', it is easy for philosophy to dismiss any idea of life after death.

Monist ideas about life after death

If dualistic ideas about life after death are not considered to be philosophically convincing, then an alternative needs consideration – this is Monism. Monism maintains that a human being is a unity – he or she cannot be divided into body and soul. This is to work within the tradition of Aristotle and when it is advocated in the Christian tradition it is an attempt to take seriously the claims that Jesus rose from the dead in bodily form.

What makes a person the same person throughout their life? What is it that makes a person the same person as when they were a fetus, a child, a teenager and what makes them the same person as the geriatric in an old age home? Bernard Williams argues that the one sure key to identity is SPATIO-TEMPORAL CONTINUITY – this means continuity of a body through space and time. Human cells are constantly changing throughout a person's life. Every day new matter is ingested as food and fluid and old matter is disposed of by urine, excretions, perspiration, or old skin simply flaking off. Yet throughout this process there is a single, changing, moving, developing person that moves through space and time. He argues that we know that the aged lady in the wheelchair is the same person as the little girl picking daisies in the photograph because the person continued without interruption through space and time from being that little girl to being that aged lady. If spatio-temporal continuity is the way that we establish identity throughout a person's life, this seems to have considerable implications for monist ideas about life after death. Williams argues that acceptance of spatio-temporal continuity as being necessary for identity would effectively rule out belief in life after death as on death spatio-temporal continuity is broken (for the monist, of course, there is no separate soul to survive).

To put it another way, to be the same person requires a single body to be continuous through time. On death the body dies and rots: it disintegrates or ceases to exist. At this point spatio-temporal continuity is broken. If the person reappears in, for example, heaven there seems to be no way of determining whether it is the same person. There is no way of establishing identity because spatio-temporal continuity has been broken.

John Hick, a modern British philosopher, seeks to address this issue and has provided one of the most convincing attempts to show that monism and life after death are not necessarily incompatible. Hick asks us to imagine the following:

- *Assume a lecturer disappears in London and reappears in Sydney. Even though there was a gap between the disappearance and reappearance surely, Hick argues, we would still say it was the same person if they looked exactly the same and had the same memories?*

- *Assume a person dies on planet Earth and, immediately after death, an identical double gets up and starts walking around on the planet Juno. Surely, Hick argues, we would say it was the same person if they looked exactly the same and had the same memories?*

- *Assume a person dies on Earth and an identical copy of the person appeared in heaven. Surely we would say that this was the same person as the one who died if they looked exactly the same and had the same memories?*

Hick asks us to suppose that, after death,

Alternative ways of arguing for identity

Some possible ways of arguing for what makes you the same person as you were ten years ago include:

MEMORY – but memory can fade and change. A person with Alzheimer's disease may have no memory of themselves as a child, but they will still be the same person.

CHARACTER – but character can change radically after, for instance, brain damage or even as a result of some psychological crisis and yet we would still want to say the person is the same person as they were before the change.

APPEARANCE – but the appearance of a baby or child may have nothing in common with the same individual when they are old – yet they would still be held to be the same person.

SPATIO-TEMPORAL CONTINUITY – this maintains that what makes a person the same person in the past and into the future is that there is a single body which continues to exist through time.

> *"I exist, not as a disembodied consciousness but as a psycho-physical being exactly like the being I was before death though now existing in a different space."*

In this case, he is claiming, I would be the same person even though there has been a gap between my death in this world and my resurrection in another. Hick's approach relies on the person who dies being recreated by God looking identical to the one who dies – so a very old person would reappear in heaven or hell looking identical to when they died. Hick then believes they would grow younger until they reached a perfect age.

Whilst Hick's approach opens the possibility of talking of life after death on a monist view, it is not without problems. How likely is it that the resurrected person is resurrected with the identical body with which they died? Jesus is the only example in any religious system of this.

The main weakness of Hick's position is that critics hold that the person who, he claims, appears in heaven could be a replica and not the same person. If the person has a new body, perhaps a spiritual body, there is no way of establishing identity with the person who died. In the Middle Ages, the importance of continuity was recognized and it was sometimes considered essential that all the parts of a person were buried together so God could re-assemble the same parts to form a person for a life after death, but no-one today holds this view.

The key question for the monist, therefore, is how identity can be established. How can the person created in a different time and space be identical with the person who died? How do we know that it is not a replica? If it is a replica how do we know that there are not two replicas? It can be argued that if God brings about the resurrected self then God would not create more than one such self and, therefore, the possibility of a second replica would not arise.[9] However, the logical possibility of such a replica still exists and, therefore, some would question whether there are sufficient identity criteria to claim that the resurrected person is the same person as the one who died.

In defence of the soul
There are severe philosophical problems with claims about life after death and, therefore, most philosophers today dismiss such claims. Those who reject life after death will argue that there is no evidence for the idea and that it is

a belief created by those who perhaps cannot face their own mortality. It might be argued that the brain is responsible for every part of a human being's experiences and there does not need to be a separate entity to explain the 'spiritual' side of life. In fact, it could be argued, spiritual experiences, which are by no means universal, are directly created in the brain by those who claim to have them. It is argued that without any empirical evidence to support the concept of the soul it is simpler to see humans as effectively intelligent animals. There is no need to suggest a separate substance called a soul as everything about a person that requires explanation can be explained in material terms.

This view is sometimes referred to as the mind state/brain state identity theory as it holds that there is an identity between mental states or events and physical states or events. For instance:

1. *Christa is happy/sad/in love or feels pain at noon.*

2. *Bunches of C fibres fire in a certain manner in Christa's head at noon.*

On this view, to talk of mental states is simply the same as to talk of physical states albeit under a different description. On this view, psychological states are simply neurological states.

Such a position is often called monism as monists maintain there is only one substance in a human person[10] – this for the materialist is the physical substance which co-ordinates a number of different brain states. Once we know enough about the workings of the brain, monists argue, we will be able to understand all mental states as well as consciousness. The materialist view of a human being is part of the Darwinian understanding of life. People are simply highly evolved animals. Life has evolved on planet Earth from rudimentary beginnings and Homo Sapiens has been the most successful of all life forms. We, as a species, have adapted incredibly successfully to our environment so that we are now able to dominate and, to an extent, control it (for good or ill). Our lives have no meaning and purpose any more than dinosaurs' had meaning or purpose.

If human beings are simply another animal species – like the dinosaurs – then the whole idea of life after death may be absurd

If talk of human beings having a soul is to be defensible today, then such a hypothesis (that there exists a soul, spiritual body, astral body or a disembodied consciousness which interacts with our bodies), needs to offer explanations for things which those who are materialist cannot provide.

There are seven possible phenomena that, whilst not provable under laboratory conditions, are nevertheless widely reported and believed and which are best accounted for if there is a disembodied consciousness:

1. *FREEDOM. If the brain is the same as the mind and if consciousness is entirely a matter of material states, then it seems difficult to explain human freedom. However complex the brain may be, if it is purely a set of complex neural firings then essentially it is no different from an incredibly powerful computer. If there is no mind (rather than simply matter) to program the computer, then it would seem that consciousness would be either entirely determined or random. The fact that most people do accept that human beings are free and that talk of moral praise or blame therefore makes sense, seems to make more likely the claim that the mind and consciousness is more than simply the product of a series of electrical impulses however complex these may be.*

2. *TELEPATHY OR ESP (Extra-Sensory Perception). This is the claimed power of one person to be able to read the mind of another, or perhaps to be able to sense their thoughts or distress, at a considerable distance when no physical means exist for this to be explained. Many people claim to be aware of things happening to close friends or relatives even though they are far away and there is no communication between them. Telepathy between some twins has often been recorded. Often this is not a power that can be exercised at will and the telepathic link is claimed to exist only in moments of high stress or danger.*

3. *THE ABILITY TO MOVE OBJECTS. This is the claimed power of some people to be able to move objects without touching them or to affect physical objects when there is no physical link between the body and the object. If there are any cases that can be verified then this points to a mental capacity that cannot be explained in material terms and greatly increases the likelihood of a spiritual self.*

4. *OUT OF BODY EXPERIENCES. In almost all societies there have been reports*

of people (a) being able to leave their bodies whilst in meditative states and (b) being able to see things which they could not otherwise have seen as they were nowhere near the events in question when they took place and had no access to the information. If these reports are true then a materialist view of what a person is cannot explain them and dualism becomes a possible explanation.

5. *NEAR-DEATH EXPERIENCES. There have been many reports of near-death experiences when people who are very close to death or who have actually died have experiences of leaving their bodies. Sometimes the person will look down at the room in which their body is lying or see doctors working on their body, quite often the person will experience leaving their body and being greeted by close friends or relatives who have died and being surrounded by a tremendous sense of light and of peace and not wishing to return to their bodies but feeling that they must do so. Often those who have these experiences are totally changed as a result. If these experiences are valid and if they cannot be explained in other ways, this dramatically increases the plausibility of dualism (see section at the end of this chapter for further discussion on this).*

6. *SIXTH SENSE. Sometimes animals are said to have a 'sixth sense' and the same can apply to human beings as well. Some people may be aware of being stared at although the person doing the staring is standing behind them and cannot be seen or they may be able to force someone to turn to look at them simply by concentrating on the back of their head. If this is possible, then it may be difficult to explain this solely in physical terms and makes a spiritual sense far more likely.*

7. *PARANORMAL PHENOMENA. Various paranormal phenomena such as Tarot cards and ouija boards have been claimed to be able to provide information that could not be obtained in any physical way. If there is any truth in these claims (even admitting that there are many frauds in the business who use these techniques to defraud people) then the adequacy of a purely material explanation for the human mind seems to be challenged.*

It must be admitted that there is no strong scientific evidence for any of these claims, but nevertheless many of these points would be accepted by a significant number of people and, if any or most of them are true, then the case for materialism is very substantially reduced. Materialist critics will reply, of course, that these claims cannot be verified in laboratory conditions and this is undoubtedly true, but this is precisely to impose as a condition for verification a scientific methodology which may actually rule out the possibility of exactly the results that are claimed to arise. If there is a spiritual side to a human person then that spiritual self or soul is not material and cannot be detected by material tests. To say, therefore, that the above claims are false because they cannot be observed under laboratory conditions needs to be challenged.

All this does not mean, of course, that a person does have a spiritual dimension – but what it may mean is that the prevailing wisdom that it is irrational or illogical needs to be challenged. There are widely attested phenomena that a materialist understanding of the mind cannot explain. This leaves room for meaningful talk of 'soul'. Because of the importance of the above seven factors, it is worth examining one of them in more detail.

Near-death experiences

In recent decades there has been an increase in scientific interest in near-death experiences. These are experiences claimed by some people who have been considered to be clinically dead – their heart has stopped beating and there is no brain wave activity recorded so that there is a 'straight line' indicating no brain activity at all – but who were subsequently resuscitated.

Some of those who are resuscitated report being aware of an out of body experience. Naturally many have been skeptical about the possibility of such experiences occurring – what is more it is not easy to demonstrate a convincing case that they have occurred in spite of the considerable similarities between the reported experiences. In his classic book *Life after Life* – American Raymond Moody records more than a hundred accounts of people who claim to have had NDEs. These anecdotal reports did not have any scientific backing but since then a number of scientists have been establishing a scientific basis for the study of NDEs.

One of Moody's former students, Professor of Psychology Bruce Greyson, developed the NDE Greyson scale which identifies the stages in a NDE to determine the type of experience a person had.

1. *Experience of being in a tunnel with a light at the end.*

2. *Changes in thinking processes – thinking gets faster.*

3. *Changes in emotional state – sense of peace, unity, love, warmth, safety.*

4. *Paranormal or psychic component – sense of leaving the body. Extra-sensory perceptions or visions of future events.*

5. *Transcendental phase; sense of being in a different dimension.*

Most of those who have had such experiences found their lives radically changed as a result so that money and material things no longer mattered to them and instead relationships and people became central to their lives. There are many who do not feel that the case for NDEs has been at all convincing. Dr. Susan Blackmore, a leading atheist psychologist, argues that there is no evidence that NDEs are anything other than a function of the brain. The brain is just billions of neurons and an NDE is an illusion created by the brain. She claims that we have all the information in our memories to create such an experience and all NDEs can be explained by brain function and chemistry.

Blackmore maintains that:

1. *The sensation of seeing a light at the end of a tunnel is due to the way the cells in the visual system are arranged. Many cells are devoted to the middle range and few to outside. If all fire randomly then with even distribution because there are more in the center it will appear brighter in the center of the visual field and darker round the edges thus giving the impression of a tunnel.*

2. *The 'feel good factor' is created by the emotional effects of the person being in the situation of being close to death. Under stress, in shock and with lack of oxygen, the body releases a massive surge of endorphins. These create good feelings, take away pain and makes the person feel positive and good about everything. The whole experience of nearly dying is therefore colored by these chemicals.*

NDEs, Blackmore says, are the product of the brain and cannot happen when the brain is dead. When do they happen? She says they can only happen during the period when the person goes into unconsciousness and in the time during which they come out of unconsciousness. They do not happen when the person is clinically dead but in these periods of borderline consciousness. She argues that unless there is evidence to verify that the experience happened in the period when the person was dead NDEs cannot be taken as indicating that a person is anything other than a material entity.

In order to answer these challenges, it would be necessary to show that, whilst unconscious and brain dead, the person had acquired experiences which could not have been obtained from memory or from the normal sense organs of a person either just before 'death' or immediately after brain activity starts once more. Producing this evidence has not been easy but there are at least two case studies that at first sight appear to answer these challenges. The BBC aired a program in February 2003 called *The Day I Died* which gave evidence from the latest studies in NDEs. There are teams of doctors researching NDEs in various centers around the world and the following example of a relevant case study is significant:

1. **Pam Reynolds**, a singer songwriter and working mother had a CAT scan that revealed an aneurysm in the base of her brain. Dr Robert Spetzler decided to operate in a procedure they called "Operation stand still". It was called this because Pam had to have her temperature reduced to 10-15° Centigrade, her heart and brain stopped and blood drained from her head for there to be any chance of success. Pam remembered being pushed into the operating theater, the squeaking of wheels of the trolley, and then nothing. She was put to sleep, had her eyes taped shut and had monitors which clicked put in her ears to register any brain activity. In this state she records that she heard a sound like being at the dentist. Then she felt a 'tingling' in her head. And then she claims that she popped out of the top of her head and was looking down at her body and didn't care. She saw an instrument in the doctor's hand which she described as being like an electric toothbrush. She had heard talk of the doctors intending to use a saw to open her head, but said that what she saw was more like a drill than a saw. She saw the "bits" of the drill, and remembered similar ones in her father's workshop. She heard the doctors say that they had a problem as the arteries were too small in her legs. She did not understand why they were looking at her legs when she was having a brain operation.

As she was watching and listening to the conversation in the room she felt a presence and saw a tiny pinpoint of light. It pulled her – a physical sensation "like going over a hill real fast." She went towards the light. The closer she got to the light the more aware she was of different figures. She saw and heard her grandmother. She said that "it felt great." She saw an uncle who passed away when she was 39 but who had taught her to play the guitar. She saw many she knew and many she did not know. But she knew she was connected to them in some way. She asked if the light was God. She was told that the light was not God but that the light was what happened when God breathed. She felt amazed to be in the presence of the breath of God.

She did not want to return to her body but her uncle brought her back down to her body. She did not want to get back in it. She knew it would hurt. Her uncle told her that she just had to do it and that it was just like diving into a swimming pool. She did not want to go but her uncle was persuading her and asked her about her children. In the end she said that her uncle pushed her back in to her body. As she went she saw her body jump, and she then felt it jump from the inside.

She says that she no longer has any fear of death and that what people say about death is a lie. It is nothing to be afraid of and is something she now looks forward to.

When Pam told her story to a doctor some time after the events took place, he sent for information about the operation and for a photograph of the type of 'saw' that had been used in the operation. The drill did look like an electric toothbrush and, when he checked with her surgeon, he found that she had accurately recorded the conversation in the room. It was confirmed that she could not have seen the drill or the bits as she went into the operation room as the surgical equipment box is not opened until the doctors are ready us use it in order to maintain a sterile environment. The conversation she heard about her leg was that the arteries in her right groin were too small to drain her blood from. They had to use the other leg. Her doctors were astounded as they agreed that there was no way that she could have observed or heard with her normal sensory apparatus whilst in that state. It was, they said, inconceivable that the normal senses could function through normal auditory pathways. Some kind of extra-sensory perception must have occurred to allow her to hear and see accurately what was going on.

If these events happened as recorded then the best explanation would appear to be that somehow the woman's consciousness separated from her physical body. This would be an extraordinary claim and would run counter to most modern understandings of how the brain works. The most interesting aspect of this account is that her experience of the drill and of the conversation in the room could not have happened in states of borderline consciousness. She had no functioning sensory apparatus to receive the data and store it in her memory. The objections of Susan Blackmore will not be overcome with a single example like this, but if research continues it may be that those who claim that the complexity of the brain can explain all phenomena may need to reassess the evidence.

2. In another case a woman, **Vicky Noratuk**, was blind from birth. She had been in a car accident and was aware of being in a hospital room. Suddenly she found herself looking down on her body. She could SEE her body but did not recognize it as she had never been able to see. She only realized that the body was hers as she recognized the engravings on her wedding ring – the engraving was on the outside of the ring to enable her to feel it. She heard the doctors saying that they could not bring her back. She then experienced going up through the ceiling, as if the ceiling did not exist. For the first and only time in her life she could see and was free and not bumping into anything. She saw trees and birds and light for the first time. She was overwhelmed by the experience as she had never been able to imagine what light or sight was like. It was very emotional for her. She then went to a place where there were people in white. She felt that this was a place of all knowledge and that she could bring forth any knowledge she wanted. Then she went back into her body and felt heavy and sick.

If the events recorded here are true then her brain could not have supplied her with sight as she had no memories on which to draw and the brain alone may not be able to explain this experience.

It may be that our understanding of the brain is far too limited. At one level this is undoubtedly the case. We really have no idea how the brain can do something as simple as arrange for a human being to walk or talk. Also there are huge areas of the brain which we do not understand. It would seem as though we are only using a small part of our brain and we do not know what the brain is capable of doing. Everyone would acknowledge this point. The second point is more controversial.

At the quantum level, the laws of common sense no longer seem to apply. Quantum particles can be in two different states at the same time and one quantum particle can affect another on the other side of the Universe even though there is no connection between them. The quantum world is bizarre in the extreme (see chapter 14). Items which seem to us to be solid are in fact made up of huge spaces with energy fields running between them. The same applies to the brain which, when observed, appears to be solid although it also generates electrical impulses. However, at the quantum level the brain is no different from any other matter in the Universe – it is mainly huge open space with energy running through these spaces. It may be that at the quantum level the brain produces quantum particles the counterparts

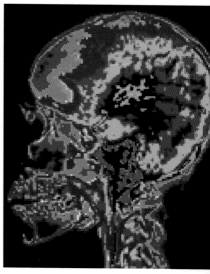

There are areas of the brain which we do not understand

of which can exist outside the brain. If these particles could remain together then consciousness in the brain could also be "quantum consciousness" outside the brain represented by the quantum equivalents of the brain events. This would enable, therefore, a person's consciousness to leave their body in a very similar manner to that in which the ancient Egyptians thought occurred or in a similar manner to the way in which Plato and Descartes talked of a soul.

In Tucson, Arizona Stuart Hameroff, Director of Consciousness Studies, is working with Dr. Roger Penrose and exploring the idea of consciousness. Hameroff has been studying microscopically small structures inside the brain – microtubials. This is the microscopic level of the brain, inside the cells. He says that inside brain cells is a network or forest of cylindrical structures that control the nervous system of the cell and control what goes on inside the cell. They also control how cells react with one another. These, he proposes, are computational devices like tiny on-board computers. He believes that they act as quantum computers. At the quantum level things can be interconnected to everything else. Particles can be in two or more places at one time and in two different states at one time. This is known as "super position in space time geometry" and is thought to be a fundamental constituent of the fundamental fabric of the Universe.

Hameroff suggests that when a person dies brain activity stops, and micro tubials stop, but that it is possible that information leaks out. Nothing is lost but it leaks out into the Universe. Quantum entanglement means that the information holds together temporarily.

What is, of course, an open question is whether this 'quantum consciousness' can retain its existence when the brain is completely dead and decayed. It could be argued that, if this scenario is plausible, the quantum consciousness could exist for a short time outside the brain but when the brain disintegrated so would the quantum consciousness.

If the theory of quantum consciousness should prove to be valid, this could support the Buddhist idea that, in life, what is needed is to train the mind so that, after death, the quantum consciousness could persist. What is clear is that there is a whole new field of science opening up which raises the possibility that ideas of survival after death which were previously dismissed now have to be re-visited and taken much more seriously.

QUESTIONS FOR CONSIDERATION

1) Do you consider that any reports of out of body experiences, near death experiences, telepathy or ESP are ever valid? If not, what explanation would you give for reports of these experiences?

2) Do you consider that human beings survive death?

3) Why do Buddhists consider that human beings need to prepare for death?

4) If human beings DID survive death, what would it be that survived?

5) What makes you the same person as you were yesterday?

6) If human beings are just made up of matter, and if human consciousness if simply a product of our brain states, then how can human beings be free?

7) Can the idea of "quantum consciousness" provide a way of understanding out of body experiences?

Notes

[1] *Socrates was sentenced to death by an Athenian court on the twin charges of atheism (because he did not believe in the state god) and "corrupting the young" because he helped young people to think for themselves and this challenged the middle class citizens of Athens whose own ignorance was revealed and who wanted their children to accept their own views. He was sentenced to death and, although he could easily have escaped, he refused to do so choosing instead to die under the laws of Athens under which he had lived throughout his life. He had to drink the poison, hemlock, but his death was delayed for a few days because of a religious festival and this gave him time to have discussions with his friends.*

[2] *The idea of an astral body has had an impact on modern psychic research and the whole idea of a spiritual realm. The astral body is held to be able to separate from the physical body but there is always a direct connection between the two and the death of the physical body leads to the death of the astral body. This idea has its origins in ancient Egypt as, without the physically mummified dead body, the astral body or Ka could not return to find sustenance.*

[3] *The influence of Zoroastrianism is also important – this is dealt with in* The Thinker's Guide to Evil.

[4] *Except for the prophet Elijah. Some Catholics today also maintain that the Virgin Mary was assumed into heaven and never died although there is no record of this in the early Church. A strong campaign is currently under way to make this belief a required belief for all Catholics to hold.*

[5] *A fourth possibility is limbo which was reserved for, for instance, unbaptized babies.*

[6] *Following St. Paul who talked of the dead receiving a new and glorified body.*

[7] *In* The Puzzle of God, *Peter Vardy fails to take account of the disputed text in Aristotle and does not, therefore, take seriously enough the possibility that Aquinas outlines.*

[8] *1 Corinthians 13.12.*

[9] *This was argued in* God of our Fathers *by Peter Vardy, DLT 1986.*

[10] *There are, in fact, monists of two types. Materialists are by far the most common but an Idealist is a monist who maintains that the only thing that exists is mind and bodies are a projection of mind.*

CHAPTER 9

MIRACLES AND PRAYER

Believers in God can be divided into two types:

1. *Christians, Jews, and Muslims are* **theists**. *They believe that God acted to create the Universe and continues to act to sustain the Universe in existence. Without God's sustaining power the Universe would cease to exist. God continues to be interested in the Universe and its people and continues to act from time to time.*

2. **Deists**, *by contrast, believe that God acted to create the Universe, but then left it to get on by itself. God does not sustain the Universe in existence. The Universe is like a clockwork toy which God has wound up and set going and which runs without further action or intervention by God. God has no interest in the Universe God created.*

The continual sustaining activity of God and God's continual involvement with the Universe is, therefore, central to the three great monotheistic faiths. However, opinions differ as to how and when God acts. Central to Islam is the idea that "everything happens by the will of Allah" and, if this is taken seriously, then God is causally responsible for every event in the world and human freedom is then a considerable problem (see chapter 7). Some Christians also accept **predestination** – the view that God decides from eternity who will be saved and who will be excluded permanently from God's presence. Again issues of freedom arise on this view. However, nearly all Christians, Jews, and Muslims agree that God can and does act in the world – the question is how and when God acts.

PRIMARY AND SECONDARY ACTION

St. Thomas Aquinas made a distinction between three types of activity by God:

1. **God's sustaining activity**. *God sustains the whole Universe and maintains it in existence. Without this sustaining activity, the Universe would cease to exist. This does not involve individual actions by God, but it does involve God maintaining the Universe and everything within it in existence.*

2. **Primary actions by God**. *This is where God directly intervenes in human history by a direct action. There are many examples but they would include:*

- *God acting to bring about the flood (the picture by Michaelangelo portrays this).*

- *God acting to send plagues on the Egyptians and then acting to protect the people of Israel after they had fled from Egypt and whilst they wandered in the desert.*

- *God acting to send Jesus and to become incarnate in the world.*

- *God acting to appear to great saints and mystics.*

- *God acting to bring about miracles at Lourdes or elsewhere or to respond to prayer.*

Michelangelo – The Flood

God acts directly either to bring about God's own purposes or else in response to prayers from those who believe in God and who make requests to God.

3. **Secondary actions by God**. *These are actions which God performs through human beings, using them as the agents who carry out God's will. Some hold that all of human history is the means through which God brings his purposes about whilst others claim that God acts through humans to bring about specific events. One of the clearest examples of this is God acting through the Babylonians to bring about the destruction of Jerusalem (see panel on next page – the picture is by Rembrandt, painted in 1630, of Jeremiah lamenting the destruction of Jerusalem).*

Jeremiah and the destruction of Jerusalem

Jeremiah was selected to be a prophet of God before he was born:

"Before I formed you in the womb I knew you, before you were born I dedicated you, a prophet to the nations I appointed you. 'Ah, Lord God!' I said, 'I know not how to speak; I am too young.' But the Lord answered me, Say not, 'I am too young.' To whomever I send you, you shall go; whatever I command you, you shall speak." (Jer. 1.5–7)

God tells Jeremiah at the start of the book that bears his name that all the nations of the world will come to take possession of Jerusalem:

"Lo, I am summoning all the kingdoms of the north, says the LORD; Each king shall come and set up his throne at the gateways of Jerusalem."

To a devout worshiper of God, this would have been scarcely credible. The people of Israel had found their identity in three key things:

1. **The promised land** – actually the boundary of David's kingdom which is recorded as being promised by God to the descendants of Abraham. This story may well have been written down at the time of David's kingdom and may have been a way of confirming that King David and his descendants did have rights to this land. Yet as soon as David died, the people of Israel began to be forced to give up some of this land. This process started under David's son Solomon and continued thereafter. The kingdom of Israel was split into two, Israel in the North and Judah in the South. Israel was overrun and destroyed leaving Judah (which included Jerusalem) still under the control of the people of Israel. Yet God was to command Jeremiah to prophesy that this kingdom would be destroyed and foreign kings would occupy Jerusalem itself. This is what happened with one empire after another seizing and controlling Jerusalem.

2. **The King** – King Saul was the first king of a united Israel and after him came David and then Solomon but from then onwards the kingdom broke into two. The occupation of Jerusalem would mean that even the king of Judah would be overthrown.

3. **The Temple in Jerusalem** – This was built by Solomon and was regarded as God's house on Earth. If Jerusalem was occupied then the Temple would be destroyed as well.

God says to Jeremiah that he remembers the faithfulness of the people of Israel in former times:

"Go, cry out this message for Jerusalem to hear! I remember the devotion of your youth, how you loved me as a bride, following me in the desert, in a land unsown...." (Jer. 2.2)

This devotion did not continue and God says he sees wickedness everywhere. He therefore tells Jeremiah that he is to prophesy that Jerusalem will be destroyed by God – but the agents who carry out this destruction will be human beings.

"See, I bring evil upon this people, the fruit of their own schemes,
Because they heeded not my words, because they despised my law." (Jer. 6.19)

Jeremiah is told by God that Jerusalem, its king and the Temple will be destroyed – and he is commanded to say this to the King himself:

"I will hand over Zedekiah, king of Judah, and his ministers and the people in this city who survive pestilence, sword, and famine, into the hand of Nebuchadnezzar, king of Babylon, into the hands of their enemies and those who seek their lives. He shall strike them with the edge of the sword, without quarter, without pity or mercy." (Jer. 21.7)

"Against you I will send destroyers, each with his axe: They shall cut down your choice cedars, and cast them into the fire. Many people will pass by this city and ask one another: 'Why has the Lord done this to so great a city?' And the answer will be given: 'Because they have deserted their covenant with the Lord, their God, by worshiping and serving strange gods.'" (Jer. 22.7–9)

The message is clear – God acts through the King of Babylon and his armies to destroy Jerusalem, the Temple and the King of Judah because of the disobedience of God's people. This is an example of "salvation history," God working through human history to bring God's purposes about. This is a secondary action by God as it is an action performed through human agency.

There are, however, a range of problems associated with the idea that God acts in the world – whether directly or through human beings.

CAN GOD ACT IF GOD IS WHOLLY SIMPLE AND TIMELESS?

Nelson Pyke and Stewart Sutherland are philosophers who consider there are insuperable problems with the idea of God acting in the world. Pyke argues that if God is outside time, then God must be impotent as any action necessarily involves time. He effectively claims that if a believer says:

a) God performed a miracle today.

This must mean that:

b) God acted today.

However, he argues, for a timeless God there is no today, tomorrow, or yesterday – there is only one, timeless "now" so action is impossible. However, this challenge portrays a basic misunderstanding of St. Thomas Aquinas and the depth of the traditional Christian understanding of God. Aquinas would say that:

a) God performed a miracle today.

means that

b) God acts timelessly to bring about a miracle in time.

In other words, God's action is timeless (there is only one, single action by God) but the effects of these actions occur throughout human history. The single action of God embraces all events in history. The act is timeless but the effects are temporal. It is, admittedly, hard to understand what a timeless action involves, but Aquinas would accept this. God is largely unknowable, God is not a human superman figure residing on the clouds. If God is beyond time and space then God is largely mysterious to those within time and space. If the existence of this God is accepted, then the possibility of God acting timlessly to produce a temporal effect is not impossible.

MIRACLES

Is the whole idea of a miracle nonsense?

David Hume was a great, atheistic philosopher. He was a Scot and had a profound respect for the power of reason. Hume was writing at a time when DEIST thought dominated and the debate about miracles had been long and protracted. Hume did not actually add much to the existing debate, but he presented ideas that had been thoroughly discussed clearly and forcibly. Hume did not quite reject the possibility of miracles as an act of God. What he did argue, however, was that it is never rational to base religious faith on miracles. Hume defined a miracle as "a breach of the laws of nature brought about by the deity or some other invisible agent"[1] and he held that it is never rational to believe reports that miracles have occurred. He says that no testimony is sufficient to establish a miracle, unless the testimony be of such a kind, that its falsehood would be more miraculous than the fact which it endeavors to establish. Hume argues that any report of a miracle confronts the hearer with two possibilities:

1. *That God or some other supernatural agent performs a miracle such as turning water into wine, Jesus walking on water, a dead man rising from the dead, or the prophet Muhammed having the precise words of the Qu'ran dictated to him by an archangel, or*

2. *That the event described did not occur.*

David Hume and the resurrection of Jesus

"When anyone tells me that he saw a dead man restored to life, I immediately consider myself whether it may be more probable that this person should either be deceived or that the fact, which he relates, should really have happened. I weigh the one miracle against the other; and according to the superiority which I discover, I pronounce my decision, and always reject the greater miracle. If the falsity of his testimony would be more miraculous, than the event he relates, and not till then, can he pretend to command my belief or opinion."

Hume says that (2) will always be more rational than (1) because we have constant experience that natural laws hold and it is always going to be more likely that reports of the breach of a law of nature were exaggerated and never, in fact, happened.[2] Hume considered that natural laws were fixed but, today, it is now accepted, based on our knowledge of quantum theory, that what we take to be fixed natural laws are no more than approximations. Nevertheless Hume could argue that the likelihood of a breach of our understanding of natural laws is so low that it is more likely that natural laws held and the miracle did not occur.

It can be held that religious faith is not based on miracles, but there are grounds for arguing that it often is. In Christianity the miracles of the resurrection and the incarnation are of central importance (as well as other miracles Jesus is reported to have performed such as walking on water and filling the fishermen's nets as shown in the picture on the next page).

In John's Gospel there is specific reference to the importance of miracles: *"...many other signs truly did Jesus in the presence of his disciples, which are not written in this book: But these are written that you might believe that Jesus is the Christ, the Son of God; and that believing you might have life through his name."*[3] In Islam the dictation of the Qu'ran is regarded as the greatest miracle of all and in Judaism the exodus of the people of Israel from Egypt is seen as miraculous, as is the promise made by God to Abraham confirming that the people of Israel would possess the land equal in area to Israel under King David.

The miracle of the large catch of fish

Anthony Flew brought David Hume's challenge up to date. Whereas David Hume effectively rules out the possibility of breaches of natural law because he considered these laws to be fixed, Flew concedes that breaches of natural law can happen. However, he argues that if a breach of our understanding of natural law does take place and the evidence in favor of this is good, then the correct reaction is not to say "God did it" but to spend money on scientific research so that an understanding can be achieved of the scientific principles which caused the event to occur.

What Hume and Flew do not take into account is the impact that a miracle can have if it is actually witnessed. If the disciples did, indeed, see Jesus rise from the dead this would have provided the transformation needed to move them from being a frightened group huddled in a locked room for fear of arrest into a confident group who were no longer afraid of death and went out with the utmost confidence and succeeded in starting a movement that converted the Roman Empire and has grown and expanded to include about a fifth of the people on the planet. To say that this was all based on a mistake (because the resurrection did not happen as Hume effectively argues) is a rather large claim. What is more, in more recent times people have claimed miracles in terms of cures of diseases that were utterly inexplicable by natural laws and, indeed, these cures often took place in a religious context. Of course, this is not a proof but it should at least give one pause before accepting that the purely rational account of reality given by David Hume is to be accepted. After all, at the quantum level most of the concepts would not make sense according to Hume's criteria – in fact common sense has to be left behind (as Einstein himself recognized[4]).

COINCIDENCE MIRACLES

Instead of miracles being seen as direct actions by God, some class miracles as events which are in accordance with the laws of nature but which are so unexpected that God is considered to have manipulated events to bring about a beneficial state of affairs. The 'Nebraska choir miracle' (see box) is a good example and others can be taken from the events of September 11 2001 in New York where some evangelical Christians held that God had specially protected them to safeguard their lives in the most unlikely circumstances.

The advantage of miracles such as these is that there is no breach of natural law to be explained. However, the disadvantage is clear – namely that because there is a perfectly good natural explanation, there is no need to bring in God to explain the event at all. God, in fact, seems irrelevant to the equation unless, of course, a person is a religious believer.

This leads to an alternative view of miracle – a view which does not even require God to act.

MIRACLES AS BENEFICIAL COINCIDENCES OR EXTRAORDINARY, UNEXPLAINED EVENTS

Because of the difficulties of deciding which events are miracles, some modern anti-realist theologians[5] reject the idea that there is any act that can correctly be described by saying "God did it." Instead a miracle is an event seen from the perspective of religious faith which is either:

Coincidence?

"Life magazine reported that all fifteen members of a Church choir in Beatrice, Nebraska, came at least ten minutes too late for their weekly choir practice which was supposed to start at 7.20p.m. They were astonishingly fortunate because at 7.25p.m. the building was destroyed by an explosion. The reasons for the delay of each member were fairly commonplace; none of them was marked by the slightest sign of a supernatural cause. However, nothing remotely resembling the situation that all members were prevented from being on time on the same occasion had ever happened before. Furthermore, this singular event took place precisely when it was needed, on the very night when they would otherwise have perished. Consequently some people were inclined to see the incident as a clear case of divine intervention and a compelling manifestation of God's care and power for everyone to see. How else could one explain such a spectacular coincidence which turned out to be the deliverance of people who were regarded as the most pious, and most intensely devoted to any church-associated work, and thus the most truly worthy to be saved, in a manner which (though it did not violate any law of nature) was too startling to be mere happenstance?"

1. **An extraordinary, beneficial coincidence.** Assume that a backpacker becomes lost in the Australian outback. She has become separated from the friends she was with and they may have believed she had decided to set out on her own as she had had a disagreement with some of them. She has run out of water and the heat beats down fiercely. There is no shade, no protection, and seemingly no hope as she is in a remote area of the outback where people hardly ever come. She staggers on but her strength is at an end and she finally collapses, scarcely conscious and awaiting death. Suddenly she hears the sound of an aircraft engine and a plane descends and begins circling. A parachute opens and a trained paramedic parachutes down with water and medicines. The plane happened to be carrying out a training exercise to see whether troops lost in desert warfare could be found using sophisticated new infra-red equipment. There is a perfectly rational explanation for her discovery but she might well consider the event to be a miracle, somehow brought about by God, because the chances of the aircraft and the new equipment being in precisely the right spot at the right time are so low that the event is incredible unless a miracle took place. She might regard the event as a miracle if she had a religious background. Note there is no suggestion in this scenario that God did anything – merely that because it was an extraordinary beneficial coincidence it might be described as a miracle by religious people. Effectively, 'miracle' is the name given by religious people to incredibly beneficial coincidences.

2. **An unexplainable event**. Assume a mother has put her young son to sleep under a cliff while she sits nearby. Suddenly a huge rock topples from the top of the cliff and hurtles down towards the child. The mother can do nothing except watch in horror. Then, instead of crushing the child, the rock comes to a halt three feet above him and hangs there in mid air. The mother rushes up and grabs the child – still the rock hovers in mid air. Scientists come out to investigate and there is no explanation. There are no wires, no force fields. After three days the rock gradually sinks to the ground. This is a totally inexplicable event. This is an example used by Fr. Gareth Moore OP and he argued that, for those within the form of life of the believing community, this would be called a miracle – to anyone else it would be an extraordinary, inexplicable beneficial event. Gareth Moore specifically denies, however, that God did anything to the boulder – it came to a halt for no known reason and the event is called a miracle because that is the word used by religious believers to describe inexplicable events.

Whilst both these are intellectually plausible ways of understanding a miracle, nevertheless they both reject the idea that God intervenes in the world. There may be various reasons for rejecting such intervention. Anti-realists, for instance, would support this view as they hold that although God is real and God exists, God is simply an idea which is central to the communities of faith (see chapter 5). There is no being or spirit called God. If the existence of a being or spirit called God is denied and if God is only an idea then, of course, these views of miracles may be plausible. However, even some who do consider that God is a being or spirit who created and sustains the world nevertheless consider that this God never intervenes in the world.

DOES GOD NEVER INTERVENE IN THE WORLD?

Professor Maurice Wiles puts forward perhaps the most convincing modern argument as to why God never acts in the Universe. Wiles, an Anglican theologian and priest, maintains that:

1. *God creates and sustains the Universe in existence, but*

2. *God never, ever acts in the world.*

Wiles claims that if God COULD act in the world, then God would not be worthy of worship. If God acted to cure a person of cancer or to help a believer in his or her life, then God would have to be condemned as if God is able to act, then God's failure to act in so many cases of extreme evil and suffering around the world means that God deserves condemnation not praise. Wiles claims that someone who can act to help those in need and who fails to do so deserves to be condemned and if God was able to help those children and adults suffering from cancer, those in danger on the seas, those in war, or those being tortured then God deserves condemnation. A God who could act and fails to do so is, therefore, to be rejected.

This, of course, has major consequences for

Responsibility

Ten year old Damilola Taylor was stabbed by a group of boys in London. He was left bleeding on the street and managed to crawl about a hundred meters toward his home. A number of people saw him and none did anything at all. They did not telephone the police or make any effort to help. Damilola died shortly afterward of his wounds. Whilst, of course, those who carried out the attack were primarily responsible, nevertheless the failure of passers by to help means that they, also, deserve moral condemnation.

Similarly, according to Wiles, if God could act and fails to do so God must be condemned.

any idea of God acting by way of miracles and answering prayer – both of these are rejected by Wiles for the reasons given. Even the incarnation and resurrection of Jesus as traditionally understood – as God acting to become a human being and of Jesus rising from the dead – are rejected by Wiles.

Sliding doors

The film *Sliding Doors* is set in London. In the opening scene a young woman just manages to board a tube train as the doors are closing. Then an identical scene is played but in this case the woman has to step round a small child and misses the train. The difference is only a second but the consequences are profound. In the second case she is delayed as subsequent tube trains are cancelled and she is forced to make a long journey home. In the first case she returns quickly, and unexpectedly, to her boyfriend whom she finds in bed with someone else. The film explores the two parallel realities brought about by the tiny chance of catching or not catching a train.

Similarly a tiny action by God would have consequences which cannot be predicted and so, Ward claims, God will only act very occasionally.

DOES GOD ONLY ACT OCCASIONALLY?

One reply to Wiles is put forward by another Anglican theologian – Keith Ward. Ward rejects the argument of Wiles but considers that God only acts very occasionally. God, Ward holds, has created a stable, law abiding Universe and any intervention has enormous consequences. This means that any action by God, even a small action, would have very great effects and, therefore, God will only act occasionally and sparingly. Ward argues that God acts to build faith and even then will only act if the action is for the best. However, he argues that if two equally good possibilities lie open, then God may be persuaded by the prayers of believers to act in one way rather than another, and therefore he maintains that the possibility of God acting in reply to prayer remains open. Nevertheless he argued that prayer must only be for what is possible given the Universe God has created and prayer should always be for the good of others.

Ward does not consider that the primary purpose of God's action is to relieve suffering. He sees much suffering as being caused by human beings and if humans are free then God has to respect the results to which the free decisions of human beings give rise. God will, therefore, save the people of Israel from Pharaoh by bringing them out of Egypt or perform miracles at Lourdes occasionally or send God's Son by a miraculous intervention into the world because these are events that build faith. The consequences of all these events are profound but the consequences are generally beneficial.

This view, although it leaves open the possibility of God acting, considerably restricts the scope for God's action. Many believers want to see God's action as far more pervasive and common than this but they then have to face the challenge of Maurice Wiles set out above.

PRAYER

Princes Charles was married to Princess Diana amidst a blaze of publicity around the world. Hundreds of millions of people across the globe watched the wedding on television. During the ceremony, the Dean of St. Paul's appeared on television and said:

"Pray for the young couple. You know it makes a difference."

The question is what kind of difference it makes. Jesus said that "The Father will give you whatever you ask in my name" (Jn. 15.16) and Muslims are instructed to pray at least five times each day, yet even when apparently worthy things are asked for such as peace or relief from suffering many prayers are not answered. There are many different types of prayer including prayer of adoration, praying for forgiveness, prayer as praise of God but it is prayer as petition to God (when God is asked for things by the believer) that generates the greatest problems.

There are three main alternative ways of understanding such prayer:

1. *Petitionary prayer as asking God to bring about some change in the spatio-temporal world as a result of the prayer.*

2. *Petitionary prayers as seeking to secure changes in the believer or the community of which he or she is a part, or*

3. *Prayer as building a relationship with God.*

The first of these positions would be rejected by both Maurice Wiles and by Fr. Gareth Moore OP for the reasons set out above. They both, for different reasons, reject the possibility that God can act in the Universe. However, even more conservative philosophers and theologians such as Fr. Gerard Hughes SJ would reject the idea that God can respond to prayer. Hughes argues that if God is wholly simple, timeless, and spaceless, then although God can act in a single creative act, nevertheless God cannot respond to prayers as a response necessarily has to take place after the act of prayer and this would mean that God is in time. God acts, according to Hughes and also St. Thomas Aquinas, once in a single, timeless act which has a multitude of effects in time. However, God cannot respond to the prayers of believers as if there is only a single act of God then there cannot be a second act after this one act – to hold this would mean that God is in time. Aquinas says about prayer that:

"We do not pray in order to change the decrees of Divine providence, rather we pray in order to acquire by petitionary prayer what God has determined will be obtained by our prayers."

Keith Ward, by contrast holds that God is in time and would therefore accept the possibility that God could answer prayers but would consider that, given the Universe that God has made, these interventions would be rare and very occasional and they would be intended to build faith and not to relieve the suffering of people.

If God cannot act in response to prayer or even if God can only act very occasionally, is there any point in prayer? Two arguments are possible which both see prayer having value in its own right:

Prayer can bring about changes in an individual. For instance if a person prays for their enemies then this, in itself, may bring about changes in attitude so that the enemy no longer remains as an enemy but comes to be seen in a different light. Alternatively if a community prays together, then this can bring about change in a community. A church community that prays for better understanding between Christian groups can, by so doing, bring about a willingness in themselves to change their attitudes and, therefore, to see other Christian groups in a better light. Similarly praying for a church member who is sick can help the church community to provide support and compassion for the individual who is ill and for their family and this feeling of being surrounded by the love and support of the community to which they belong may itself have beneficial consequences.

In a human love affair, the two lovers want nothing more than to communicate with each other. They will telephone, text, e-mail, or see each other as frequently as they can and their urge to be with each other takes precedence over almost anything else. It can be and is argued by some that the human need of God is the greatest good that any human being can seek and that, in seeking God, they are seeking what is needed more than anything else for human fulfillment. If this is the case, then prayer is not about "getting things out of God" or getting God to act, but about being in the presence of God and giving the individual time to be still and silent before God. Christianity, on this view, is a love relationship with God and prayer is the means that human beings and God use to communicate and strengthen the bond of love between them.

C.S. Lewis in *Letters to Malcolm* explores the issue of prayer from the viewpoint of a committed Christian. He points out that even Jesus' own prayer was not answered when, shortly before his death on the cross, he asked his father to spare him but nevertheless added, "not my will but yours be done." Prayer, for Lewis, is about a relationship with God. In prayer, each individual becomes known by God as a person and is no longer simply an animal. Prayer builds each individual up until they become something more. Each person, through prayer, can become known by, accepted by and loved by

The real point of prayer?

The Scots theologian, George MacDonald, argues that the point of prayer is not to get things from God but, in prayer, the greatest need of human individuals is satisfied. He puts it like this.

"What if God knows prayer to be the one thing we need first and most? What if the main object in God's idea of prayer be the supplying of our great, our endless need – the need for himself?... Hunger may drive the runaway child home and he may or may not be fed at once, but he needs his mother more than his dinner. Communion with God is the one need of the soul beyond all other needs; prayer is the beginning of that communion, and some need is the motive of that prayer... So begins a communion, a talking with God, a coming-to-one with him, which is the sole end of prayer, yes, of existence itself in its infinite phases. We must ask that we may receive; but that we receive what we ask in respect of our lower needs, is not God's end in making us pray, for he could give us everything without that; to bring his child to his knee, God withholds that man may ask."

God as an individual. For Lewis, therefore, prayer is not about asking God to do things but about beginning and then deepening a relationship with God. Lewis claims that the prayer life of most people is incredibly shallow. Lewis discovered after talking with a priest that, "the overwhelming majority of his parishioners mean by 'saying their prayers' repeating whatever little formula they were taught in childhood by their mothers." He contrasts this shallowness of prayer with those called mystics. They seem to have a depth of prayer that is very real and meaningful to them. Something most people never experience (*Letters to Malcolm* chapter 12).

St. Teresa of Avila described her own mystical journey using the image of a castle – each person has to make an inward journey which starts with a basic level of prayer and then going through seven stages of deepening involvement with God. The first stage begins when the material things of the world appear to be the most important and prayer is hard and difficult. By the third stage, prayer has become a central part of the life of the person and it is an integral part of their life. The person will be stable and will be able to pray for prolonged periods but they will also feel a call to move on. The fourth stage is intermediary – it is the middle of the seven stages of St. Teresa's spiritual journey. It is necessary in this stage to deepen prayer life or else all vitality and energy for the journey will be lost here. In this stage, the individual becomes more passive in prayer and a real faith and confidence in the service of God starts to emerge. Teresa's castle portrays this by two troughs supplied with water. One trough is filled via aqueducts which require human skill and ingenuity (these represent prayer begun and maintained by the efforts of the individual) whilst the second trough is filled directly from the spring and is always flowing (this represents prayer that begins with God and ends in the person – in other words in this stage God takes the initiative in the relationship which prayer represents). This fourth stage is the beginning of true mysticism. In this stage, the individual becomes more passive in prayer and a real faith and confidence in the service of God starts to emerge. The final stage involves the person with a very deep prayer life achieving close fellowship with God and then coming back into the world, out of compassion, to help others on the same path. Prayer, for most Christians with a deep faith is not, therefore, about asking God to do things but is concerned with a deepening of a relationship with God. It is significant that Carl Jung studied Teresa's inner journey and concluded it was something that every person has to take for themselves – whether or not they consider that prayer is involved. Jung maintained that unless this is done psychological problems will emerge.

QUESTIONS FOR CONSIDERATION

1) The prophet Jeremiah prophesied that God would destroy Jerusalem because of the wickedness of the people of Israel. The actual destruction was carried out by the Babylonians. In what sense can God be said to have carried out Jeremiah's prophesy?

2) Do you agree with David Hume that it is never rational to believe that miracles, defined as a breach of natural law brought about by God, have ever occurred?

3) If a person claims that God has acted but no natural law has been broken, on what basis could this be described as a miracle?

4) Maurice Wiles considers that if God could answer prayer, God would not be worthy of worship. Do you agree? If not, why not?

5) What do you consider to be the main purpose of prayer?

Notes

[1] *Aquinas held a very similar definition. He wrote "those things are properly called miracles which are done by divine agency beyond the order commonly observed in nature."*

[2] *"A miracle is a violation of the laws of nature; and as a firm and unalterable experience has established these laws, the proof against a miracle, from the very nature of the fact, is as entire as any argument from experience can possibly be imagined."*

[3] *John 20.30–31.*

[4] *Einstein described common sense as the series of prejudices accumulated up to the age of 18.*

[5] *Such as Fr. Gareth Moore OP, The Revd. Don Cupit and others – see chapter 5 on anti-realism for an explanation of its significance.*

CHAPTER 10

JESUS, THE TRINITY, AND CHRISTIAN THEOLOGY

"The only point of human reason is to drive itself into the buffers"
Rowan Williams, Archbishop of Canterbury,
The Kierkegaard annual dinner at the Danish Church,
London on November 18, 2002

The three monotheistic religions – Judaism, Christianity, and Islam – all share one fundamental belief: belief in a single God, the Supreme Being, the Creator and Sustainer of the Universe. This concept of the Oneness of God is stressed by Moses in a biblical passage known as the "Shema" which is fundamental to the Jewish faith:

"Hear, O Israel: The Lord our God is one Lord." (Deuteronomy 6.4)

Jesus was to repeat this about 1500 years after Moses when he said:

"...The first of all the commandments is, Hear, O Israel; the Lord our God is one Lord." (Mark 12.29)

The Prophet Muhammed approximately 600 years later brought the same message in the Qu'ran which was held to have been dictated to the Prophet over a period of years and thus is held to represent the exact words of God:

"And your God is One God: There is no God but He, ..." (The Qu'ran 2:163)

This great similarity is the clearest mark of the shared belief and commitment of the three monotheistic religions – indeed the very word 'monotheist' means 'believer in one God' and Jews, Christians, and Muslims are all monotheists.

It is the oneness of God, central to the simplicity of God, (see chapter 2) that underwrote much philosophical theology in the Middle Ages. God does not belong in a category along with other created beings. God is one, indivisible, and without parts. This conviction was shared by great theologians like Ibn Al Arabi (Muslim 1165–1240), Moses Maimonides (Jewish 1136–1204), and Thomas Aquinas (Christian 1206–1280) (notice the overlap of their dates).

Christians, however, whilst clearly affirming the oneness of God, hold that God is a Trinity. St. Augustine said "In no other subject is error more dangerous, or inquiry more laborious, or the discovery of truth more rewarding." But there

Moses Maimonides

is probably no subject that the average Christian priest is more nervous of preaching about than the doctrine of the Trinity because it is far from easy to understand. Christianity agrees that God is one but also maintains that God is three persons. This chapter will first explore how Christian claims about Jesus and the Holy Spirit developed from the experiences of the earliest Christians to the agreement found in Christian creeds.

The incarnation

The first Christians witnessed the death and then the resurrection of Jesus. After the resurrection appearances were over they felt that Jesus was somehow still alive and with them. Their experience of Jesus was of someone who continued even after death to communicate with them. He mysteriously revealed to them the nature, the person, and the will of God. It is in attempts to rationalize these experiences that the doctrine of the incarnation emerged. The experiences of Christians and the living traditions of the church were sources of great authority in the formulation of doctrine. The other source of authority was Scripture. In the earliest years after the death of Jesus,

The Roman Emperor Constantine declared that Christianity was to be the official religion of the Roman Empire in **318 C.E.** He recognized that there were divisions about the Christian doctrine of the Trinity, led by Arian, which would lead to discord. He therefore summoned a great Council of the Church which met at Nicea in **325 C.E.** At this Council a statement about the Trinity was approved although many continued to challenge it.

The 'Arian heresy' was contained by the agreement at Nicea but it continued to be influential. It was not until **451 C.E.** at the Council of Chalcedon that the Creed agreed at Nicea in 325 was finally held to be binding on all Christians. From then on, few rejected the Trinity – although Unitarians still do so today.

Islam is the major religious movement that refused to accept the Trinity and it is specifically rejected in the Holy Qu'ran [Sura 4.17].

Christians looked to the Hebrew scriptures for prophecies that would help them to understand their experiences and the conclusion that Jesus was the expected 'Messiah' was immediately affirmed. It was however far more difficult to reach universal agreement about his exact relationship with God. Once the texts which later became known as the New Testament were formed and established as authoritative Christian documents any doctrinal statement had to be shown to concur with both tradition and the scriptural record.

BIBLICAL EVIDENCE AND THE INCARNATION

Although biblical critics highlight the difficulty of regarding the biblical texts as historical documents the existence of Jesus as a historical figure is not in dispute. There is a great deal written about the person and work of Jesus in the New Testament and the real issue is not whether the texts can be regarded as historical but whether the claims they make about Jesus are true. Some scholars argue that the texts, whilst containing some historical detail, should not be regarded as historical texts but as documents that record the reflections of the earliest Christians on the person of Jesus. The texts certainly point to Jesus as having been a good man, one in a long line of good men who have shown the world how human life can be lived. If this interpretation alone is right, then Jesus is essentially no different to Socrates, Ghandi, Mother Teresa, Martin Luther King, or Nelson Mandela. If it was possible to travel back in time then Jesus would be seen teaching and preaching – obviously a remarkable man who could attract a crowd. Yet it is possible to claim that there was nothing about him that was substantially different to the other people with whom he mixed and other great people who have lived in history before or since. There was nothing particularly unusual about his appearance. He had a family and friends, he wore clothes, ate meals, walked, and talked and there seemed to be nothing about him to indicate that he was anything other than an exceptional human being. However, this is a long way from the picture of Jesus presented in the New Testament. The picture here is of a man who was substantially different from other human beings because he was the Son of God.

The incarnation

The incarnation is the claim that God chose to become an ordinary human being. The doctrine of the incarnation maintains that Jesus was both fully God and fully human. This doctrine holds that Jesus is not in a subordinate relationship with God but that he is of the same substance as God. That he is indistinguishable from God and that when he acts, God acts. If this is hard to understand, this is not surprising as the language of paradox is required. The claim is that Jesus is both:

God and man

Finite and infinite

Limited but all powerful

Weak and yet incredibly strong

Creator of the Universe but also a creature within the Universe.

The Annunciation *by Tissot*

The birth narratives

Do the biblical texts support the doctrine of the incarnation? The records of the birth of Jesus suggest that Jesus was born as a human being through a normal, young, innocent woman – Mary. The story of the virgin birth is well known and accounts can be found in the Gospels of Matthew and Luke. Mary was engaged to a young man called Joseph but before they were married and whilst Mary was still a virgin, Mary was discovered to be pregnant. In Matthew's Gospel it is Joseph who is told that the child is of God and in Luke it is Mary who is visited by the angel. Both accounts, in recording this, are recording the very earliest Christian beliefs that Jesus was not an ordinary person but that God was his father in a special way. Picturing the "annunciation" (the moment when the angel announced to Mary what was to happen to her) is difficult, but perhaps Tissot's painting captures this well. Mary must have been frightened and overawed but her trust, faith, and willing acceptance of what the angel had said was going to happen to her have singled her out for a unique place in Christianity and in Islam.

Nativity painting by Josi Williamson

Joseph, instead of rejecting Mary, believed in the angel's message and made her his wife. According to both Matthew and Luke Mary gave birth to Jesus in Bethlehem, the town of King David's birth and the place where, according to tradition, the Messiah would be born. The birth was hailed by angels and shepherds in Luke's Gospel and by kings in Matthew's Gospel who come to worship the newborn baby. There have been innumerable paintings of the nativity, but this painting by the Australian artist Josi Williamson portrays an aboriginal nativity set outside the town of Albury-Wadonga in New South Wales/Victoria and, instead of shepherds and kings, ordinary people surround her. This painting, as all records of the nativity, is trying to express something about the importance of the birth of Jesus – it attempts to say something about the significance of the birth of Jesus for the whole Earth and to say that the birth of Jesus is as important to Australians today as it was to people who were alive at the time. The animals shown are a wombat and a horse – both very much part of the Australian scene. The use of symbolism in the painting as well as in the birth narratives is clearly signposted with both the adoration of the child by strangers and the shining of a bright star as common symbols pointing to the significance of Jesus in heaven and on Earth. There is a long tradition of nativity paintings which make the birth of Jesus relate personally to the viewer. In Poland there is a famous painting of Mary as a colored lady – the "Black Madonna". This and the Australian painting both point to a truth claim that cannot be undermined by challenges about the historical authenticity of the biblical narratives. At the time of Jesus' birth it was believed that the man implanted his seed into the woman and that the seed grew inside the woman's 'nest' into a child. They did not understand the genetics of baby making as we do today. To say that Mary was a virgin is a way of saying that Jesus is God's child, conceived by the power of the Holy Spirit. In other words it is saying something about Jesus and who he is. No-one believes that Mary was actually black or that a wombat was present at Jesus' birth, but these are ways of saying that the birth of Jesus has universal significance, for all people for all time. The truth claims of the birth narratives are like this.

The birth narratives reflect the beliefs of the earliest Christians that Jesus was from God and of God – that he was the son of God. Does this amount to a belief in the incarnation? If Jesus was from God and of God did he have to BE God? If Jesus was the "son of God" does that mean that he was fully God himself?

Miracles and the resurrection

The evidence in the New Testament about the person of Jesus is not limited to the accounts of Jesus' birth and there are allusions to his nature throughout the accounts of Jesus' earthly life. Accounts of Jesus doing miracles and his resurrection from death are well attested throughout the New Testament and many argue that these events point to his divine nature as only God himself could do the miracles Jesus did and only God himself could conquer death. It is worth noting, however, that the miracles and the resurrection did not constitute proof of Jesus' divine nature to those who witnessed them and that this is recorded in the Gospels themselves:

- *When Jesus performed miracles, he often told people to say nothing about what he had done as he did not want people to follow him just because of the miracles they had seen. Jesus did not do miracles with the hope of proving to people who he was. The story of the temptations in the desert tells of how he met this challenge to do remarkable things in order to prove who he was and that he knew this was not the right way to get followers. Even those who did witness miracles did not necessarily conclude that he himself was divine – they were open to interpretation and some people attributed his ability to do miracles to the devil rather than to God. The scribes in Mark 3.22-23 said, "He is possessed by Beelzebub, and by the prince of demons he casts out demons." Miracles were not offered by Jesus as proof of his identity and the reason for this is that the miracles themselves were not clear signs of his divine nature. They had to be interpreted as signs of God's activity and it was possible to interpret them another way.*

- *That Jesus did miracles cannot be proven but even if they did happen they did not show that Jesus was divine. The disciples, who saw many miracles, did not conclude that Jesus was divine. It was not until the resurrection that the disciples came to believe in Jesus as being more than an extraordinary man.*

- *Moses, and many others in Jewish history, performed miracles which showed that they were men of God – but nobody claimed that they were themselves divine. The claim that Jesus is divine in many ways depends on the willingness of the witness to see through the events to what they indicate about Jesus' identity. Most people, even the disciples, were not able to do this until after Jesus' death.*

- *The resurrection appearances, it can be argued, did not constitute proof of Jesus' divine nature either. In the resurrection appearance in Galilee in Matthew's Gospel, chapter 28, it is recorded that when the disciples saw Jesus they, "worshiped," him. This is an appropriate response to Jesus if in that moment it became obvious to them that he was in fact God. However, the very next phrase in Matthew's Gospel is that, "some doubted." This suggests that even the appearance of a man risen from the dead was not enough to prove to some that Jesus was divine. It still required a level of faith. In the parable of the rich man and Dives (Luke 16.19) the same truth is told by way of story. When in the parable the rich man dies he asks to go back and tell his brothers what tortures lie ahead of them if they do not change their ways. He is told "If they do not hear Moses and the prophets, neither will they be convinced if some one should rise from the dead."*

Biblical claims, inside the New Testament, for the identity of Jesus vary, and it is evident that the New Testament speaks with a number of different voices.

St. Paul

St. Paul was not a disciple but became Jesus' most famous apostle. He established many churches and wrote to them after he had left to spread the Gospel further. His letters contain some of the earliest records of what the earliest Christians believed about Jesus' life and work. In St. Paul's letter to the Colossians he describes Jesus in language that seems to imply equality with God: "He is the image of the invisible God, the firstborn of all creation. For in him were created all things in heaven and on Earth, the visible and the invisible, whether thrones or dominions or principalities or powers; all things were created through him and for him. He is before all things, and in him all things hold together." (Col. 1.15–17). Critics might reply that this is St. Paul's view of the importance of Jesus but does not give grounds for the doctrine of the Trinity. The argument would be that Paul talks of Jesus as "the firstborn of creation." This suggests that he was created by God. God is self-created, self-existent and if Jesus was created by God then he is not equal to God. Paul also talks of Jesus as the "image of the invisible God." Again, if Jesus is only the image of God he is not God himself. The doctrine of the incarnation maintains Jesus was God Himself, which means that Jesus did not need to be created by God and was not just the image of God – he was God.

St. Paul

John's Gospel

The Gospel of John presents a very high Christology and is far more explicit in the claims it makes about Jesus' person. It is in the prologue of St. John that the first explicit claims to the incarnation are made. Jesus is talked of as the pre-existent word of God who was with God from the beginning.

"In the beginning was the Word, and the Word was with God, and the Word was God. He was in the beginning with God.
All things came to be through him, and without him nothing came to be. What came to be through him was life, and this life was the light of the human race; the light shines in the darkness, and the darkness has not overcome it.
A man named John was sent from God. He came for testimony, to testify to the light, so that all might believe through him. He was not the light, but came to testify to the light. The true light, which enlightens everyone, was coming into the world.
He was in the world, and the world came to be through him, but the world did not know him. He came to what was his own, but his own people did not accept him. But to those who did accept him he gave power to become children of God, to those who believe in his name, who were born not by natural generation nor by human choice nor by a man's decision but of God.

And the Word became flesh and made his dwelling among us, and we saw his glory, the glory as of the Father's only Son, full of grace and truth."

Here Jesus is seen as the WORD of God. It was the WORD of God which created the Universe in Genesis. The WORD of God came to the prophets in the Hebrew scriptures and St. John has God's WORD becoming human ("become flesh") in Jesus. In Matthew and Luke's Gospels Jesus is portrayed as God's son born of the Virgin Mary, but in John's Gospel there is no record of Jesus' birth but simply the statement that Jesus was the Word of God become human. This in no way contradicts, of course, the birth stories but it is a difference of emphasis. In John's Gospel Jesus is recorded as describing himself as "I AM" – this was the name God gave himself in the Hebrew scriptures when God spoke to Moses out of the burning bush (Ex. 3.14). If Jesus said this, this would certainly imply that Jesus saw himself as God: *"So the Jews said to Jesus, 'You are not yet fifty years old and you have seen Abraham?' Jesus said to them, 'Amen, amen, I say to you, before Abraham came to be, I AM.'"* (Jn. 8.57–58)

Critics might reply that the Gospel of John was the latest to be written and this could easily have been the writer of the Gospel imposing on Jesus the Church's interpretation of his divinity. Other passages in John also seem to imply that Jesus rejected equality with God, for instance: *"You heard me tell you, 'I am going away and I will come back to you.' If you loved me, you would rejoice that I am going to the Father; for the Father is greater than I...but the world must know that I love the Father and that I do just as the Father has commanded me."* (Jn. 14.28, 31) Jesus also prays to his Father as if to a superior; says that only God should be described as good and not himself and also sees himself as fulfilling the will of the Father.

The Hebrew scriptures
In the Hebrew scriptures generally there is very little clear evidence pointing to the idea of the Trinity and Jewish scholars reject this doctrine. Nevertheless some Christians see the story of the visit of three strangers to Abraham as representing the Trinity, and as being the first recorded instance of the tri-partite nature of the Trinity.

It would seem, therefore, that the biblical evidence for the incarnation is not clear but, in the mind of the early Christian Church, it was almost universally accepted within four centuries of Jesus' death.

The tradition in the early Church

The Christian Church in the first five hundred years after Jesus' death was responsible for deciding which beliefs about Jesus were true, and thus orthodox, and which were untrue and were thus heretical. There were fierce battles between competing viewpoints and the outcome was decided by great 'Councils' of the Church (see panel earlier in this chapter) which brought together the leading Bishops from across the Roman Empire. Christianity grew in a Roman Empire which persecuted and oppressed the new religion exceptionally fiercely – thousands were thrown to the wild beasts to be eaten alive for the enjoyment of the spectators (the Christians often responded to this by standing in the arena and singing hymns and refusing to resist – much to the anger of the crowds who had come expecting a fight) whilst other Christians were imprisoned or put to death. In spite of this the number of Christians kept growing at an extraordinary pace. When the Emperor Constantine become a Christian and declared that thereafter the Roman Empire should be Christian – Christianity moved from being a persecuted sect to being the official religion of the greatest empire on Earth. Once Christianity became established it became even more important to decide between the many competing ideas about Jesus circulating at the time and to separate what was true from what was false.

> ### Two heresies
>
> The most important errors to develop concerning the person of Christ were held by the Ebionites and Docetists. **Ebionites** believed Christ only had a human and not a divine nature whilst **Docetists** believed exactly the opposite – that Jesus was divine and only appeared to be human. This term was derived from the Greek word dokeo, meaning to "seem," or to "appear." Thus Docetists held that Jesus appeared to be human but was actually a divine being and was not human at all.

The idea that Jesus was fully God and fully human was not immediately obvious within the early church and there were a variety of alternatives – the idea that he was simply a good man, another great Jewish rabbi or teacher was held by some Jews. Some early Christians maintained that Jesus was really God but only appeared to be a man and others that he was a man but not really God. All the various alternative ideas about the nature of Jesus which are considered today were around at the time of the early Church and were discussed and debated in great detail. Great Christian theologians took various positions.

The Adoptionist heresy

Christians firmly resist the claim that Jesus is simply another human being, however special. Some have held this view but it has been formally condemned by the Church as a heresy. If Jesus was simply a human being, then he could not have had the power that Christians maintain was central to him – namely the power to forgive sins and to bring all human beings who follow him to salvation. Those who say Jesus was an ordinary human being accept what has come to be called 'the Adoptionist heresy' – this claims that Jesus was born as an ordinary human being but was adopted by God and that God's Spirit descended upon him. Supporters of this view hold that Jesus was the son of God, but an adopted son – not physically related to God. They argue that when St. John the Baptist baptized Jesus in the river Jordan, what really happened was that God adopted Jesus as his son because Jesus was so faithful to God and was so willing to be God's messenger. The painting by Pierro della Francesca painted in 1442 shows John the Baptist baptizing Jesus with the dove, representing the Holy Spirit, hovering above Jesus' head. This, Adoptionists would argue, was the moment when Jesus was adopted by God and when Jesus became God's special messenger. This can be supported by reference to Mark's Gospel where there is no birth narrative and it appears that Jesus was unaware of who he was before his baptism. The early Church, when faced with these claims had to respond and out of this and other controversies the orthodoxy of the incarnation was developed.

The heresy of Docetism

Within the Graeco-Roman world the idea that a god could suffer was unacceptable, as was the idea that God could become matter. Docetism was the claim that Christ's manhood and his suffering were unreal. Docetism is first mentioned early in the second century after the death of Jesus, but it influenced many later heresies such as Marcionism and Gnosticism. Ignatius and Polycarp argued against the Docetists in the second century and held that Jesus was fully human and that his suffering was real. This heresy is the opposite end of the scale to Adoptionism as it argues from Jesus' divine nature to the conclusion that as a divine person he could not truly become flesh and blood, but that he only appeared to.

The Arian heresy

The Arian heresy was a far more serious challenge to Christianity. It began with Eusebius of Nicomedia and Arius, a presbyter of Baucalis in Alexandria, who both held that Jesus must, as a matter of logic, be subordinate to God. Their starting point was the Christian claim to be a monotheistic faith. They argued that IF God is unique and transcendent, an indivisible monad, who is above and beyond reality, the cause of all things, and self-existent and without beginning then Jesus cannot be God as well – there is only one God.

Arianists argue that Jesus is a distinct person/substance made by God and used by God as his intermediary for creating and governing the Universe. As the Father's offspring he differs from all creatures and carries in himself the image of the ineffable Godhead. It is because of this that he is entitled to be called God but is not truly God because he is only the image of the one true God. Whilst Jesus might have existed before all ages before eternity began, Eusebius and the Arians refused to acknowledge that Jesus was 'co-eternal' with the Father. The Father alone they argued is self-existent and without beginning. The Father existed before the Son and therefore precedes him. The Son's existence depends on a specific act of the Father's will. God is self-existent and unoriginate but Jesus is originate having his origin in the Father. The Son is not part of the substance of the Father and is not derived from the Father as this would mean a compromise in the indivisible nature of God. The being of God is unique, transcendent, and indivisible, and the being or essence of God cannot be shared or communicated – for God to do this would mean he is divisible and subject to change which is inconceivable. If any other participated in the divine nature in any valid sense this would result in a duality of divine beings whereas God is by definition unique.

This was a serious challenge to Christianity. Arius was effectively saying that either God is one OR God is a duality. If Jesus is God and equal to God then either **God has divided in two** – this preserves the identity of Jesus but challenges the nature of God – or **God is one** and Jesus is a creation of God, in which case the uniqueness of God is preserved but the status of Jesus is undermined. Arius and Eusebius were saying that the Church could not have both a single monotheistic God and affirm the divinity of Jesus without a contradiction.

It was Bishop Athanasius who dealt in part with this heresy. Recorded in Athanasius' polemical writings are the fundamental claims of Arius:

God is one

1. *The Son must be a creature begotten by God out of nothing. He owes his being wholly to the Father's will. He is a creature above other creatures because he is perfect but he is a creature. He does not share the essence of the Father he has no direct knowledge of or communion with the Father, "The Father remains ineffable to the Son" (Athanasius, ep, ad epics. Aeg. Et Lib 12:cf de syn, 15).*

2. *To suggest that Jesus is in some way an emanation from God or consubstantial with God is to reduce God to a thing which may be divided, and God cannot change. Jesus on the other hand was human and could and did change and had the capacity to sin, which is fundamentally at odds with the divine person of God.*

3. *Jesus cannot be self-existent because only God is self-existent and therefore Jesus owes his existence to the will of the Father. If Jesus was co-eternal this implied that there were two self-existent principles and that meant the end of monotheism.*

The catchphrase of the heresy was that even though Jesus was born outside of time and brought time and all things in it into being, "**There was when he was not.**" It is straightforward to move from this to the subordination of Jesus to God.

The Arians had no difficulty supporting their position from Scripture: Acts 2.36 "God has made Him Lord and Christ" Romans 8.29 "the first born among many." Col. 1.15 "the first born of all creation" Hebrews 3.2 "Who was faithful to Him who made him." John 17.3 "this is eternal life, that they should know Thee the only true God, and Him Whom Thou didst send, Jesus Christ." All of these were used to demonstrate that the son is a creature created by God and that "there was when he was not."

The challenge of Arianism was massive. It challenged the Christian doctrine of God, it made a nonsense of baptizing in the name of the Son, and offering prayers to Jesus, and it undermined the idea of redemption – if Jesus was not divine then he could not be the mediator of salvation.

The Emperor Constantine was keen to maintain doctrinal unity in the church and planned an ecumenical council at Nicea in 325 C.E. The following is a translation of the Creed which the council drafted and required all the bishops present to sign (J.N.D. Kelly *Early Christian Doctrines* A&C Black London 1980 p.232):

We believe in one God, the Father almighty, maker of all things, visible and invisible; And in the one Lord Jesus Christ, the Son of God, begotten from the Father, only-begotten, that is, from the substance of the Father, God from God, light from light, true God from true God, begotten not made, of one substance with the Father through Whom all things came into being, things in heaven and things on Earth, Who because of us men and because of our salvation came down and became incarnate becoming man, suffered and rose again on the third day, ascended to the heavens, and will come to judge the living and the dead: And in the Holy Spirit. But as for those who say, There was when He was not, and, Before being born He was not, and that He came into existence out of nothing, or who assert that the Son of God is from a different hypostasis or substance, or is created, or is subject to alteration or change – these the Catholic Church anathematizes.

Arianism is condemned. Jesus is begotten but not made. He is affirmed as true God, not a demi-God or God just in name. He is not a creature or subject to moral change or development. Jesus is affirmed as fully God, in the sense of sharing the same divine nature. The view of the official church was that Scripture and tradition attested the divinity of Jesus. BUT the central problem raised by Arius concerning the unity and uniqueness of God if Jesus is "out of the Father's substance" is not dealt with at all and so Arianism did not go away. In what sense can Jesus be divine unless there is a division in God? The controversy continued for many years after the council of Nicea and it was not until 381 at the council of Constantinople that the Nicene faith under the formula "of like substance" was agreed and Arianism finally put to bed.

This heresy whilst hundreds of years old is of particular interest as the identity of Jesus as God is the single most powerful stumbling block for many today. In this sense it has a very contemporary ring to it.

The Place of the Holy Spirit in the Trinity

After the doctrine of the incarnation had been accepted as an official doctrine of the Church the debate about the place of the Holy Spirit in the Trinity emerged. The evidence from Scripture is diverse on the person, work, and status of the Holy Spirit.

Biblical evidence and the person of the Holy Spirit

In the Acts of the Apostles the coming of the Holy Spirit to the disciples is recorded as having taken place on the day of Pentecost which was fifty days after the crucifixion of Jesus. It is described as being like a "mighty wind" and that there appeared "tongues as of fire" resting on each one of them. In the Hebrew scriptures both wind and fire are symbols associated with the presence of God. This was the turning point for the disciples and the moment when they changed from being afraid to go out of doors into brave men who were prepared to go out and preach the Gospel. The first declaration that Peter made on the day of Pentecost was that the prophecy of Joel in the Hebrew scriptures had been fulfilled:

"And in the last days it shall be, God declares.
That I will pour out my Spirit upon all flesh,
And your sons and your daughters shall prophesy,
And your young men shall see visions,
And your old men shall dream dreams:
Yes, and on my menservants and my maidservants in those days
I will pour out my spirit; and they shall prophesy' Acts 2.17-18/Joel 2.28-31

St. Peter clearly identifies the Holy Spirit as God's Spirit and that the Spirit of God had come upon them in a mighty way on this day. The prophecy indicates that the gift of God's Spirit is now available to all flesh – sons and daughters but also servants and that this is the signpost of a new age. Further on in the speech Peter says that Jesus, "having received from the Father the promise of the Holy Spirit, he has poured out this which you see and hear." This indicates that the Holy Spirit is a gift from God but that it is given by Jesus to the disciples. At the end of the speech he calls people to "Repent, and be baptized...in the name of Jesus Christ for the forgiveness of your sins; and you shall receive the Holy Spirit." The Holy Spirit is a gift, given freely to those who repent and are baptized in the name of Jesus. The Holy Spirit is only given to those who first turn to Jesus, thus confirming that the Holy Spirit is given through Jesus. Whether this is a speech original to Peter or a creation of Luke need not worry us here. This is a very early piece of Christian literature revealing the way the early Christian Church talked about and explained their experiences of the Holy Spirit. The Holy Spirit is seen as a catalyst for action and is used to explain the transformation that the disciples have experienced in themselves. It is a HOLY spirit because of its relationship to Jesus and to God. Some scholars argue that the picture here is that the Holy Spirit, whilst incredibly special and powerful is nonetheless inferior to God and to Jesus as:

The coming of the Holy Spirit at Pentecost

- *It is sent by God.*

- *It is given through Jesus.*

- *It is in a passive role as the agent of God, sent through Jesus; it has things done to it rather than doing things itself.*

- *It is through the Sprit that God acts in the world. (The Holy Spirit is seen in Acts guiding the growth of the Church and giving the apostles power to convert people and to do miracles.)*

St. Paul and the Holy Spirit

Paul, whose writings are perhaps earlier than the above accounts, records how the Spirit is active in the Church. In particular he describes how the church at Corinth is a church endowed with many gifts of the Spirit and how the spirit makes itself known in their communal worship.

John's Gospel and the Holy Spirit

John offers a different type of picture of the Holy Spirit than Paul. John is concerned to explore the nature of the relationship between Jesus, God, and the Holy Spirit. This is discussed by Jesus in John's Gospel at the Last Supper. Jesus teaches the disciples about the Spirit. He teaches that when he dies and leaves his disciples he will not leave them permanently but only temporarily as he will send the Paraclete, or the Spirit, to be with them. The work of the

Spirit is described – it will remind them of things that he taught them and reveal to them all things. There is very little distinction between the work of Jesus and the work of the Spirit. Gifts, such as prophecy or speaking in tongues are not mentioned at all, and neither is the Spirit said to give believers the ability to do miracles. The work of the Spirit is to "take what is mine and declare it to you." The Spirit is described as the one **"whom the Father will send** in my name" in 14.26 but also as the one **"whom I shall send** to you from the Father…who proceeds from the Father" in 15.27. John is not clear who sends the Spirit, whether it is Jesus or God. What is clear is that the Spirit is the one who is sent, which again indicates a subordinate role. Just as 'M' sends James Bond into the world and is his superior, so God and/or Jesus send the Spirit into the world to do their work and are superior to the Spirit.

In these early texts the teaching about the Spirit is multi-dimensional and it is not at all clear whether the Spirit is the Spirit of Jesus or the Spirit of God. The Spirit is seen to be regarded as passive and not an independent agent but sent only to do the work of Jesus.

There is no clear and unambiguous evidence in the New Testament for the idea of the Trinity but, once the idea had been developed by the early Church Fathers, then there was seen to be many passages in the New Testament that could give support to the idea. Tertullian, a leading lawyer and theologian from Carthage, in the 3rd century after Jesus, was the first to use the word "Trinity," but it can be argued that he was giving expression to ideas that were already widely accepted in the Christian Church. Thinking on the person of the Spirit took some years of mature Christian reflection to enshrine in a formula of words that was acceptable and cohered with the experiences of the community.

Development of ideas regarding the person of the Holy Spirit in the Early Church

In the Arian struggle the controversy was over the full divine status of Jesus. This was an essential part of the journey to the doctrine of the Trinity. The Nicene Creed affirmed belief in the Holy Spirit but the position of the Holy Spirit in the Trinity did not develop until the latter part of the 4th century C.E. The key figures in developing ideas about the Holy Spirit in the East were the Cappadocian fathers: Basil the Great, Gregory of Nazianzus, Gregory of Nyssa, and in the West, Augustine of Hippo.

Eusebius of Caesarea argued that the Spirit was in the third rank, a third power. He used the Gospel of John to show that the Spirit had come into existence through Jesus. This was the basic position taken up by others before him, and many after him. Athanasius, Bishop of Alexandria from 328 C.E. argued that the Spirit is fully divine and of the same substance as the Father and the Son. He argued that the three are indivisible and that this can be seen in the work of creation and in the way the prophets were inspired. Most importantly, however, Athanasius argues from the experience of many Christians. He says that the Holy Spirit was the means by which individuals experience themselves becoming a part of God – to do this the Holy Spirit must himself be divine.

"The holy and blessed Triad is indivisible and one in Itself, When mention is made of the Father, the Word is also included as also the Spirit Who is in the Son. If the Son is named, the Father is in the Son, and the Spirit is not outside the Word, For there is a single grace which is fulfilled from the Father through the Son in the Holy Spirit."[1]

This was discussed at the Council of Alexandria in 362. Those opposing the divine nature of the Spirit – the Pneumatomachians (spirit-fighters) argued that the Spirit was "like" God in all things, but essentially occupies a middle position being neither God nor a creature. Once again those who opposed the line which would become orthodoxy were able to quote Scripture in support of their thesis – the absence of any claim in Scripture for the divine status of the Spirit and some texts which appear to subordinate the Spirit.

There were many others who did not commit to the full divine status of the Spirit but the Cappodocian fathers were central in bringing the Church toward the full Athanasian statement. They argued that the Holy Spirit sanctifies a person and so must be divine. They also argued to the divine nature of the Spirit from the logic of his relationship with Jesus:

It is a basic principle of logic that if:

- *A is identical to B, and*
- *B is identical to C, then*
- *A must be identical to C.*

If, therefore:

- *God is identical to Jesus*
- *Jesus is identical to the Holy Spirit*
- *The Holy Spirit must be identical to God.*

The Arians accused the Cappadocians of claiming that God had two sons. Gregory of Nyssa was to provide the definitive statement on the origins of the spirit – The Spirit is "out of God and is of Christ"[2]: he uses the analogy of a torch imparting its light first to another torch and then through it to a third to illustrate the three persons. This lacks a trace of subordinationism as it recognizes that the person of the Holy Spirit is of the same substance as God and of Jesus. In 381 at the Council of Constantinople the equality of the Spirit was affirmed and the doctrine of the Trinity was established as orthodox Christian belief.

The Holy Trinity *by El Greco*

THE CENTRAL PROBLEM OF THE TRINITY

The main problem in the Christian idea of the Trinity is that it wants to hold two positions which are far from easy to reconcile:

1. God is one with no distinctions within God.

2. God is three persons – Father, Son, and Holy Spirit.

These are far from easy to reconcile and the picture on the left makes this difficulty clear. The picture was painted by El Greco in 1577. El Greco uses the white dove to represent the Holy Spirit (the Holy Spirit is generally represented as a dove, as a dove came down to Jesus when he was baptized in the River Jordan). The Father figure supports Jesus in his arms whilst the Holy Spirit hovers above.

The difficulty is that when a painter depicts the three separate persons of the Trinity, it becomes hard to show the unity – in other words the more the personality of God as Father, Son, and Holy Spirit is emphasized the more difficult it is to show the unity and the more the unity of God is emphasized the more difficulty there is in understanding God as three persons. The normal theological reaction to this is to say that this is a mystery – but, of course, Islamic and Jewish critics will reply that this supposed mystery in fact represents an

incoherence as God cannot both be three persons and yet one. The ikon above – painted in 1390 by Luca di Tomme makes the problem even more clear. Jesus is on the cross but behind him are the three heads representing the Trinity. Here the three persons of God are all given human expression (i.e. there is no dove) but the shape of the central part of the picture is meant to illustrate that the three are nevertheless one.

The Protestant theologian Karl Barth maintained that the only way that the doctrine of the Trinity could be known to be true was through revelation. Any attempt, therefore, to understand the Trinity using reason was to be rejected. For Barth, the whole basis for the truth of the doctrine of the Trinity rests on the claim that this has been directly revealed by God in Scripture. The only way of coming to knowledge of God is through the revelation of Jesus as God's son. Barth freely accepts that the idea of the Trinity is a mystery and holds that this is a mystery precisely because God conceals himself within this. Barth was reluctant to talk about any of the three persons of the Trinity separate from the other two because of the dangers of implying three gods. He insisted on the oneness of God but God could be correctly spoken of as Father and as Son and as Holy Spirit.

It should, perhaps, not be surprising that doctrines such as that of the Trinity should be difficult to conceptualize – at the quantum level all the normal laws of science break down and scientists are left with the language of paradox and contradiction, yet what they are saying is still readily accepted by most people today as being true. For instance light is held to be a wave and not to be a wave – both are in some senses true and it is helpful to think of light as a wave BUT if it is thought of as literally a wave then immediate errors creep in. If at the quantum level, within the created Universe, the language of paradox, contradiction, and mystery is necessary then perhaps it should come as little surprise that the language of paradox, contradiction, and mystery is also necessary in representing what may be an infinitely more complex idea of the nature of God.

But Christian claims are, for the atheist philosopher, offensive for this reason. The claim that Jesus was God incarnate is singularly offensive. Offensive because it is logically impossible. Philosophically speaking to talk of a human being as also being at the same time a spiritual being does not make any sense. The idea that a person can be conceived but have no earthly father, the idea that a person can rise from the dead, come out of the tomb in which his dead body had been laid and walk, eat, and talk with his friends are also absurd claims, which go against all human experience. To claim that God is one, but then to maintain that there are three persons in the Godhead is absurd. It is here that the atheist and the monotheist may unite against Christianity. For the philosopher it is illogical and for the monotheist these claims appear to go against the basic tenet of faith that God is one. The Christian claim that this man, Jesus, was both a normal human being and also God, that he was both a creature and the Creator of the Universe is a clear challenge to the idea that there is one indivisible God.

The basic claims about Jesus, founded on the experience of believers, are enormously challenging and the problems associated with these claims face modern day people just as much as they faced those to whom Christianity was first preached.

Mother of God
The status of Mary was much debated in the early Christian Church and one of the great Councils was called at Ephesus (where previously the goddess Diana had been worshiped) to decide once and for all on her status. The logic of the position was clear – since Jesus was held to be God and since Jesus was held to have had no earthly father and was deemed to be the son of God, then Mary was decreed to be **THEOTOKOS – THE MOTHER OF GOD**. The picture of the ikon opposite is of Mary as Theotokos (literally this mean "God bearer").

One of the early Church Fathers set out Mary's status in the following hymn:

"All creation rejoices in you: the assembly of angels and the human race. O Sanctified Temple and Spiritual Paradise, from whom God, Who is before the ages, was incarnate and became a Child! He made your body into a throne, and your womb He made more spacious than the heavens. O full of grace, glory to you."

God, therefore, who existed before the Universe was created was nevertheless born of Mary's womb and became incarnate with the birth of Jesus.

Christian doctrines about Mary: of Mary as the Mother of God, of the annunciation to Mary, of Mary having conceived Jesus without human agency, of Mary's quiet and gentle acceptance of God's will, and of Mary having been kept free from original sin by the special grace of God, are teachings that point toward a deep and profound mystery which lies at the heart of Christianity – that God is held to have chosen a poor, ordinary girl to be the mother for God's son, and that her faith and gentle and willing compliance with this provides an example for all people throughout the centuries.

One of the reasons that Muslims venerate Mary and hold her in such high esteem is because she willingly submitted to God's will. The word 'Muslim' means, literally, to submit to God and this is why Mary is seen as being a faithful Muslim – even though born before the Prophet Muhammed. The first Muslim was, of course, not Muhammed but Abraham as Abraham is held to have been the first person to submit to God and Mary is held to have done precisely the same.

Crucifixion and resurrection

The incarnation and nature of Jesus as God and man are two of the central teachings of Christianity – the third is based on the claim that Jesus died on the cross under the Roman governor Pontius Pilate. Although the Gospels allocate blame to different figures – sometimes to the priests and religious leaders of the Temple in Jerusalem – Christian teaching is clear that the death of Jesus

was a historical event. He died the death of a common criminal, crucified with iron nails driven through his wrists and feet which was the common Roman means of killing people at the time. He was crucified with two criminals, one on either side of him. According to Luke one of these men mocked him and made fun of him saying that if he was so wonderful and a prophet why did he not save himself and them as well. The other criminal, however, rebuked the first and said that they, at least, deserved to die whilst Jesus was an innocent man and he then asked Jesus to remember him when he came into his kingdom. Jesus said to this second man "Today you will be with me in paradise." Something of the pain and isolation of the cross is portrayed in many paintings of the crucifixion.

Christians, therefore, portray Jesus dying a terrible death but also a shameful death as a common criminal. When Christianity began to be preached around the Roman world, many people could not understand this idea – how could God die on a cross? For those with a background in Platonism this was offensive as matter was regarded as the antithesis of the spiritual realm. Why preach Christ crucified? The idea that a man who was condemned as a criminal under Roman law could be proclaimed as the Lord of all the world was absurd. Who would believe that? And who could possibly be expected to believe the extraordinary claim that he rose from the dead? Even the disciples who had lived and worked with Jesus himself found it hard to believe this. St. John's Gospel records that one of his closest friends and disciples, Thomas, refused to believe the reports of the resurrection unless he saw Jesus for himself – not only that, he demanded to put his finger in the holes where the nails had pierced his hands and his feet and also where a Roman spear had pierced his side. Once the resurrection appearances were over how could anybody else be expected to believe such wild claims without any evidence?

It is probably fair to say that nothing appeared to be so completely finished as the mission of Jesus on the day that he died. Why and how has Christianity survived at all? What transformed the disciples? What inspired the Church? What drove St. Paul to establish churches? If the stories of the resurrection are not true, "We are of all men most to be pitied."[3] The continued existence of Christianity is a remarkable fact. From a small band of frightened men hiding away in secret came the conversion of the whole Roman world and more than 2000 years of Christianity. People

gladly laid down their lives because of their belief that Jesus had risen from the dead and that his death on the cross was a seminal moment in history when God revealed himself and offered himself for their sins. If the reports were not true, then one of the world's major religions is based on a lie and many have staked their lives on empty claims and died for nothing.

How Christian beliefs have been defined

Christian confessions of faith or creed come from different sources: (1) **From the authority of the great Councils of the Church (see below).** (2) **From the teachings of a particular church** (such as the decrees of the Council of Trent or the Second Vatican Council in Catholicism; the Westminster Confession in the Presbyterian Church or from Church catechisms). (3) **From a number of theologians specifically commissioned for such work by ecclesiastical authority** (such as the Thirty-Nine Articles of the Church of England; or from an individual, such as the Catechisms of Luther).

The Apostles' Creed was seen as the original creed as it was held to have been derived from the Apostles themselves. Modern scholars now accept that it was developed over the first few hundred years of the life of the Christian church but it is still one of the earliest formulations of Christian belief. This creed is as follows: *"We believe in God, the Father Almighty, the Creator of heaven and Earth, and in Jesus Christ, His only Son, our Lord: Who was conceived of the Holy Spirit, born of the Virgin Mary, suffered under Pontius Pilate, was crucified, died, and was buried. He descended into hell. The third day He arose again from the dead. He ascended into heaven and sits at the right hand of God the Father Almighty, whence He shall come to judge the living and the dead. I believe in the Holy Spirit, the holy catholic church, the communion of saints, the forgiveness of sins, the resurrection of the body, and life everlasting."*

This creed is accepted by almost all Christian Churches – particularly Protestant Churches who accept it because of its age and its connection with the Apostles.

The great Councils of the Christian Church are as follows

1 **The First Ecumenical, or Council of Nicea (325)** – lasted two months and twelve days. Three hundred and eighteen bishops were present. The Emperor Constantine called this Council soon after the Roman Empire became Christian. This Council produced the Nicean Creed and also said that Jesus was truly divine, being the Son of God.

2 **The Second Ecumenical, or First General Council of Constantinople (381)** – under the Emperor Theodosius I. This was attended by one hundred and fifty bishops. This council confirmed that the Holy Spirit was also divine and thus laid the foundations for the doctrine of the Trinity.

3 **The Third Ecumenical, or Council of Ephesus (431)** – more than two hundred bishops, presided over by Cyril of Alexandria representing Pope Celestine I. It defined the true personal unity of Christ and declared that Mary was the Mother of God ("Theotokos" – God bearer) against Nestorius, the Bishop of Constantinople, who held that Mary was "Christokos" – bearer of Christ. Nestorius rejected the idea that God was born of a woman as the Word of God has always existed and, he held, came to Jesus as he grew. Nestorius is alleged to have said: "I find it very difficult to worship God three weeks old in a manger." Nestorius held that Mary was the source of Christ's humanity but not of his divinity. Cyril of Alexandria, who was president of the Council demanded agreement from the Council that Nestorius' views should be rejected even though seventy bishops from the Eastern Church who would have supported Nestorius had not yet arrived. The resolution was duly carried in their absence but there was much controversy about it later and most scholars today hold that Cyril's Presidency was unjust and, indeed, devious. This Third Council also condemned even more strongly Pelagius who had held that it was possible for a person to be good and to attain salvation by their own efforts and without the grace of God.

4 **The Fourth Ecumenical, or Council of Chalcedon (451)** – attended by one hundred and fifty bishops under Pope Leo the Great and the Emperor Marcion. This defined Jesus' two natures (both divine and human) and again rejected the position held by Nestorius and his supporters. The Council was necessary as, after the Third Council, there was much unhappiness about the way agreement had been reached without all the bishops being present.

5 **The Fifth Ecumenical, or Second General Council of Constantinople (553)** – of one hundred and sixty five bishops under Pope Vigilius and Emperor Justinian I, condemned errors of Origen and certain writings of Theodore

Bishop of Mopsuetia.

6 **The Sixth Ecumenical, or Third Council of Chalcedon (680)** – under Pope Agatho and the Emperor Constantine Pogonatus, was attended by the Patriarchs of Constantinople and Antioch, one hundred and seventy four bishops, and the emperor. It said that Christ had two separate wills – one divine and one human and these operated independently of each other.

7 **The Seventh Ecumenical, or Second Council of Nicea (787)** – was convened by Emperor Constantine VI under Pope Adrian I. This regulated the veneration of holy images.

In the 6th and 7th centuries, the Western Church began to insert into the Creed the claim that the Holy Spirit came not only from the Father but from the Father and the Son together. This became known as the FILIOQUE CLAUSE (because the words "and from the Son" were inserted into the creed) and was to be one of a number of reasons that led to the great split in Christianity between the Western Church centered on Rome and the Eastern Church centered on Constantinople (now Istanbul). The Eastern Church could not accept this amendment to the original Christian creed since it had not been agreed by a Council of the whole Church, and to them it implied that the Spirit was subordinate in the Trinity. Cardinal Humber, in 1054 C.E., placed on the altar of the great Cathedral of St. Sophia in Constantinople the Papal "Bull of excommunication" which excluded all the Orthodox Christians from the Catholic Church – partly because they did not use the Filioque clause.

QUESTIONS FOR CONSIDERATION

1) What is a heresy and what is orthodoxy?

2) What were the most important heresies in the early Church about?

3) Place the following in time sequence: crucifixion, annunciation, incarnation, resurrection. What do each of these mean?

4) If you had lived in the time of Jesus, what evidence would have convinced you that the resurrection story was true?

5) What was the "adoptionist heresy"? What are the strengths and weaknesses of this theory?

6) What is Arianism and why was it seen as such a threat by the young Christian Church?

7) Why is Mary revered in Islam?

8) What is the significance of the early Councils of the Church today?

Notes

1 *Athanasius Ib. 1,14*

2 *C. Maced. 2:10*

3 *1 Corinthians 15.19*

CHAPTER 11

FAITH AND REASON

"What has Athens to do with Jerusalem?" Tertullian

"Reason, my dear Zoe, is just a way of being wrong with authority." Dr. Who

BELIEF AND KNOWLEDGE

There is a difference between:

- *Believing a statement to be true, and*
- *Knowing a statement to be true.*

Both belief and claims to knowledge aim at the truth, but a claim to knowledge is a claim to have arrived at the truth and, therefore, if this claim is to be publicly acknowledged, some justification for the claim will be required. If a person claims to know something and can produce no reason as to how they know and cannot demonstrate that they know, then their claim may reasonably be treated with some suspicion. Whilst a dubious response is reasonable to such claims, it may be that the person does "know" and is absolutely right, even though no one accepts this to be the case. If, for example, the Qu'ran was dictated to Muhammed by the angel Gabriel, then the claim to know that the Qu'ran was dictated to Muhammed by the angel Gabriel is not just "belief," it is knowledge of something that is true. This does not mean "true for a Muslim." Lack of empirical, scientific evidence cannot invalidate this knowledge as, if it happened as claimed, it is knowledge and not just belief.

The same may be said about the claims of the disciples of Jesus about his resurrection. If they did, indeed, see Jesus rise from the dead then their belief that he did rise was not just a belief, it was rational, based on their own experiences and was absolutely true. That others will doubt this kind of knowledge is not surprising, because although it was rational and reasonable for those who experienced the events first-hand to claim "to know," for others it is not compelling. For those who accept the testimony of the first Muslims and Christians such claims are accepted as knowledge, and this knowledge is based on the acceptance that the original witnesses were telling the truth. Belief may therefore be true but requires acceptance, without proof, of earlier testimony. The same kind of acceptance is found about historical incidents and historical figures from every age and culture. For those who do not believe that claims about the Qu'ran or Jesus are true, further evidence is needed before the accounts can be accepted. It is worth noting that the same kind of "hard" evidence might not be required for acceptance of events surrounding figures such as Julius Cesar, although the nature, quantity, and quality of the evidence is identical.

Religious claims to "knowledge" can seem to some to be rather like the child who is absolutely convinced that Father Christmas exists. The child has all the evidence it needs – crumbs from the mince pie, carrot chompings in the garden, sooty footprints leading from the chimney to the Christmas tree, gifts delivered, and perhaps far more important than any of these pieces of empirical data, all of which undoubtedly point to the existence of Santa, there are the reliable witnesses whom the child trusts – Mom and Dad. Yet Santa does not exist. Some will argue that religious "stories" about God and Jesus and Muhammed and Moses are like stories about Father Christmas – nice stories and part of every healthy childhood, but passed on by authority figures whom the gullible choose to believe. Once one has grown up, they are something to be realistic about and certainly not the sort of tale to stake one's life on. It is precisely the fact that people do stake their lives on such claims that challenges this account of religious "knowledge." In addition religious people make claims about spiritual truths, which go far beyond historical events, but for those who are skeptical far more is needed to ground such claims than pure testimony.

Wittgenstein points to the need to examine how the word belief is used. There is no single usage – for instance (to use Wittgenstein's examples):

1. *"I believe there is a German aeroplane overhead,"* and

2. *"I believe in the Last Judgment."*

These function in very different ways. The first is tentative and can be shown to be either true or false, whilst the second cannot be proved and yet may involve a life-commitment that affects everything the individual does. One cannot assume that the word "belief" has a single meaning. The Christian creeds start "I believe in God, the Father Almighty...." but this is not a tentative commitment.

THE BASIS FOR FAITH CLAIMS

Many people stake their lives on their religious beliefs but, on the face of things, the evidence for the truth of these claims seems meager. The arguments for the existence of God may be persuasive to those who already have faith but to anyone else they are unlikely to bring anyone to faith. In today's world, science seems to be able to explain a great deal and what it cannot at present explain many scientists maintain will be explained in due course. The natural world seems to be a cruel place based on random factors and on evolution which is wasteful and seemingly cruel as well as being extended over incredibly long periods of time. Can it any longer make sense to hold onto belief in an omnipotent and wholly good God? Some religious believers are willing to fully accept that there are no rational grounds for belief – they instead maintain that **faith goes beyond reason**.

W.K. Clifford is one philosopher who totally rejects any idea of basing beliefs on other than good grounds. He maintains that:

"It is wrong, always, everywhere, and for anyone, to believe anything upon insufficient evidence.... It is never lawful to stifle a doubt; for either it can be honestly answered by means of the inquiry already made, or else it proves that the inquiry was not complete."

Clifford's is the best known example of **STRONG EVIDENTIALISM** – he emphasizes the serious consequences both for the individual and for others of not taking doubts seriously:

"A shipowner was about to send to sea an emigrant ship.... Doubts had been

expressed to him about the possibility that she was not seaworthy. These doubts preyed upon his mind... Before the ship sailed, however, he succeeded in overcoming these melancholy reflections.... He watched her departure with a light heart... and he got his insurance money when she went down in mid ocean and told no tales. What shall we say of him? Surely this, that he was verily guilty of the deaths of those men. It is admitted that he did sincerely believe in the soundness of his ship; but the sincerity of his conviction can in no wise help him, because **he has no right to believe on such evidence as was before him.**"

On this basis, all religious beliefs should be rejected as, it can be argued, there is insufficient evidence for any of them.

When some religious groups today justify their treatment of others by their religious convictions (whether this is in terms of some Islamic fundamentalists bombing the World Trade Center, Jewish fundamentalists excluding Palestinians from their lands, Hindu fundamentalists in India burning mosques and killing Muslims or Christian fundamentalists rejecting those who have abortions or are homosexual) then Clifford is effectively saying that to act in any of these ways without strong evidence that one's beliefs are right is a morally wrong thing to do.

STRONG EVIDENTIALISM is based on the view that human reason is neutral between conflicting theories and can therefore judge between them. However, this can be

Evidence

In November. 19, 2002, the oil tanker Prestige broke apart and sank off the northwest coast of Spain releasing an estimated 3-4 million gallons of its 20-million-gallon cargo of oil and soiling approximately 125 miles of the Spanish coastline. This oil is classified as "residual fuel oil" and is the bottom of the refining barrel. It is thicker than crude oil and is incredibly hard to remove. Huge numbers of sea birds, fish, dolphins, and other animals died as a result of this oil spill. The tanker was very old and had a single skin hull. Tankers of this type are going to be phased out because they are considered dangerous. Assume (and there is no evidence for this) that the tanker owners thought that the tanker was vulnerable but believed that they could "get away with" keeping it operating in order to make money. Would they be wrong to do this even though there was no solid evidence for their belief? Clifford's claim is that they would be wrong as they held a belief without sufficient evidence.

challenged – perhaps there is no such thing as a philosophy which does not have presuppositions.

Opposing the view that good evidence is required for religious belief is the claim that RELIGIOUS BELIEFS ARE NOT SUBJECT TO RATIONAL EVALUATION. This is a **fideist** view and it maintains that all systems of thought rest on assumptions and the assumptions cannot be justified from some neutral standpoint. Possibly the best known advocate of this position is Blaise Pascal.

BLAISE PASCAL

Pascal put forward **The Wager Argument** for belief in God. This is often presented as claiming that so much hangs on whether a person believes in God or not, that it is sensible to try to acquire belief:

1. If God does not exist and you do not believe in God, then you win nothing and lose nothing.

2. If God does not exist and you believe in God, then you win nothing and lose very little (at the most, you may live a virtuous life which may cause you some loss of enjoyment, but not a great deal).

3. If God does exist and you choose not to believe in God then you may end up in Hell – Hell is terrible and whatever else you do you should try to avoid it.

4. If God does exist and you choose to believe in God, then you may end up in Heaven which is the best possible outcome.

If you balance these factors, it is argued, then if nothing else will persuade you to believe you should be able to see that to reject belief in God carries very few advantages and could have the most major disadvantage of going to Hell, whereas to believe in God could carry the most tremendous advantage. Self-interest, therefore, should prompt you to believe. However, Pascal's position is not as simple as this. Pascal did not think that one could just will to believe in God – this is a position which is called DIRECT VOLITIONISM. Direct volitionism maintains that a person can just decide to believe, without any evidence and just by willing to do so. Cardinal Newman is meant to have been a direct voluntarist – he said:

"Assent is an act of the mind, congenial to its nature; and it, as other acts, may be made both when it ought to be made and when it ought not. It is a

free act, a personal act for which the doer is responsible."

The Catholic theologian Bernard Lonegran agrees when he says:

".....believing is a free and responsible decision of the will."

This is not easy however – does a person really have the ability, by force of will, to force themselves to believe something even though they feel that the evidence is inadequate and they consider that the thing which they wish to believe is false? Could one really make oneself believe in Father Christmas?

Pascal, however, is not a direct volitionist even though he is often presented like this.

Instead Pascal is an INDIRECT VOLITIONIST. Indirect volitionism maintains that one can decide to place oneself in a position where one might come to believe. For instance, a person might go to church, mix with believers, read books about religion and hope that they might come to believe. This is very different from direct volitionism which means you can will yourself to believe – under this heading the most you can do is to place yourself into a position where you may (or may not) come to believe.

Pascal maintained that both reason and faith were required, neither one could be excluded:

"There are two excesses: to exclude reason, to admit nothing but reason."[1]

Both extremes had consequences:

"If we submit everything to reason our religion will be left with nothing mysterious or supernatural. If we offend the principles of reason our religion will be absurd and ridiculous."[2]

Pascal is, however, unashamed of putting his faith in Christ at the center of his understanding of faith:

Imagine you are sheltering from the rain outside a modern art gallery. The rain has set in so you decide to go into the gallery for half an hour. You see a pile of bricks in one corner with a note saying the gallery paid $750,000 for these. On another wall is what look like a child's daubs but a notice says that the "paint" was elephant dung and the work of art was purchased for $1.4million. You think to yourself "That's mad! Any child could do better." But then you reflect that this IS a major international gallery and perhaps you are missing something. You see a course on modern art advertised running over six weeks – you could either decide to ignore it and walk outside once the rain had cleared convinced that your judgment about modern art as meaningless was right, or you could decide to take the course and, possibly, you might then come to see the real value of modern art.

Pascal is claiming that the same applies in the case of religion. A person can choose to inquire further into religious belief, to take part in  services, to read and receive instruction or they can walk away and ignore the possibility. His "wager" argument is intended to persuade people to at least investigate the possibility of religion further.

"Not only do we only know God through Jesus Christ, but we only know ourselves through Jesus Christ; we only know life and death through Jesus Christ. Apart from Jesus Christ we cannot know the meaning of our life or death, of God or otherwise."[3]

This type of theological language would not be likely to be accepted by the non-believer and this is what Pascal's wager argument is addressing – he is trying to get people to take seriously the search for faith knowing that there is no certainty that faith will be achieved. Pascal points to the primacy of faith over reason:

"...the heart has its reasons of which reason knows nothing" and also *"It is the heart that perceives God and not the reason. That is what faith is: God perceived by the heart and not by reason."*[4]

Perhaps it would be fair to say that Pascal sees reason as providing an impetus to seek faith and challenging the view that reason and philosophy can decide what is true.

SØREN KIERKEGAARD

If one instead abides by Clifford's maxim (set out above) then the question arises whether faith in God is against reason. **Catholic natural theology** claims that belief in God is not opposed to reason and, indeed, that it is possible to argue for the existence of God (through Aquinas' "Five Ways" and other proofs for the existence of God, see chapter

6). Natural theology, it is claimed, is able to arrive at the existence of God and certain basic knowledge of God's attributes by the use of reason alone.[5] Revealed theology can further amplify the findings of natural theology but nothing in revealed theology goes against reason.

This position, however, was rejected by Kierkegaard[6] and also by Karl Barth who, in the Protestant tradition, rejected any attempt to arrive at the existence of God using reason. Faith, they claimed, went beyond reason. Kierkegaard in particular holds that Christianity is based on the **ABSOLUTE PARADOX** of Jesus who is both God and man. Kierkegaard claims that this is a paradox because how can God be man? How can creator be creature? How can the infinite be finite? Philosophy and reason, he claims, cannot understand this and when reason comes into contact with the Absolute Paradox (i.e. with the claim that Jesus is fully God and fully man) then only two approaches are possible:

1. *OFFENSE – in which case reason rejects the Absolute Paradox and says it is unreasonable and cannot therefore be true. This will lead to the rejection of Christianity as reason insists on remaining in the driving seat and judging faith claims. Reason will say "Either Jesus was an ordinary human being, in which case he was not God OR Jesus was God but in that case he could not have been an ordinary human being – he cannot be both." Jesus was often confronted with people who were "offended" by him.*

2. *FAITH – in which case reason accepts that it cannot understand and accepts that there is something that goes beyond reason. This is where faith comes in – it involves the acceptance that reason has limits.*

Kierkegaard would say that faith is not **IRRATIONAL** – however, faith may be **NON-RATIONAL**. It may not be based on reason but it does not necessarily go against reason, rather it may go beyond reason. Merely because reason does not understand something, does not mean that it is irrational – it just may not be able to be understood. Something may appear to be irrational but may actually not be if one understands things at a deeper level.

Philosophy tends to put reason into first place, but maybe there are things that go beyond reason (like falling in love – which is rarely a matter of rational evaluation). Falling in love and getting married means committing oneself to another human being knowing that marriages often go wrong and that there

St. Paul's letter to the Corinthians

The message of the cross is foolishness to those who are perishing, but to us who are being saved it is the power of God. For it is written:

"I will destroy the wisdom of the wise, and the learning of the learned I will set aside."

"Where is the wise one? Where is the scribe? Where is the debater of this age? Has not God made the wisdom of the world foolish? For since in the wisdom of God the world did not come to know God through wisdom, it was the will of God through the foolishness of the proclamation to save those who have faith. For Jews demand signs and Greeks look for wisdom, but we proclaim Christ crucified, a stumbling block to Jews and foolishness to Gentiles, but to those who are called, Jews and Greeks alike, Christ the power of God and the wisdom of God. For the foolishness of God is wiser than human wisdom, and the weakness of God is stronger than human strength." (1 Cor. 1.18–25)

is no proof that all will go well. In fact there is a 40% chance of divorce and a considerably higher chance that the marriage will be mediocre and the couple will "stay together for the sake of the kids" – nevertheless many people DO get married and trust that their marriages will succeed.

CRITICAL RATIONALISM will hold that it IS possible to evaluate belief systems but that it is not possible to arrive at a convincing, universally accepted proof that any one system is correct. This requires the individual to choose the most probable approach and argument can certainly contribute to an assessment of this probability.

REFORMED EPISTEMOLOGISTS

Modern Protestant philosophers who reject the supremacy of reason and instead rely on God's revelation as the basis for faith are called "Reformed Epistemologists". Reformed epistemologists argue that the effects of sin have hampered human reason and that it is, therefore, impossible for sinful human beings to use reason, philosophy, and argument to arrive at the existence of God. The alternative, they claim, is to hold that God has revealed God's truth in Jesus Christ and through the Bible and what people have to do is to accept this. Failure to accept this truth is equivalent to sin and is the result of pride and a willful assertion of reason against the revelation of God. (See also page 71.)

This view has a long history going back to St. John's Gospel and also the writings of St. Paul. John's Gospel portrays the world as a place of darkness and only those who believe in and accept Jesus as the Christ sent by God dwell in the light. The choice, then, is sin, darkness, and ignorance or being willing to accept the Christian revelation and thereby dwell in the light of truth.

St. Paul, also, holds that faith in Jesus is central and, indeed, says:

"We proclaim Christ crucified, a stumbling block to Jews and foolishness to Gentiles."

The Gentiles would have been the philosophers of St. Paul's time and Paul considers that faith gives knowledge that goes beyond reason and is based not on philosophy but on revelation. This is the position of modern reformed epistemologists. They hold that the truth of Christianity is self-evident to those who believe and there is simply no need for philosophic argument. The reality of God is so clear to the believer when he or she is at prayer or reading their Bible that talk of justifying God's existence is out of place. It is as if someone asked for justification of your claim to have met your father, mother, brother, sister, wife, or husband. There simply would be no question in your mind that you had met them and even to attempt to justify it would be considered foolish and inappropriate. Similarly for the believer, God's reality is unquestioned as they experience God in prayer and at other times. God's presence is such a reality to them that talk of justification is out of place.

> ### Imagine
>
> Imagine that you were St. Paul and the experience recorded in Acts actually happened. You have been persecuting Christians and suddenly there was a blinding light, a voice from heaven and you were struck blind. The experience might be so overwhelming that you simply could not fail to believe in God and Jesus. Talk of trying to prove that God existed would not make sense. This is rather like the reformed epistemologist's position – they claim to be so clearly aware of the presence of God that doubt is almost impossible and talk of proof is out of place.

Reformed epistemologists maintain that believers have "a properly ordered noetic structure" – this means that their whole way of seeing the world (including their belief in God) is correct, valid, and true. Non-believers, because of the effects of sin, fail to see the world correctly – they are therefore in the darkness and sin of which John's Gospel speaks.

The problem, however, is how does one decide which of the many claimed revelations are true?

1. *Should one accept the Muslim view that the Holy Qu'ran was the revelation of Allah to the Prophet?*

2. *Should one accept the Christian claims that Jesus revealed God to human beings?*

A page from the Qu'ran

3. Should one accept the Jewish claim that God's will for human beings is set out in the Torah?

4. Why accept one revelation rather than another?

In a multi-faith world, to claim (as the reformed episte-mologists effectively do) that one group is right because they are totally certain that they are right and that they need no justification for their claims is not persuasive to the millions of people who hold different positions and who adhere to different revelations. At most, reformed epistemology may provide reassurance to those safe within their own religious communities that they do not need to seek to justify their faith claims but it cannot do any more than this. The skeptic will not be convinced and the reformed epistemologist will not feel any threat to his or her position because of this as, of course, the skeptic will be held to be in sin and to be asserting their own rational autonomy rather than accepting the "obvious" truth of the revelation that is proclaimed to them.

There is also debate over what is revealed and how revelation takes place:

- *The Protestant Christian will see God speaking through the pages of the Bible when the individual Christian prayerfully reads the Bible.*

- *The Catholic may see God speaking through the wisdom of the Catholic tradition and the teachings of the Roman Catholic Magisterium (this is the teaching office of the Catholic Church in Rome).*

- *Orthodox Christians will see God revealed in the declarations of the Councils of the early Christian Church.*

The criteria as to which type of revelation to accept are by no means clear and, in the absence of rational grounds for preferring one claimed revelation to another, the problems of faith and reason remain.

"Belief in" and "Belief that"

H.H. Price has an important article[7] which throws light on what it means to believe. Price distinguishes between "Belief that" which is equivalent to factual or propositional belief and "Belief in." He maintains that "Belief in" can be of two types:

1) The **REDUCIBLE** *form of "Belief in" is where "Belief in" can be reduced to "Belief that." For instance "I believe in fairies at the bottom of my garden" can be reduced to "I believe that there are fairies at the bottom of my garden." Price maintains that most "Belief in" statements are like this (e.g. "I believe in wholemeal bread" would reduce to "I believe that wholemeal bread is good for you"). "Belief in God" under this heading could be reduced to "Belief that God exists."*

2) The **IRREDUCIBLE** *form of "Belief in" is where "Belief in" cannot be reduced to "Belief that." This is where an evaluative sense is being employed and would cover such cases as "belief in a friend" meaning trust in a friend. In the religious arena, on this view, "Belief in God" would amount to "trust in God" and this operates in a different way to "Belief that" statements.*

Price holds that "Belief in God" cannot simply be reduced to acceptance of statements about God's existence. Price's claim is that religious belief involves trust and commitment of a different order from factual belief. While factual beliefs may be a part of religious beliefs, they are by no means the only or even the major part.

St. James' epistle puts Price's point well:

"You believe in God? You do well. The devils also believe, and tremble."

In other words the devils believe THAT God exists, but they certainly do not believe IN God in that they do not trust their lives to God. To bring a person to factual belief that God exists is not, therefore, the same as bringing them to believe in or to trust God. Trust and commitment to God may be present in very simple people who have little knowledge of the detail of propositional claims (i.e. "Belief that" claims) about the nature of God.

Søren Kierkegaard made a very similar point in much of his philosophy by making a distinction between objective and subjective claims to truth. Most philosophy is concerned with whether statements are objectively true. Most schools and universities are concerned with the transmission of objective or factual claims to knowledge – these are the sort of knowledge claims that can be communicated in a text book or in a series of lectures. A person can show

It is one thing to stand on the side of a pool containing killer whales or sharks and to say "I do not believe they would harm me if I went into the water" and quite another to get into the water with them and to say 'I do not believe they will harm me."

Similarly belief in God that is simply a matter of saying the words "I believe in God" is very different from staking one's life on this belief.

they know the truth claims concerned by either reciting them or showing how these claims can be applied (for instance one can show that one knows how to fly an aeroplane by actually doing so!). However, the really important issue in religious truth claim is not, according to Kierkegaard, developing rational proofs that God exists – indeed he considered these to be impossible. What was vital was to bring individuals to take on board for themselves what a religious life is like and then to follow the religious path. Reciting creeds and dogmas of a Church or particular religion does not make a person religious – this only comes when the truth claims are internalized and the individual is subjectively affected by the claims being made.

People stake their lives on religious truth claims which generally cannot be proved and may often seem unreasonable. This does not, however, mean they are foolish. Some of the most intelligent people in history have placed God at the center of their lives and have attempted to live lives of radical obedience to God. To say that such people are deceived simply because they cannot prove their convictions is to be naïve in the extreme. Kierkegaard contrasted:

- *The philosopher who might be an expert in theories about survival of death but who the idea of life after death did not affect personally in any way, with*

- *Socrates who said that he could not prove the immortality of the soul but was ready to stake his whole life on the 'if' that the claim to survive death was true.*

It is the person who stakes their life who may be closer to the truth than a disinterested observer – although, of course, it is possible that they may be wrong. This is why the person who takes religion seriously may be "suspended over 70000 fathoms"[8] – staking their lives on truth claims that they know could be mistaken but which they passionately believe to be true. St. Paul recognized this when he said:

"If Christ has not been raised, then empty (too) is our preaching; empty, too, your faith." (1 Cor. 15.14)

St. Paul admits the possibility that Christian claims could be false although, of course, he is in no doubt that they are true and is willing to go to his death in defense of his beliefs. Perhaps religious claims can only be known by those who stake their lives on the religious quest and the disinterested observer will always, of necessity, remain a mere spectator without understanding or insight.[9] To rely, therefore, solely on reason may be to exclude oneself from the whole religious enterprise and the quest for truth that this involves.

Notes

[1]   *Blaise Pascal.* Pensées *p.85.*

[2]   Pensées *p.83.*

[3]   Pensées *p.148.*

[4]   Pensées *p.154.*

[5]   *This position was held by the First Vatican Council in 1879 based largely on Aquinas'* Five Ways.

[6]   *For an introduction to Kierkegaard's thought see the volume* Kierkegaard *in the HarperCollins Fount Christian Thinkers series by Peter Vardy. The U.S. edition of this is available through the Amazon website.*

[7]   Belief in and Belief That. *Religious Studies 1965.*

[8]   *This phrase was used by Søren Kierkegaard to portray the person who stakes their life on religious claims that cannot be proved. They invest their whole lives in their commitment to the truth of the position they hold, but they are "suspended over 70000 fathoms" because they also know that it is possible that they could be mistaken. See also discussion on Kierkegaard in chapter 5.*

[9]   *This approach is developed more fully in* What is Truth? *by Peter Vardy, John Hunt Publishing 2003.*

QUESTIONS FOR CONSIDERATION

1) Should beliefs only be based on strong evidence? If this position was accepted, what would the consequences be?

2) What is the difference between belief and knowledge?

3) What was the purpose of Pascal's "wager" argument?

4) Can one believe in God just by willing to do so? If not, could God condemn someone who did not believe?

5) What is the difference between someone who says "I believe in aliens" and "I believe in my best friend"? Which of these is closest to "I believe in God"?

CHAPTER 12

ATTACKS ON GOD – DARWIN, MARX, AND FREUD

Various significant attacks on God and religious belief have been formulated over the last two hundred years. One of the most influential was the rejection of God as not being worthy of worship. This was based on the existence of innocent suffering and was put forward by Dostoyevsky in his novel *The Brothers Karamazov*. Further significant attacks have been put forward by atheists such as David Hume, A.J. Ayer and Bertrand Russell who tried to demonstrate that the existence of God was indefensible by rational inquiry (for a further discussion of the above see *The Thinker's Guide to Evil*). Such challenges were debated widely but it is fair to say that their impact on religious belief and society as a whole was, and is, limited. By contrast the work of Darwin, Marx, and Freud not only challenged religious belief in their own day but their impact is still very much present. Such has been the power of their ideas that even today their challenges are seen by many as valid and conclusively damning for religious belief. An agnostic or an atheist today may still argue their case from one of or a combination of these positions. Between them they prepared the way for Post-modernism, by attacking not only religion but the established social order.

Their work has little in common but each was able to put before a largely religious and increasingly well-educated public a view which was acclaimed as "scientific." This was a time when there was faith in science and the techno-logical advances it brought. The advent of rail travel and steam-driven ships, of electricity and greatly improved medical care made this time seem like a time of positive progress. Improved printing techniques meant books were widely accessible and affordable. There was a great deal of interest in scientific inquiry and anybody who was interested could read the work of Marx, Freud, or Darwin in their own home. The "scientific" work of these three would disrupt the fundamental assumptions of society and present an alternative, coherent, view of the world that appeared to be incompatible with religious belief. This chapter will outline each of these challenges and assess their validity for today.

CHARLES DARWIN –
The survival of the fittest

The work of natural science[1] first challenged the authority of religious accounts of creation. The geologist Lyell showed that the traditional date of 4004 B.C.E. given by Bishop Ussher for creation was wrong. Ussher had worked out the date of creation from the biblical narratives but this could no longer hold given the findings of geology. The creation of the Earth had to be millennia earlier than the biblical dating, as the Earth needed eons to develop. The stratification of rocks occurred through the slow cooling and liquefying of gases to become solids. The fossils of plants and animals existed millions of years before the date of creation accepted by the Church.

In the 19th century, geology was developing as a popular hobby and there were constant newspaper reports of new *Animal and plant fossils*

fossil discoveries which seem to show that the world was far older than the Bible indicated. The discovery of dinosaur bones, for instance, raised real questions in the minds of many thinking people. There is no mention of dinosaurs and woolly mammoths in the Bible which seemed to suggest that the writer of the Bible did not know about them. If God was the authority and inspiration of the Bible it was not unreasonable to expect each of God's cre-ated works to be listed in the account of creation, but fossil finds showed that there were generations of animals not mentioned. More and more evidence accumulated of many creatures that must have lived and died out far in the

Some definitions

Various terms need to be defined:

- Atheism is the rejection of belief in God – it is based on the claim that God does not exist.

- Naturalism claims that there is nothing beyond nature – there is no supernatural being and no spiritual realm.

- Materialism is committed to the view that there is nothing but matter and energy. Human minds are simply material objects and consciousness is a product of neural activity.

- Humanism starts from the assumption that God does not exist and human beings are at the center. It attempts to work out what it means to live in a world devoid of God.

Although all these share their rejection of God, it is a mistake to see this rejection in entirely negative terms – naturalism, materialism, and humanism all seek to develop a positive vision of the world in which God did not create the Universe.

distant past and not been included in the biblical account. Initially efforts were made to reconcile these discoveries with the biblical account but this proved more and more difficult as the discoveries increased in scale.[2] This was a major challenge to the biblical view of creation, as geology made it clear that the biblical view of seven days of creation was wrong.

As geological finds continued the **Lamarckian version of evolution**, popularised by Robert Chambers in *The Vestiges of the Natural History of Creation*, 1844, was published and suggested that CHANCE was underneath the present order of the world and not God or any kind of design. This idea, that human beings evolved over thousands of years from other life forms, has a long history before Darwin and was particularly prevalent amongst French philosophers in the 18th century. The French philosopher Montesquieu wrote about the close similarities between species in 1721 and by the mid 18th century these ideas were widely accepted by a number of French philosophers including Voltaire and Diderot. Ideas about evolution in France were usually coupled with anti-religious beliefs, including materialism and a faith in scientific progress. These ideas had a significant impact on the French Revolution. French society was feudal with the King, great Lords, and the Church in power and the mass of poor people disempowered. The idea of evolution questioned this social picture. If the theory of evolution was right, human beings had evolved – this meant that their place in society was not necessarily "God-given" and that the poor did not have to accept their lot. This contributed to the violent overthrow of the French feudal order. The French Revolution of 1789, with its accompanying violence and the mass killing of many French aristocrats and their supporters, brought Napoleon to leadership in France. The theory of evolution was, therefore, making an impact long before Charles Darwin. The key problem that the theory of evolution faced was that there seemed no mechanism which could explain how evolution occurred. The action of God still seemed to many the best explanation to account for the great variety of different species of birds, animals, and plants. The significance of Charles Darwin was his discovery of the means by which evolution took place – this is the **theory of natural selection through the "survival of the fittest".**

The challenge to religion of Darwin's theory of natural selection is not to be viewed in isolation. Darwin built on the work of earlier scientists who had worked extensively in the field of geology. In order to understand the magnitude of Darwin's challenge it is important to understand a little about the society in which these ideas appeared.

Up until the time of Darwin, religious scriptures and religious leaders were viewed as authoritative. Most world religions have an account of the origin of the world in which the deity usually has a major part to play in the creation of the Earth and all things in it. Within the tradition the story may be regarded as a myth – that is as a story containing truth about the human condition – or it may be understood literally by some.

Darwin worked in a world where most people assumed a divine origin of the Universe and believed that the Universe was unfolding by a divine plan. The rightness of the capitalist system was assumed and conformity to the system was prized and considered to be God-given. As one hymn puts it:

"The rich man in his castle
The poor man at his gate
God made them high and lowly
And ordered their estate."

There was a feeling that not only was the Earth here by divine order but that the structures of society were approved of by God. This belief system was common throughout much of the world.

In *The Origin of the Species,* 1859, Darwin argued for his theory of "natural selection." This holds that those members of a species whose characteristics are best suited to enable them to survive in their environment go on to breed whilst those ill suited die off before breeding. Whenever an advantageous characteristic appears – such as greater capacity for speed in a predator or greater reach in a carnivore, those animals who display this characteristic have a survival advantage over others. They survived to pass on the characteristic to their offspring. In this way a species naturally evolves by the principle of the survival of the fittest.

Darwin's carefully researched theory, following the voyage of *H.M.S. Beagle* to the Galapagos Islands, showed not only how evolution had happened in the past but how evolution was continuously at work. Darwin observed differences between the Galapagos animals and others he had studied and in some cases entirely different species had developed. He concluded that the fittest animals and plants survived to mate and to pass on their genes.[3] Those random adaptations occurred through sexual reproduction which mixed the genes of the two parents (whether these were plants or animals) and those parents which were most successful survived to breed and to pass on their successful characteristics. Species, therefore, adapted over generations by random changes and those which successfully met the changing conditions survived.[4] Darwin did not consider that there was any end to which evolution was directed. In nature, it was simply a case of the "survival of the fittest." The theory of evolution and Darwin's explanation for the mechanism of evolution posed a very serious challenge to a number of accepted religious doctrines:

- **Darwin challenged the authority of the Bible.** *The Bible, in the story of creation, pictured God creating humans and all animal species directly. If the biblical story of creation was false then so, many considered, was the rest of the Bible. The Bible could no longer be regarded as the divinely given "word of God" and the authority of the Church was therefore undermined. This particularly applies in the case of Protestants who based their faith on the Bible but also for Catholics as the teaching authority of the Church depended on the Bible and the Church had always strongly defended a literal reading of the biblical texts.*

- **Darwin challenged the place of humanity.** *Fundamental to the creation stories of many world religions is the idea that humans are somehow unique or special. Evolution and the theory of the survival of the fittest contradicted this. Humans are not special and not made in the image of God, or with a divine spark. It is just a matter of blind chance that humans have managed to adapt successfully to their environment. Humans are not the pinnacle of* *creation at all but are just animals that have adapted well to their environment. Furthermore man is not "of God" but "of ape." Instead of being a little lower than the angels, mankind is seen as a little higher than the apes. Theologically humankind had been held to be the pinnacle of creation but Darwin's theory led to the conclusion that there may be a greater creation yet to come. Man may be the fossil of the future. The blind world of nature was seen as incompatible with a loving creator God.*

- **Darwin challenged the religious concept of providence.** *He drew attention to the apparent lack of purpose in creation. In most religious traditions the Earth has been created by God for a divine purpose and each human life has an end or a goal. Darwin was able to demonstrate that nature discards entire species and that there is a war between the species. Nature*

Did humans evolve from apes?

was now seen to be "red in tooth and claw." The survival of the fittest entailed the destruction of huge numbers of animals and plants as well as entire species as part of the random nature of evolution. Such a cruel, random system seems to be at complete variance to any idea of a loving God and the Universe seems meaningless and without purpose in the face of this randomness. Competing successfully to survive, in the Darwin model, is the only purpose of any life form.

- **Darwin challenged the idea of an immutable law operating.** *In many world religions there is the idea that God has set the pattern of creation and fixed the laws of nature. There now emerged the idea of constant change in the world. The world, argued Darwin, is full of developing creatures and plants. Religion often pictures the world as inhabited by plants and animals carefully crafted by God. Darwin challenged the idea that different animal species had been designed by God. They are designed, so that only those most successful in the environment survive. Darwin also argued that all animals had a common ancestor which again suggested design by success at adaptation and not design by a creator God.*

- **Darwin challenged ideas about God's action in the world.** *God could no longer be seen as the designer of species, each with its own unique attributes.*

The claim that each animal had its own unique and special design, made to suit its environment as part of a divine plan was seriously undermined. Darwin argued that it was the environment that had shaped the species, and that those best suited to the environment had survived whilst others had not. Over time, things had designed themselves – it was not God who did the designing. Evolution recognized that there was an element of design in the world but gave a purely naturalistic explanation for it.

Responses to Darwin

For many who feel that the authority of the religious scriptures is central to their faith, Darwin was and remains a decisive challenge to belief in God. Equally for the atheist or the agnostic who thinks that a literal reading of sacred scriptures ought to be central to a believer's faith, Darwin is a barrier to religious commitment.

The first reaction of many religious leaders, especially Christian leaders, was to reject evolution as well as the mechanism by which evolution was brought about.[5] Today, however, most accept the theory of natural selection and do not see it as a challenge to religious belief at all.

1. *Evolution and the survival of the fittest is seen as the means God uses to bring about God's purposes. Evolution and natural selection can be seen as a way of explaining differences and deviations in nature, but is not a way of discarding God. The mechanism for evolution, it is argued, comes from God and is part of a divine plan.*

2. *The religious person can argue that even if God did not design the individual species, God did create the conditions necessary for the formation of the planet Earth and may have initiated the beginnings of life itself. No scientist has yet created the mechanisms for "life" in the laboratory, which arguably leaves room for God.*

3. *The mystery of how life came from "random chaos" is still an unanswered question. Many scientists argue from the principle of entropy that the natural world tends towards chaos, and this means that the ordering of matter in such a way as to create life is against the natural tendency of raw matter. It is held that the degree of chance needed for the creation of life is against all probability. (See chapter 13 for a more detailed argument on this.)*

4. *It can be argued that the "accidents" of evolution that have led to the diversity of life on Earth and the evolution of men and women are not accidents at all and that the hand of God may be seen turning the hand of fate. This means that the world and human life can still be seen to have ultimate purpose.*

That Darwin leaves room for religious belief is often met with the counter "belief" that science will one day explain these things too. Richard Dawkins develops this idea and his arguments are dealt with in chapter 13. The point is that belief in God is by no means ruled out by the work of Darwin, as is often held.

Darwin's work did shake the foundations of religious believers who depended for their faith on a literal reading of sacred texts. However, for most religious believers this was by no means a decisive blow. For many people today Darwin is still seen as a significant challenge to belief, and it is true that the shock wave of Darwin's challenge to religion can still be felt. Darwin undoubtedly provided a scientific explanation for the development of life on Earth but many are happy to accept the theory of evolution alongside religious belief and see no contradiction. In fact for many religious believers it has been a very positive experience as it has triggered a new, and arguably a more profound, way of understanding and interpreting sacred scriptures. However, whilst natural selection is not seen as a contradiction to religious belief the world view of the pure Darwinian is totally at odds with the religious world view. For those who believe that there is a totally naturalistic explanation for life on Earth – the materialist – there is no purpose or goal to human life. The ethic that arises out of this purposeless existence is an ethic which justifies a great deal of competition in the name of "survival of the fittest." The ethical imperatives once taken for granted were challenged by the drive to compete – validated by social Darwinism. It was in Nazi Germany that natural selection was given a helping hand by the "evacuation" of those considered to be weakening the gene pool. This is the law of the jungle and the religious outlook is very different to this. The religious world view is one in which the whole world has a purpose and a meaning. Life is not purely about the self, and fighting for supremacy, no matter who is downtrodden along the way. Life is a special and unique gift that can be squandered or lived well in service to others. The problem of Darwin for the religious person is not the idea of natural selection but the way that this idea can be used to undermine the ethic of a caring society and turn it into a culture where the individual is encouraged only to look after themselves and has no sense of responsibility for the wider community. As Bishop Gore said – "It is a case of each for himself, as the elephant said when it danced among the chickens."

KARL MARX (1818–1883) Religion as a Product of Society

Born in 1818 and ethnically a Jew, although formally a Christian Karl Marx was brought up in a free-thinking family. He spent his life escaping from prosecution for his radical ideas and ended his life in London working to expose the unsatisfactory nature of capitalism. As a youth he was religious but by the time he went to Berlin to study he had abandoned religion. Karl Marx therefore worked with the underlying assumption that religion is a human creation. He believed that his task was to reveal the causes of religion, which he thought could be found in society, in order to free people from the myths that ensnare them.

Alienation

Marx believed that people experience what he calls alienation, and it is the cause of this feeling of alienation that Marx is most curious about in the human condition. In his exploration of the cause of this feeling of alienation he was influenced by Feuerbach.

- *Feuerbach placed human self-consciousness at the center of his philosophy.*

- *He said that humans were alienated because they created a God and then felt alienated from their own creation.*

- *They created God but this mythical creation supported by formal religion provided a standard which could never be lived up to.*

- *The source of alienation for Feuerbach was therefore the creation of an illusion, God, with which a person could not then feel at home.*

Marx agreed with this, and accepted that God was a human construct, but then asked the question – **why do people create this God to feel alienated from?** He concluded that the political, economic, and social reality of human life and the existing conditions of society were the true cause of alienation and the real reason that people create God.

- *Religion he saw as an expression of distress caused by the social conditions in which people lived and as a protest against these conditions. It was also a means for those who are distressed to find comfort.*

- *The real source of alienation for Marx is to be found in the class structures in society, and religion is a symptom of that alienation. The societies in which people live are so alienating and dissatisfying that in order to cope with conditions in society people live by projecting or creating the illusion of religion.*

- *What is needed is a change in society to overcome the illusion.*

- *If the social conditions change to allow people to be more authentic and more who they want to be then religion, he says, will go away naturally.*

- *The real struggle for Marx is not with religion but with society. It is society that alienates people and gives rise to the need for religion. Religion is only a problem in so far as it distracts people from the root of their alienation.*

Why is society so alienating?

For Marx both human beings and religion are social products. It is people who make society BUT they are also made by society. Men and women are social beings who live in particular historical circumstances and these circumstances form people into what they are and will become.

Religion, which has been produced by society as a way of dealing with alienation, is then used by those in society who are best served by the distraction religion brings – the ruling classes. The ruling classes own all the factories and the means of production and take all the profits. They do not share the profits with the workers who give their lives to the factories. The workers spend their lives working and have little money and leisure time. Religion supports the ruling classes in their oppression of the poor. Religion is an ideology that legitimates the social status quo in the interests of the ruling classes, but alienates the poor from the benefits of their labor and from any sense of autonomy or freedom in determining how they live their lives. The ruling classes benefit from the myth of religion because it keeps poor people happy with their lot in life.

How religion contributes to social alienation

It is true that religion the world over has served this conservative function. Hindu society is organized around the caste system in which people are born into a certain caste and may not move up the social ladder because that is the way they are born. In the Bhagavad Gita the great God Vishnu speaks, through Krishna:

The four-caste system did I generate
With categories of constituents and works;
Of this I am the doer, know thou this.
Bhagavad Gita IV. 13

This kind of oppression for Marx is the hallmark of religion. It works with the ruling classes to oppress ordinary workers. Men and women are denied the opportunity to develop as human beings and they are thwarted in their attempts to express, affirm, and authenticate themselves by such a society. At the time of Marx, the Christian Church identified itself with the ruling social elite and effectively gave it God's seal of approval. This was part of a long process – in the Middle Ages the Church was generally on the side of the kings and lords and was a major landowner and power in its own right. The Church was grounded in a feudal past and after the Industrial Revolution, the Church switched to serve its new capitalist masters. Based on this analysis it is easy to see why Marx saw the Church as being on the side of the "haves" against the "have nots" and saw the role of the Church as being to pass on a message of submission and obedience to those with power, wealth, and authority. Marx was fiercely critical of the Church and saw religion as a profound human response and protest against the terrible conditions in which most ordinary people had to live. Marx said:

"Religion is the sign of the oppressed creating the feelings of a heartless world and the spirit of conditions that are unspiritual. It is the opium of the people."[6]

It is important to read this quotation in its entirety – often the only part of the quotation that is given is the last part: "religion is the opium of the masses." Marx recognizes the cry that religion represents from the suffering mass of humanity.

Release from alienation

People, for Marx, make themselves. There is no creator God and there is no higher purpose than their own, "Man is the highest being for man" but full realization of human potential cannot be achieved without a change in social conditions to allow people the freedom and opportunity to self-create. A society which prevents people from fulfilling their potential alienates individuals and people will find ways of coping with this. Religion is, therefore, a means of coping with alienation.

The solution to the alienating influence of society is to re-create society so that it allows people to fulfill themselves as human persons. If the underlying cause of religion has not been tackled, alienation will remain. To criticize religion but not to criticize its secular base for Marx would achieve nothing.

In Marx's thesis on Feuerbach he wrote, "Philosophers have only interpreted the world...the point, however, is to change it." Unless the world changed, argued Marx, there would be no hope of release from the feeling of alienation.

Marx's philosophy of history

Marx developed Hegel's idea of a philosophy of history and considered that the overthrow of capitalism was inevitable with the workers rising up to take control of the means of production. This was what was intended by the Russian Revolution in 1917 when the communist government came to power. Marx analyzed history in terms of class struggle and he saw the working class being suppressed. In Marx's analysis, the working class were certain to rise up to take control away from the wealthy and those who owned the factories. It was only a matter of time. If a modern Marxist was asked why this has not yet happened, he or she would reply "it will." Marx has a great faith in the inevitability of the historical processes which he analyzed.

St. Francis came from a wealthy family but renounced his family and dedicated himself to a life of poverty and service to the poor. The Franciscan movement, and the thousands of people who have followed in his footsteps, have sought to serve the poor and to live lives of great simplicity. Their example is not one that Karl Marx considered when he was so critical of the institutional Church and yet the Franciscan movement has, arguably, had as great an effect in history as Marxism.

Is Marxism compatible with religious belief?

It has to be recognized that many who believe in God would agree with Marx's criticism of institutional religion as a means of supporting social structures. There is a sense in which Marx gave the world a timely reminder that religion can easily be distorted so that it becomes, as he argued, a means of maintaining social structures rather than about issues of justice and concern for the poor. This concern is at the heart of most world religions. In Islam believers must give one tenth of their income to the poor and Jews are encouraged to give similar sums. Within the Christian tradition St. Francis of Assisi and his friend and companion St. Clare sought to bring the Church back to an identification with the poor and the outcasts of his day and, throughout its history, Christians have constantly sought to identify with those who suffer and those who are marginalized. Francis always identified with the outcasts of his society whether these were lepers, robbers, or simply the poor. Today, Liberation Theology – influenced by Marx – is a Christian theology which is actively on the side of the poor in what is seen as a struggle against those in power.

Many religious people today affirm the "option for the poor" and see it as part of their faith commitment to identify with those who have nothing in worldly terms.[7] Religion and Marxism, at first sight, seems a contradiction in terms but, in fact this is not necessarily so. It is possible to bring together Marx's social analysis with a religious commitment to those on the fringes of society – the dispossessed and those with no power or influence. The poor were of great concern to Jesus as recorded in St. Luke's Gospel and in Islam there is a very strong emphasis on giving to the poor – indeed prayer and alms-giving are constantly linked in the Qu'ran and prayer without alms-giving is considered of little worth. Pope John Paul II made clear the importance of the "option for the poor" in 1994:

"If we recall that Jesus came to 'preach the good news to the poor' (Matthew 11.5; Luke 7.22) how can we fail to lay greater emphasis on the Church's preferential option for the poor and the outcast? Indeed it has to be said that a commitment to justice and peace in a world like ours, marked by so many conflicts and intolerable social and economic inequalities, is a necessary condition for the preparation and celebration of Jubilee."[8]

Communism

Marx is often hailed as the first communist. For Marx communism meant the creation of a new type of society based on co-operation, community, and wealth held in common. He was, however, not the first to have such an idea. Indeed this communistic approach was the type of society that the first Christian communities tried to establish. The New Testament records an early Christian community where wealth was shared:

"And all who believed were together and had all things in common; and they sold their possessions and goods and distributed them to all, as any had need." Acts 3.44-45

This is precisely in accordance with one of Marx's best known phrases which sums up the communist approach:

"From each according to his ability to each according to his need."

The communistic experiment in the Christian Church failed but it is recognized as being an "ideal" way of running communities. The great religious orders such as the Benedictines, Dominicans, Jesuits, and others give up all personal possessions and share property. In the 17th century there were a whole series of groups who shared their possessions including the Levellers and the Diggers. More recently, Christian-based communities in Latin America and communities such as that of Taizé in France aspire to a form of communist shared ownership. Much, therefore, of Marx's insights are not intrinsically challenging to religion, but can be seen as compatible. Marx himself, however, is quite clearly an atheist and attacks institutional religion when it is used to support the social order.[9]

In the Soviet Union, which claimed to be a Marxist state, religion was forbidden and every effort made by the communist government to suppress religious belief. However, communism does not have to be anti-religious and after the collapse of communism in the Soviet Union, other communist parties have been much more open to religion being compatible with communism. For example, the South African Communist Party accepted that belief in God was compatible with the communist ideal and religious belief was not a rival system to be dismissed and rejected. In the Tenth Congress of the party in July 1998 the following declaration was made:

"Our class approach to reality (a bias toward the poor), our struggle for a society based on social need and not on private profit, our condemnation of selfishness, and personal greed, and our refusal to give way to demoralization (in other words our espousal of hope) are closer to the core values of all the world's major religions than the ethos of globalization, imperialism, and the Johannesburg Stock Market. Dogmatic errors from the side of Marxists, and the class abuse of institutionalized religion by many reactionary forces, have historically contributed to a dichotomy between socialists and believers that should never have happened."[10]

Fidel Castro is President of one of the few remaining communist states in the world – Cuba. He recently recognized that Marxism – on which the communist revolution depends – does not necessitate the rejection of belief in God:

"From a strictly political point of view I believe that it is possible for Christians to be Marxists as well and to work together with Marxist communists to transform the world. The important thing is that in both cases they be honest revolutionaries who want to end the exploitation of man by man and to struggle for a fair distribution of social wealth, equality, fraternity, and the dignity of all human beings – that is, that they be the standard-bearers of the most advanced political, economic, and social ideas, even though in the case of the Christians their starting point is a religious concept."[11]

How far is Marx a challenge to religious belief today?

- *One of the reasons that Marx's ideas can sit comfortably within a religious framework is that he did not actually produce philosophic arguments against God – his starting assumption was that God does not exist and that all religion is based on a self-created illusion. This is an assertion similar to a religious faith assertion and is based on his own beliefs about the world. However he could well have worked out much of his theory about the need for a revolution of existing social structures and for a sharing of wealth within traditional religious categories. Without some justification for these assumptions Marx does not really challenge religious belief.*

- *Furthermore a religious person could argue that the true source of alienation – to use Marx's words – is not society. They might argue that spiritual thirst and enrichment are human needs that must be satisfied. If a person does not acknowledge the spiritual side of their nature they will remain alienated from themselves as they truly are. Those who believe in a creator God will argue that the feeling of alienation is due to a person refusing to meet with their natural inclination to acknowledge God as their Father and until their maker is recognized they will be truly alienated from the source of all being.*

- *It might also be argued that the hopes and aspirations of humans can never be fulfilled in this world. What form of society can bring about fulfillment of human nature? Perhaps humans can only be truly satisfied with a meaning that transcends the everyday world. This is essentially a question about what it is to be human and it is a question that will be returned to in the final chapter.*

- *Marx's definition of what it is to be human and Marx's explanation of the phenomena of alienation is not science. It can only be accepted on "faith". Whilst Marx offers a radically different and coherent view of the world and the place of humanity in it, there is no way of establishing that Marx's view is true.*

Marx did offer an account of religion but how coherent is it? He claims that religion is created to assuage feelings of alienation that come from living in society. This is something of a circular argument which requires one to believe that human beings create societies from which they subsequently feel alienated and this in turn causes them to create a God to comfort them in their social alienation. If one starts with the same assumptions as Marx about religion then it can be seen as a challenge to religion – but it is important to recognize that the assumption is being accepted on faith and that Marx offers no justification for it. It is at least as probable that religion has its origins in God as that it has its origins in society.

There is an increasing awareness that Marxist ideas are not incompatible with religious views, but this is not to say that the two are wholly compatible. They can exist alongside one another, but they are not bedfellows. They start with completely different views about the world, the existence of God, and the origins of religion, but this is not all. The religious person would not accept that social conditions are the sole deciding factor in a person's beliefs and patterns of behavior. For the religious person Marx places too much emphasis on "society" and not enough on the responsibility of the individual for their own fulfillment and behavior. For the religious person it is the free will of the individual that is crucial in how a life is lived, and it is their responsibility. If a person fails to live well this it is not the fault of society and social conditions. Many people from the poorest homes have led good, honest, and "authentic" lives, have died quietly and been completely fulfilled. This is not to say that religion does not have a mission to the poor, but it is to say that, "the poor will always be with you"[12] and that being poor is not a hurdle to a good and fulfilled life and that belief in God may be a highly positive contributor to this.

SIGMUND FREUD (1856–1939) Religion As a Psychological Construct

Freud was born in 1856 in Freiberg, which was then part of the Austro-Hungarian Empire, in the modern-day Czech Republic. His father was a Jew but Freud did not have a particularly Jewish upbringing. In 1859 the family moved to Leipzig and then to Vienna. He studied in Paris under the neurologist Charcot, and from here he moved into psychopathology. Impressed by the techniques he had developed for uncovering repressed memories he moved into psychoanalysis. His special interest was the interpretation of dreams as a way of understanding the subconscious mind. He worked in Vienna until the anti-Semitic policies of the Nazis forced him into exile in London where he died in 1939.

As in the case of Marx, Freud agreed with Feuerbach that religion is essentially a human construct with its origin in the individual, although the individual would not recognize this. He developed these ideas further and claimed that:

- *Religion is a projection, an objectification, an externalization of subconscious desires. Once this desire is objectified into "God" it is mistakenly taken to have an autonomous existence independent of its human creators.*

- *Religion is therefore a coded way for human beings to talk about themselves and their desires. Human beings have desires and human beings with desires invent gods who are able to fulfill these desires. If the fundamental human desire is happiness then religion offers happiness – if not in this world, then in the next.*

- *Religion is therefore born of wish fulfillment. It is desire, fulfilled.*

- *Freud was interested in what drives humans to create these idols and to expose the irrational factors of the unconscious mind. Exposure of these factors, he believed, would liberate humans to act in a more informed, freer way.*

In *The Future of an Illusion* Freud wrote;

"This is a fresh psychological problem. We must ask where the inner force of those doctrines lies and to what it is that they owe their efficacy, independent as it is of recognition by reason."

In other words Freud saw his task as exploring the subconscious motivation that he believed must lie behind religious ideas and doctrines. What are the hidden triggers for religion within the personality? He believed that psychoanalysis could uncover these triggers. For Freud religion is nothing more than the product of a psychological process. This is where he begins his account of religion: religious claims are false and psychoanalysis can explain why religion has persisted for so long.

Freud's account of religion

Freud's first attempt to account for religion in psychological terms is found in *Totem and Taboo*, 1915, where he suggests that religion arose during pre-history as an act of expiation for a primeval murder of the male father by the male adolescents because they desired the mother. Today this is seen as a somewhat bizarre idea but in later works he developed his idea that there was a connection between "the father complex" and the belief in God. He believed that he could show that God is psychologically constructed as a magnified father figure.

Freud's understanding of a person's development in childhood lies behind this claim. For Freud the human infant is a bundle of instinctive desires and each person undergoes a process of modifications to these instinctive desires as they move from infancy to childhood and from childhood to adulthood. The basic primal desires of the baby are modified in the light of their experiences and in the light of parental encouragement and criticism. The path of modification is, for Freud, easy to track and each person goes through a series of identifiable phases. However, no child passes through all stages completely smoothly. Difficulties and conflicts occur and some are too painful for the person to keep in the conscious mind. Therefore these painful childhood experiences are locked into the subconscious mind. But they emerge in dreams and in slips of the tongue (hence a "Freudian slip") and sometimes will emerge in neurosis. If there is a situation in later life that places the person in a situation to trigger the memory then the person may regress into a childhood response.

For Freud **the religious response to the world is a neurosis** which has its roots in childhood. It is an infantile regression into childhood but may be triggered by any stage of development that did not go smoothly. If that problem area can be identified by psychoanalysis the religious neurosis should disappear.

1. Religion is the **defense mechanism** of the religious person to the experience of living in a hostile world. The world is a fearful place to the child and if

learning how to deal with the world is not accomplished in childhood it reveals itself in later life in the form of religious neurosis. The person creates a great father figure in the sky who will defend them and protect them. God is therefore the magnified father figure on whom the religious person wishes to be able to depend in adult life. The religious person is, therefore, someone who has not grown up. This, Freud argued, explains why young people often lose faith in God when they realize that their father is only human and can make mistakes.

2. *Religion is a **form of wish fulfillment** – the wish of the child for a loving father in a hostile world who will look after them and upon whom they can depend leads them to create God. God is the ideal projection of what a father should be. Religion, as part of what Freud terms "wish fulfillment," is therefore an illusion and a mass-delusion that shapes reality for religious believers. Individuals feel the need for one upon whom they can rely and create a god with whom they can share all their troubles. Religion enables people to feel comforted and secure as the God they worship is all-powerful, loving, and totally trustworthy so whatever happens in an individual's life they can be confident that all will work out well in the end.*

3. *Freud noted that in religion there are **repetitive patterns of behavior** in rituals and services. He considered these to be similar to the neurotic behavior patterns that some of his clients exhibited. He argued that this neurosis also had its origins in childhood. He said that babies develop very complex feelings about their parents. They see their fathers as a threat as the father often takes over the priority which the mother initially gives to the baby and this creates jealousy in the baby. This is particularly the case with males who develop a wish to kill their father and to make love to their mother because the father is seen as a rival and a threat. This gives rise to the "Oedipal complex" stemming from the Greek myth of Oedipus when the young man, Oedipus, ends up killing his father and making love to his mother (albeit without knowing at the time that the woman was his mother). The "Electra complex" is the reverse of the Oedipal complex and applies to girls. **Religion and religious rituals, argued Freud, provide a mechanism to work out these early tensions**. He regards the repetition of religious rites and rituals as exactly like other repetitive neurotic behavior patterns.*

CHALLENGES TO FREUDIAN
ANALYSIS OF RELIGION

- *Freud's views on the origins of religion have been consistently challenged and criticized from immediately after he put them forward to the present day. Many of the so-called "facts" on which his theories were based are not facts but opinions. Like Marx, Freud starts with the assumption that there is no God rather than arguing for this and, once this assumption is made, he then seeks to explain what makes people accept the idea of God. However, he does not put forward an argument against God – his claim is as much a faith claim as that of the religious believer.*

- *Freud explained God as a projection of the earthly father figure. The religious person may want to say that it is not God who is a projection of the earthly father, but the earthly father who, in the mind of the young, is always a disappointment because he can never live up to God. In other words it is because of the reality of God that the earthly father is destined to be a disappointment by comparison.*

- *If Freud is to be taken as a serious attempt to explain the phenomena of world religions he needs to account for the existence of God in cultures which are matriarchal not patriarchal and also to account for religions such as Buddhism that has no "god" figure at all. He does not explore these issues.*

- *Freud's view of reality is that there is no God, and he does not even consider that the "projections" of God in the human psyche might correspond to something transcendent beyond the individual. Freud's arch rival, Jung, considered that all human beings have within them a number of archetypes including the archetype of God – but Jung was open to the possibility that this archetype represented the "imprint" of the God who does exist. Jung believed in God and starts from a different point from Freud – both starting points may be valid but they both need justification and cannot be accepted without analysis. Many of those today who reject religion because of Freud do not recognize this.*

Freud's account of religion, therefore, rests on an unjustified assumption. Although it is often held today that psychology has "explained" religion this is far from being the case. However, it is common to hear the agnostic or the atheist argue that religion is "all in the mind" and only for those who "need" it. The impact of Freud on religion must not be underestimated as he offered an explanation for religion that has had an enormous impact, even if the details of how Freud reached his conclusions are not always fully appreciated.

CONFLICT OR COLLABORATION

There are two basic models of the relationship between psychology and religion – the first is a "conflict" model where religion and psychology are seen as being opposed and in tension. The second model is a "collaboration" model where religion and psychology are seen as potential collaborators in the search to help understanding of what it is to be human. Freud made no attempt to disguise the fact that he belonged to the first of these – his approach is to reject religious belief and to reduce the religious impulse to one that can be explained entirely in materialistic terms. As an example, Freud wrote at the end of his psychological study of Leonardo da Vinci:

"Psychoanalysis ... has taught us that the personal God is psychologically nothing other than a magnified father; ... "

Elsewhere he wrote that religion is:

"...nothing other than psychological processes projected into the outer world."

Two words appear in both these statements – "nothing other." Freud is putting forward a reductionist view by which religion is reduced to psychological states – this is "psychological reductionism." Religion can, it is held, be explained entirely in psychological terms. Many modern psychologists share with Freud a reductionist approach coupled with commitment to the view that human beings are essentially material and that there is no spiritual dimension to their lives. Psychology, the reductionist believes, will soon be able to explain the existence and the mechanisms of consciousness, just as medicine explains the workings of the body. B.F. Skinner was the leading behavioral psychologist of his generation, and he maintained that human beings could be entirely analyzed in terms of behavior – he was thus another member of the "conflict" school. He achieved great success with techniques for shaping and modifying behavior and he went on to consider how such techniques might be harnessed to influence the future of society. Skinner maintained

Are humans "nothing but" psychological machines?

that similar principles, based on the effects of rewards and punishments, could explain how religion functions psychologically. "The religious agency," he said, "is a special form of government under which 'good' and 'bad' becomes 'pious' and 'sinful'." He argued that good things, personified as a god, are reinforcing, whereas the threat of hell is an adverse stimulus. These two impulses shape the behavior of religious people. God, he considered, could be reduced to a positively reinforcing psychological impulse. Skinner is, therefore, another reductionist in the wake of Freud.

Roger Sperry on the other hand, a distinguished psychologist, neuroscientist, and Nobel laureate, rejected the psychological reductionist and behaviorist position. Sperry was a leading member of the "collaborative" school seeing religion and psychology as allies in a joint enterprise. Sperry maintained that it was too simple to reduce humans to "nothing but" psychological machines and that both religion and psychology could illuminate the complex issue of what it is to be human. The one cannot replace the other. The issue, therefore, of the relationship between psychology and religion is still very much an open one – Freud and those after him who rejected religion without argument or evidence were premature.

BRINGING THE THREADS TOGETHER

Darwin, Marx, and Freud each challenge religious belief and have been used to justify a materialist way of looking at the world. Whilst those who are not religious may regard these attacks on religion as definitive it is clear that the religious believer will not accept this. The work of Darwin was based on good science but the work of Marx and Freud was based on presuppositions that, for the religious believer, were never justified, and certainly do not qualify as good science. Ultimately the question is whether one opts to live life according to the creed of a world religion or according to the modern-day creed of post-modernism which has been heavily influenced by these three key figures. The modern-day creed might go something like this poem written by Turner.

Creed – Steve Turner

We believe in Marxfreudanddarwin.
We believe everything is OK
as long as you don't hurt anyone,
to the best of your definition of hurt,
and to the best of your knowledge.

We believe in sex before during and after marriage.
We believe in the therapy of sin.
We believe that adultery is fun.
We believe that sodomy's OK
We believe that taboos are taboo.

We believe that everything's getting better
despite evidence to the contrary.
The evidence must be investigated.
You can prove anything with evidence.

We believe there's something in horoscopes, UFO's and bent spoons;
Jesus was a good man just like Buddha
Mohammed and ourselves.
He was a good moral teacher although we think his good morals were bad.

We believe that all religions are basically the same,
at least the one that we read was.
They all believe in love and goodness.
They only differ on matters of
creation sin heaven hell God and salvation.

We believe that after death comes The Nothing
because when you ask the dead what happens they say Nothing.
If death is not the end, if the dead have lied,
then it's compulsory heaven for all
excepting perhaps Hitler, Stalin and Genghis Khan.

We believe in Masters and Johnson.
What's selected is average.
What's average is normal.
What's normal is good.

We believe in total disarmament.
We believe there are direct links between warfare and bloodshed.
Americans should beat their guns into tractors
and the Russians would be sure to follow.

We believe that man is essentially good.
It's only his behaviour that lets him down.

This is the fault of society.
Society is the fault of conditions.
Conditions are the fault of society.

We believe that each man must find the truth that is right for him.
Reality will adapt accordingly.
The Universe will readjust. History will alter.
We believe that there is no absolute truth
excepting the truth that there is no absolute truth.

We believe in the rejection of creeds.

(This poem is by Steve Turner, and appears in his (out of print) *Up To Date anthology*
(Hodder & Stoughton). It also appears in Ravi Zacharias' book, *Can Man Live
Without God*.)

Notes

[1] *Lyell's* Principles of Geology *published in 1830–33.*

[2] *George Cuvier, in* Essay of the Theory of the Earth *published in 1813 argued for
a whole series of extinctions of animals and plants in the history of the Earth.
He maintained that the biblical Flood was historical and occurred about five to six
thousand years previously and was the most recent cataclysm. The attraction of this
theory to theology was that different creatures discovered as fossils were not related
to each other and so the idea of species as being unchanging was not challenged.*

[3] *Darwin did not talk of genes but of inherited characteristics but today we know that
it is the genetic code that contains these characteristics.*

[4] *Darwin held that all animals evolved from primitive life forms and all the great
variation resulted from random natural selection: "...not only are the various
domestic races, but the most distinct genera and orders within the same great class –
for instances mammals, birds, reptiles, and fishes – are all the descendants of one
common progenitor and we must admit that the whole vast amount of difference
between these forms has primarily arisen simply from variability." (Darwin,* Variation
of Animals and Plants under Domestication*)*

[5] *Bishop Samuel Wilberforce at a meeting of the British Association in 1860 said that:
"The principle of natural selection... is absolutely incompatible with the word of God."*

[6] *Preface to a* Critique of Hegel's Philosophy of Right *(1844) – Karl Marx.*

[7] *The hymn sung by most Christians based on the song attributed to the Virgin Mary
before the birth of Jesus set out the commitment to the poor, "He has put down the
mighty from their seats, and exalted the humble and meek. He has filled the hungry
with good things, and the rich he has sent empty away."*

[8] *Pope John Paul II's encyclical* Tertio Millenio Adveniente.

9 *The article "Re-opening the debate on Marxism and Religion by Geoff" Bottoms influenced the writing of this section.*

10 *SACP Programme 10th Congress July 1–5, 1998.*

11 Fidel and Religion – Conversations with Frei Betto, *1990. Ocean Press.*

12 *Mark 14.7.*

CHAPTER 13

GOD AND SCIENCE

I n a world dominated by science, some argue that God is irrelevant. In more primitive times many events seemed to be inexplicable and it therefore made sense to suggest that gods or a God was responsible.

1. *In Greek and Norse mythology there was a whole pantheon of gods and their disputes and desires affected everything on Earth. Zeus was the god of thunder, Aphrodite/Daphne the goddess of love. Infertility was thought to be curable by praying to the right god and warfare was often seen as a battleground between different gods. We can now explain thunder scientifically and even, perhaps, get closer to understanding love so the gods seem irrelevant. We can admire the picture by Poussin of the goddess Selene[1] who saw a shepherd, Endymion, asleep in a cave. She fell in love with him, and began to neglect her duties to lie beside him as he slept. In some stories, Zeus grants Endymion perpetual sleep with perpetual youth, so that Selene would resume her duties. In others, Selene herself puts him to sleep. However, whilst admiring the genius hardly anyone accepts the reality of the gods they depict.*

2. *Little used to be known about the human body so when someone became ill, prayer was likely to be as effective as the primitive medicine available at the time. Relics of saints and prayers to particular gods were thought to be part of most healing processes. When people recovered they gave thanks to the appropriate gods and when they died then this was either the will of god or the person had not made the right sacrifices or had not led a sufficiently holy life.*

Goddess Selene *by Poussin*

3. *The Earth was seen as the center of the Universe, placed there by God, and the stars rotated round the Earth in perfect circles. Human beings were created in the image of God and were God's direct creation. We now know that human beings have evolved from other animals over millions of years and that the Earth is a minor planet circling a minor star in an average sized galaxy.*

Many people today are **CLOSET VERIFICATIONISTS** – they have adopted a "scientific" mindset which rejects anything not empirically verifiable. They assume that the only statements that have meaning are those that can be verified and, therefore, science is their new god because the statements of science are all held to be verifiable. Religion is dismissed because they consider it to be meaningless or, at best, to be an activity indulged in by groups of people who may get together for companionship on Sundays or because they have psychological needs which religion may fulfill.

Many people today consider that as no evidence can be given for the existence of God, God can be rejected. The real power of science is to encourage a verificationist mindset about life and to reject any alternative ways of understanding reality and the world. In fact the claim that belief in God has no basis fails to take into account the various arguments that have been put forward for God's existence (see chapter 6) and whilst none of these may, in themselves, be convincing, together they may put up a persuasive case that the existence of God makes better sense of human experience of the world than any rival theory. It is precisely here, however, that some scientific critics of God will object. They will say that God is an "ad hoc" hypothesis which no serious scientists would entertain. One of the fiercest of such critics of religion in Richard Dawkins.

Richard Dawkins and the design argument

Richard Dawkins is a passionate, persuasive writer, speaker, and broadcaster. He is Professor of the Public Understanding of Science at Oxford University and he is vitriolic in his dismissal of religious belief and the idea of God. In a series of books Dawkins has launched devastating attacks on the evils of religion, the inadequacy of religious believers, and, as he sees it, the bankrupt and irrelevant idea of God. Dawkins is a modern Darwinian – he is a biologist who considers that "the survival of the fittest" can explain all aspects of this world and all aspects of human behavior and purpose. For Dawkins life has no meaning and no purpose – human beings are simply the creatures that have most successfully evolved to suit the conditions available and they have now moved on to be able to dominate and alter their environment. They are no longer simply products of the environment, they have transformed their environment and the ability to do this is something that has itself evolved.

One of Dawkins' early books was entitled *The Blind Watchmaker*. This referred to the famous argument put forward by William Paley in the 19th century which runs as follows:

1. *Imagine you are crossing a heath and you find a watch. You might not know what the watch was for, but you would recognize that it has all the marks of contrivance and design. It is made up of wheels and cogs (this, of course, was before the days of digital watches) and, unlike a stone, it had clearly been made with care and with intelligence.*

2. *The world is rather like a great watch – it is even more complex than a*

watch and bears similar marks of contrivance and design. Birds, bees, butterflies, and the whole natural order show every sign of design and intelligence.

3. *Just as the design of the watch clearly implies an intelligent designer, so the great design in the world implies a great designer.*

4. *This designer is God.*

Dawkins ridicules this argument as he maintains that the only "designer" that is needed is the principle of natural selection. All the beauty and order in the world is simply the product of evolutionary forces. The delicate intricacy of a coral reef with its myriad colored fishes is merely the product of evolution which guides particular fish to evolve in particular ways to find niches in which they can survive and breed and avoid predators. As Dawkins puts it:

"Evolution has no long term goal. There is no long term target, no final perfection to serve as a criteria for selection... The criteria for selection is always short term, either simply survival or, more generally, reproductive success. The 'watchmaker' that is cumulative natural selection is blind to the future and has no long term goal."

Instead, therefore, of a God who has carefully produced an orderly and beautiful world in which human beings can live and develop, Dawkins sees a world that works according to the inexorable forces of natural selection.

In another book, *The Selfish Gene*, Dawkins maintains that the only basis for human actions is so that human genes can survive – indeed men and women are nothing more than the "machines" constructed by genes to enable the genes to replicate and live on. The genes of each species are in competition and within each species genes are in competition – the drive is, therefore, to reproduce successfully so that the genes may be passed on and thus survive. Dawkins says:

"We are survival machines – robot vehicles blindly programmed to preserve the selfish molecules known as genes."

Does a human life have meaning?

Human beings have evolved to meet the conditions available. There is no purpose and no meaning to our existence except to replicate. Religion is based on a sense of personal inadequacy and the unwillingness to face the clear evidence of science. Human beings are unwilling to recognize their position as highly evolved animals and therefore have sought, from primitive times, to tell themselves stories that they have been created by a great father figure in the sky – this enables humans to think that their lives have meaning and significance when in fact this meaning is entirely lacking.

Dawkins understands human beings strictly in terms of biology – we have about 5 billion cells each containing 46 chromosomes. Each chromosome contains tens of thousands of genes. Our DNA is passed on through our genes and, therefore, there is a sense in which the real essence of who we are, our DNA, is transmitted when we breed. Our DNA lives on in our children and we preserve our DNA by breeding. Our DNA represents the very essence of who each human being is just as it represents the essence of every living thing in the world. Dawkins puts this as follows:

"It is raining DNA outside. On the banks of the Oxford canal at the bottom of my garden is a large willow tree and it is pumping downy seeds into the air.... not just any DNA but DNA whose coded characteristics spell out specific instructions for building willow trees that will shed a new generation of downy seeds. These fluffy specks are, literally, spreading instructions for making themselves. They are there because their ancestors succeeded in doing the same. It's raining instructions out there. It's raining programmes; it's raining tree-growing, fluff-spreading algorithms. This is not a metaphor, it is the plain truth. It couldn't be plainer if it were raining floppy discs." (The Blind Watchmaker 1986 p.111)

Peter Williams, a modern theistic philosopher, agrees with Dawkins that there is a strong analogy between DNA and a computer disc but he maintains that just as we know that computer programs come from minds, we should similarly assume that DNA comes from a mind – the mind of God. Science, he argues, falls silent when asked for an explanation for the ultimate nature of the natural laws that give rise to order and that generate the processes that brings DNA about. He quotes Michael Behe:

"If you search the scientific literature on evolution, and if you focus your search on the question of how molecular machines – the basis of life – developed, you find an eerie and complete silence." For example, the Journal of Molecular Evolution *was established in 1971, and is dedicated to explaining how life came to be at the molecular level. None of the papers published in* JME *has ever proposed a possible route for a single complex biochemical system to arise in a gradual step-by-step Darwinian process."*

This, however, is not a good argument against Dawkins – it is effectively a "God of the gaps" argument as it is maintaining that as scientists have not yet discovered how organic life forms from inorganic, then God must be responsible. This type of argument has been put forward by generations of theistic philosophers and scientists but it is vulnerable to the next scientific discovery which may discover the explanation for what is presently inexplicable.

Williams maintains that a supernatural origin is required not for the DNA itself but for the processes which bring the DNA about:

"To say that Darwinian evolution cannot explain everything in nature is not to say that evolution, random mutation, and natural selection do not occur; they have been observed (at least in the case of microevolution) many different times..... I believe the evidence strongly supports common descent. But the root question remain unanswered; what has caused complex systems to form?" (Michael Behe *Darwin's Black Box* pp.175-6)

In other words, the principle of natural selection does not rule out belief in God – the question still remains as to where the whole system comes from and this, it is claimed, science cannot explain. This is a much stronger argument and it needs development and detailed consideration later in this chapter.

Dawkins sets up religious perspectives which are banal and then finds these an easy target to knock down. He shared a platform with John Polkinghorne and Peter Vardy in Manchester and London Universities in 2001 and in his presentation Dawkins gave the example of a U.S. Christian web site which pointed to the following features of a banana as being designed by God:

- *Outward indicator of inner contents: green – not ready; yellow – ready; and black – over-ripe.*

- *It is curved toward the mouth.*

- *Has non-slip surface.*

- *Bio-degradable.*

- *Tab for removal of wrapper.*

- *Shaped for human hand.*

- *Perforated for ease of access.*

- *Pleasing to taste buds.*

- *It has a specially designed "unzipper" for ease.*

- *It is nutritious.*

Dawkins then proceeds to mock religious believers who hold such banal and foolish positions. Of course he is right, but challenging religious belief on the basis of an argument that a child of seven would not accept is hardly a position worthy of a serious thinker. He does the same in his argument against believers who claim their position is rational because it cannot be disproved:

"Theists say: 'You can't prove a negative… Science has no way to disprove the existence of a supreme being.' (This is strictly true.) Therefore, belief or disbelief in a supreme being is a matter of pure, individual inclination, and both are therefore equally deserving of respectful attention! When you say it like that, the fallacy is almost self-evident; we hardly need spell out the reductio ad absurdum. As my colleague, the physical chemist Peter Atkins, puts it, we must be equally agnostic about the theory that there is a teapot in orbit around the planet Pluto. We can't disprove it. But that doesn't mean the theory that there is a teapot is on level terms with the theory that there isn't. Now, if it be retorted that there actually are reasons X, Y, and Z for finding a supreme being more plausible than a teapot, then X, Y, and Z should be spelled out."

This simply will not do – as Wittgenstein said "for a blunder, that's too big."[2] There is not a single serious theologian in Christianity, Islam, or Judaism who thinks that God is in any way whatever like a teapot or any other sort of physical object located at a particular space and time. As this book has made clear, theologians are far more sophisticated than this. God is the god of the Universe and transcends the normal categories of objects within the Universe. God is *de re* necessary, necessary in and of God's self and in a completely different category to physical objects. Also, no religious believers speak as Dawkins portrays them as speaking. It may be true that there is no good scientific evidence for God (and in demanding this Dawkins is showing that he is a closet verificationist) but that does not mean that there are not good reasons to believe in God and that these reasons cannot be evaluated, probed, examined, and questioned – as this book has attempted to do. Dawkins' lack of awareness of theology and also of the profound philosophical thought that, for more than 2000 years, has engaged with and been preoccupied by the issue of God's existence radically undermines the effectiveness of his attacks.

In his latest books, Dawkins has developed a real spiritual sense grounded in a feeling of awe and wonder at the Universe:

"The spotlight passes but, exhilaratingly, before doing so it gives us time to comprehend something of this place in which we fleetingly find ourselves and the reason that we do so. We are alone among animals in being able to say before we die: Yes, this is why it was worth coming to life in the first place..." (*Unweaving the Rainbow* pp.312-3)

"After sleeping through a hundred million centuries we have finally opened our eyes on a sumptuous planet, sparkling with color, beautiful with life. Within decades we must close our eyes again. Isn't it a noble, enlightened way of spending our brief time in the Sun, to work at understanding the Universe and how we have come to wake up on it." (op. cit. p.6)

Dawkins, however, is quick to refute suggestions that this sense of wonder has anything in common with religion – indeed he is dismissive and highly critical of those scientists who he sees, as "cashing in" on religious interest in science and who connect a sense of wonder and awe at the Universe with some form of religious imperative. For Dawkins, the Universe is a blind accident, but nevertheless something about which human beings can rightly wonder in the short time that we are alive.

Dawkins is dismissive of those theistic philosophers who argue that the sheer improbability of the world makes it likely that there is a God. Richard Swinburne is one philosopher who asks his reader to imagine a madman who kidnaps his victim and ties him to a chair underneath which is some explosive. This explosive is attached to ten machines, each of which shuffles a pack of playing cards. The madman leaves his victim saying to him that the explosive will detonate unless each of the randomly shuffled packs of cards comes up with an ace of hearts. The chances of this happening are incredibly small – 144,555,105,949,057,024 to one.[3] The victim waits, watching the cards. When the explosive does not go off and the victim sees that every single one of the cards has come up with the desired ace, he will be convinced, argues Swinburne, that this could not have happened by chance. The card shuffling machines must have been fixed in some way, it cannot just be an accident. Similarly, argues Swinburne, the chances of the exact conditions being present for human beings to exist are so slim that there must have been a designer – namely God.

Russell Stannard, former Professor of Theoretical Physics at The Open University gives a similar example. Imagine that a prisoner is blindfolded and taken before a firing squad. The firing squad is made up of trained marksmen – they never miss. The marksmen all take aim at point blank range and they all fire, and every single one of them misses. Surely, Stannard argues, the prisoner would be right in thinking that this was not merely chance – someone must have given orders that the marksmen would miss. It is simply too improbable that every single one could do so as a result of chance.

Dawkins rejects these arguments and sees them as being based on a false and naïve premise. The difference between Swinburne and Dawkins can be explained by the following example. Imagine that ten packs of cards are shuffled and the cards that appear are:

5H; 7C; 2S; AD; 2D; QS; 9C; KH; 2D; 5H

1. The odds of this combination coming up are astronomical. Swinburne and Stannard claim that the chances of human beings having evolved are similarly slim and, therefore, an intelligence must be assumed that arranged

conditions so that this incredibly unlikely scenario comes into being.

2. *Dawkins, by contrast, maintains that the cards are just what happened to come up. Similarly human beings are just what happened to evolve to suit the conditions available. The error, he would maintain, made by Swinburne is to work back from the existence of human beings and to wonder at the unlikelihood that the conditions are just right for us whereas, for Dawkins, we are the accident of evolution. In fact, to talk of the "accident" of evolution is slightly misleading as evolution, based on survival of the fittest, favors those species that are best adapted to the conditions that exist and that is why human beings are here now.*

What Dawkins fails to address is the question why there is a Universe at all and why there are natural laws that enable evolution to take place. He fails to ask why the natural laws are as they are and why they are so finely balanced to produce life. He fails to address the issue of why the world is saturated with beauty[4] not just at the macro but also at the micro level. These are questions about which science falls silent and atheists have to say, as Bertrand Russell does, that the Universe is simply a brute fact which does not require an explanation. David Hume put this position well when he said that the Universe may be **ordered** but this does not mean that it is **designed**. Hume, as an atheist, accepts that the world is ordered but considers that this order results from mere chance – his position is, therefore, very similar to that of Richard Dawkins. Given modern developments in science, however, this position is becoming increasingly difficult to hold. Two factors, in particular, need to be assessed before the "brute fact" hypothesis can be considered:

a) The origin of the Universe

There is no firm agreement to explain the origin of the Universe. The "Big Bang" theory still seems the most likely, but there are now a range of competing theories.

The Big Bang, it is suggested, was an initial singularity which exploded at a rate faster than the speed of light. Nuclear explosions took place giving rise to concentrations of hydrogen and helium and some of the lithium found in inter-stellar space. After about

300,000 years, the initial fireball dropped to a temperature a little below the present temperature of the Sun allowing electrons to form orbits around atoms and releasing photons or light. The Big Bang theory first came to prominence as the initial explosion can today be measured as background radiation at microwave frequencies equivalent to a temperature of about 2.7 kelvin (the kelvin scale begins at absolute zero and this temperature is equivalent to 273.16 degrees centigrade).

The Big Bang theory appears to explain a great deal, but recent observations also cast doubt on it:

1. The Hubble Space telescope has been measuring distances to other galaxies and these observations suggest that the Universe is much younger than the Big Bang theory implies. This is because the Universe is expanding much faster than previously assumed – this implies a cosmic age of as little as eight billion years – about half the current estimate. On the other side, other data indicates that certain stars are at least 14 billion years old.

2. Big Bang theorists maintain that the initial explosion was extremely smooth – this is based on the uniformity of the background radiation left behind. However Margaret Geller, John Huchra, and others at the Harvard-Smithsonian Center for Astrophysics have found a great wall of galaxies about 500 million lights years in length across the northern sky. These seems difficult to explain based on a uniform Big Bang.

Nevertheless the Big Bang theory still seems the most plausible explanation for the origin of the Universe. What is extraordinary, however, about the Big Bang is that for any stars and galaxies to be formed, the initial explosion had to occur within incredibly tight limits. If the initial explosive force of the Big Bang had been a tiny fraction less then the Universe would have collapsed in on itself in a comparatively short period of time – certainly before stars could form. If the initial explosive force had been a tiny fraction more than it was, then the Universe would have expanded at such a rate that, again, no stars could form. What is more, the elements making up the Big Bang had to be in such a fine balance that even the slightest deviation would have prevented the nuclear fires that cause stars to give off heat and, therefore, prevented planets forming. All these factors have to be so finely balanced for any stars and planets to form and the chances of them being present in just the right balance are correspondingly astronomically small. There are only two plausible ways to explain this:

1. *That there are an infinite number of Universes and this Universe just happens to be the one, out of the infinite number that exist, where stars can form and where life can be possible. A number of scientists take this view but this is no evidence for it in that, as Professor Stannard points out, it is not possible to provide evidence of alternative Universes other than the one we inhabit. The claim to there being alternative Universes is, then, a faith claim – it is not a scientific claim.*

2. *To claim that there is an intelligence that brings about the precise conditions necessary for stars, planets, and the Universe itself to form to provide the conditions necessary for life. This intelligence, of course, is the God claimed to exist by Christians, Muslims, and Jews.*

The situation today, therefore, is that far from God being a far-fetched hypothesis put forward by religious believers who fail to engage with science, the existence of an intelligent designer for the Universe is highly persuasive.

b) Conditions for life to evolve on Earth

Richard Dawkins argues that natural selection and evolution can explain the existence of all life on Earth. This may well be the case, but this leaves open wider questions which Dawkins does not address. First there is the issue of why evolution and natural selection exist at all. If these are as effective as many, including Dawkins, claim, then why does such a sophisticated arrangement exist? It is one thing to argue, as the previous section did, that the conditions needed for the Universe to form have to be incredibly precise and are thus incredibly unlikely in the absence of a guiding intelligence, but even more unlikely (if that is possible) is the existence of the forces necessary for life to form.

One group of scientists, under the leadership of James Lovelock, have put forward the GAIA hypothesis (the name "Gaia" comes from the Greek Earth-goddess of that name) which sees the world as a single entity and makes the extraordinary claims that Gaia herself manipulates and engineers the conditions necessary for life. This is a quite remarkable claim. It maintains that planet Earth, Gaia herself, is engaged in planetary engineering to foster the conditions necessary for life. Clearly scientific argument is needed to support this.

Life first appeared on Earth more than a hundred million years ago yet in this time the Earth's climate has changed very little. The chemical composition of the seas and the atmosphere runs quite against what we would expect. Lovelock argues that the atmosphere is a biological construction – a living system engineered to maintain a chosen environment. The whole is maintained at an equilibrium from which even a tiny departure could have disastrous consequences for life. This is the reverse of randomness – the chosen environment is maintained within very tight limits to provide the ideal conditions necessary for life and the Gaia scientists maintain that these conditions are the result of manipulation and engineering. Instead of Nature being seen as a primitive force that needs to be subdued, Gaia should be seen as a complex entity involving biosphere, atmosphere, oceans, and soil – a living organism, maintaining and sustaining itself.

Lovelock claims that if evidence is required for the work of Gaia-type processes, in other planets than Earth this evidence would be found on other planets where entropy is reversed. Entropy is based on the second law of thermodynamics and sees the Universe gradually moving to a state of equilibrium where all heat dies out and complexity declines. On Earth exactly the reverse is happening and this can only occur, according to the Gaia scientists, because planetary engineering is taking place. James Lovelock cites a whole series of factors that provide evidence for this planetary manipulation and engineering including:

AIR – OXYGEN

If there is less than 12% oxygen in the atmosphere then no fires could be lit. If there is more than 25% oxygen then fires would never go out – even damp leaves will go on burning once a fire is started so the whole planet would burn. Unless oxygen is between 12–25% life would not be possible. Gaia scientists argue that the planet Gaia has "designed" the oxygen level to be as it is (21%) and alters the conditions necessary to sustain this. On Venus and Mars there are only trace percentages of oxygen – indications of worlds where

Gaia does not operate. As Lovelock puts it:

> *"The chemical composition of the atmosphere bears no relation to the expectations of steady-state chemical equilibrium. The presence of methane, nitrous oxide, and even nitrogen in our present oxidizing atmosphere represents violation of the rules of chemistry to be measured in tens of orders of magnitude. Disequilibria on this scale suggest that the atmosphere is not merely a biological product, but more probably a biological construction; not living, but like a cat's fur, a bird's feathers, or the paper of a wasp's nest, an extension of a living system designed to maintain a chosen environment. Thus the atmospheric concentration of gases such as oxygen and ammonia is found to be kept at an optimum value from which even small departures could have disastrous consequences for life."* (James Lovelock, *GAIA: A new look at life on Earth,* p.9)

Sources of high potential, whether chemical or electrical, are dangerous. Oxygen is particularly hazardous. Our present atmosphere, with an oxygen level of 21%, is at the safe upper limit for life. Even a small increase in concentration would greatly add to the danger of fires. The probability of a forest fire being started by a lightning flash increases by 70% for each 1% rise in oxygen concentration above the present level. Above 25% very little of our present land vegetation could survive the raging conflagrations which would destroy tropical rain forests and arctic tundra alike (*Gaia: A new look at life on Earth,* p.65). What is more, this percentage has remained unchanged for hundreds of thousands of years and this is not an accident.

TEMPERATURE

The Earth spins before the vast heat of the Sun whose temperature has risen by 30% in 350 million years. Yet throughout this same period the overall temperature of the Earth (in spite of Ice Ages in some places) has not varied by more than a few degrees and life has always been able to survive. Even the ice ages only affected 30% of the planet. The Gaia scientists maintain that the planet actively manages the temperature – even though they are not yet clear on the mechanisms that achieve this result. It could not have been a random process. If, for instance, methane had been produced to retain more heat, runaway heating would have occurred which would have destroyed life. Darker plants absorb more heat and these may well have been present in the early days with gradual change over the eons to reflect more sunlight – thus regulating the temperature by reference to how much heat is absorbed.

SALT

If there is more than 6% salt in tissue, life is not possible. Even in brine pools (pools with very high salt contents) the forms of life have a watertight membrane to keep the internal saline levels below 6%. For hundreds of millions of years rivers have poured over the land taking incredible quantities of salt into the sea (when this does not happen there are devastating effects as salt builds up and almost all plant life dies – as happens, for instance, in areas of Australia where dams and irrigation schemes prevent water flowing to the sea). One would therefore have expected the level of salt in the sea to keep rising inexorably so that life in the sea would become impossible – yet the reverse has happened. For 350 million years the percentage of salt in the sea has been 3.4%. We know that salt is continually running off from rivers into the sea and being thrust up by undersea volcanoes. The percentage should have at least doubled. It has not.

So where does the salt go to? The amount of salt washed off the land every 80 million years is equal to the amount of salt in the sea now – but the oceans have existed for well over twice as long as this. A means must exist for salt to be removed from the sea. The mechanisms that make this happen are still unclear but Lovelock suggests the following:

1. *The falling shells of tiny marine creatures act like a continual rain through the sea – these may take salt with them as they fall, just as dust is removed from the air by rain.*

2. *Gaia itself may construct lagoons and "cordon off" parts of oceans which then dry out (thus removing huge quantities of salt).*

We have no more than partial answers and do not understand the processes but there seems no doubt that the processes are happening. Gaia is engineering the Earth to maintain its suitability for life, the processes it is using are as yet barely understood, but we now know they are there. As Lovelock says:

"The keynote, then, of this argument is that just as sand-castles are almost certainly not accidental consequences of natural but non-living processes like wind or waves, neither are the chemical changes in the composition of the

*Earth's surface and atmosphere which make the lighting of fires possible.
....how does it help us to recognize the existence of Gaia? My answer is that
where these profound disequilibria are global in extent, like the presence of
oxygen and methane in the air or wood on the ground, then we have caught a
glimpse of something global in size which is able to sustain and keep constant
a highly improbable distribution of molecules."* (p.35)

If Lovelock and the Gaia scientists are right, then this world is not a random
event. The Earth, Gaia herself, is manipulating and engineering the conditions
necessary for life to emerge and to sustain and develop life once it does emerge.

When the above two arguments are put together (the sheer improbability of
the precise composition of the singularity represented by the Big Bang and
the Gaia hypothesis claiming that there are mechanisms at work to enable life
to evolve) then Richard Dawkins' analysis seems to be not just inadequate, not
just increasingly improbable but simply wrong. There are processes in place
that demand an explanation. What is the origin of these processes? Why do
they exist at all? Religious believers, of course, will be able to point to the
activity of God but for those who reject God it is far more difficult as there is
no obvious explanation of why these forces should be in place or even exist.

Conclusion

Even if a unified theory which formulates total knowledge of how the
Universe operated is developed, then this would still not explain why there is
a Universe or why it is orderly or why the conditions make it possible for life
to evolve. These questions, philosophers and theologians maintain, are "too
large" for science.

Scientific language marginalizes a whole way of looking at the world and of
engaging with human beings with disastrous consequences (see overleaf).
It is not just that scientific and religious languages are different – it is
that science of the Dawkins variety seeks to reduce religious language to
scientific language. It is thus reductionist and this reductionism impoverish-
es what is of profound significance for the human spirit.

Human beings seek constantly to exercise control over their lives but this
control is at best illusory. Death is still inevitable and, in spite of scientific

advances, so are illness, disease, and broken relationships yet the scientific paradigm minimises the importance of these or claims that, one day, they can be overcome. This, however, is a fiction and is a denial of a central part of what it is to be human. Talk of God and of human beings in relation to God provides a different priority and a different way of locating human beings in the world in which they live.

If you start with the assumption that the material world is all there is and by saying this you will be satisfied to understand why things work as they do and are not interested in wider questions such as why they are there at all, then the atheist's position may be satisfying. However most people who think deeply about these issues will be not satisfied with these limited explanations and, if further reasons are demanded, then the existence of a guiding intelligence behind the Universe becomes far more plausible and this, of course, is precisely what Christians, Jews, and Muslims maintain is the case.

Those who reject this have to claim that:

1. *There "just happens" to be an infinite number of Universes.*

2. *It "just happens" that we are in one of the few Universes, of the infinite number that exist, where not only stars and planets can form but where the precise conditions for life become possible.*

3. *It "just happens" that Gaia has the precise conditions needed for life to be developed and sustained.*

4. *It "just happens" that the world is incredibly beautiful at every level when there seems no good reason why this should be the case, and*

5. *It "just happens" that human beings have evolved to be capable of space flight and advanced science but also with a religious sense which is common across all human beings and which some psychologists maintain is an essential part of human fulfillment.*

There perhaps comes a point when "ad hoc" assumptions that are individually so highly implausible become cumulatively difficult to sustain. At the very least, the idea of God is no longer one that can be regarded as a discredited and outmoded conception – it remains a live option which science does not in any way threaten and, perhaps, can increasingly sustain.

1) Why are many people today "closet verificationists"?

2) What are the strengths and weaknesses of Paley's argument from design?

3) Explain the significance of the title of Richard Dawkins' book *The Blind Watchmaker*.

4) Why does Dawkins consider that humans beings are the "robot vehicles" constructed by their genes?

5) What explanation can be given for the precise conditions necessary at the Big Bang for stars and planets to form?

6) What is the possible significance of the Gaia hypothesis when considering whether or not God exists?

Notes

1   *The Greek goddess of the full Moon, Selene is the daughter of Hyperion and Theia and one of the deities of light during the dynasty of the Titans. She represents the full Moon phase of the lunar cycle, along with Artemis (the crescent new moon) and Hecate (the waning moon). Like her brother Helius, she drives a chariot through the sky each night; hers is usually drawn by two horses. Selene is often closely identified with Artemis and Hecate, both of whom are Moon goddesses as well.*

2   *Wittgenstein said this in the context of a non-Catholic grabbing the consecrated bread and wine at the eucharist, taking it off for laboratory analysis and then effectively saying "You see, Catholic claims to this being the body and blood of Jesus are absurd because it analyzes as bread and wine." This is, Wittgenstein points out, too big a blunder – the Catholic accepts that the material will analyze as bread and wine but still maintains that it is body and blood. Language is being used in a more sophisticated and complex way than the non-believer allows.*

3   *This figure is arrived at by multiplying 52 (the number of cards in a pack) by 52 by 52 up to ten times for the ten packs of cards. The result is the number given.*

4   *The early master of the Franciscan order, St. Bonaventure, put forward the idea that every creature is an expression of the Word of God – the divine fecundity outpouring from the love-relationship at the heart of the Trinity. The Word of God is the divine art – "ars suprema, ars Patris." Bonaventure, as Edwards points out, specifically talks of the Word of God as the Wisdom of God who bears in her womb the eternal thoughts of God (The God of Evolution p.120). Wisdom in creatures is like "a ray of light which penetrates through the window panes breaking up into many colors" (Lignum Vitae 46)   "... every creature is of its very nature a likeness and resemblance of eternal wisdom" (Itinerarium 2.12). In the Franciscan tradition beauty is placed in the world to lure people toward God – it therefore has an explanation. For science, it is largely a matter of symmetry and has no meaning and no purpose.*

CHAPTER 14

QUANTUM REALITY, MULTI-DIMENSIONS, AND GOD

"The certainties of reason, however real and tangible, eventually come to an end, and thus one is forced to rely on other certainties, based on a different scale of values regulated by love and illuminated by faith."
John Paul II, 9/1989

"The fairest thing we can experience is the mysterious. It is the fundamental emotion which stands at the cradle of true art and true science. He who knows it not and can no longer wonder, no longer feel amazement, is as good as dead, a snuffed-out candle."
Albert Einstein 'The world as I see it'

"Religion without science is blind,
Science without religion is lame."
Albert Einstein

In a novel written by Edwin Abbott, called *Flatland,* it told the story of a flat kingdom where there were only two dimensions. There was a hierarchy of "people" in Flatland (who were all flat shapes) – the more sides an individual had, the greater his or her social position.

Squares were low down this hierarchy and those individuals with multiple sides – which therefore came closest to a circle – were the lords. No building could be in the shape of a triangle because these would be too dangerous as they were too pointed and could have harmed the inhabitants of Flatland. There was no idea of height and, indeed, the whole idea of a third dimension was completely dismissed. The novel develops, outlining what would happen if a sphere were to come into the world of Flatland. The Flatlanders could not experience it as a **sphere** as they could only experience the world in two dimensions – and so the sphere was experienced as a line or a point which moved along the two dimensional world. The point which they experienced represented the place where the sphere rested on the Flatlanders' world. The whole science of this world was based on two dimensions. No one could conceive of or contemplate the idea of a third dimension. A modern book, *The New Flatlanders* by Eric Middleton (Highland Press, 2002) resurrects this original story but in the form of an excellent debate between science and religion. There are close links between the Flatlanders, many who reject any transcendent reality or any transcendent aspect to life and those who reject God – but this needs explanation.

The science of Sir Isaac Newton was firmly based on three dimensions. The assumption behind Newtonian physics is that the world is orderly and predictable, if the rules of physics are understood. Physics was dominated by Newton's ideas and, by the end of the 19th century, a number of professors of physics were confidently predicting the end of science as it seemed that almost all the answers to the riddle of the physical world were either solved or were well on their way to being solved. Into this secure, predictable, three dimensional world came quantum theory – rather like the sphere coming into the world of Flatland.

Quantum science[1] turned the whole of physics and the whole way in which the Universe is understood on its head. Suddenly everything that was previously seen to be so obviously true was either false, vague, or uncertain. Common sense was almost completely wrong – indeed Einstein described common sense as:

"The series of prejudices we acquire by the age of 18."

Holbein's famous enlightenment painting *The Ambassadors* portrays confidence in the enlightenment period in progress and science. The two ambassadors, surrounded by their scientific instruments, were confident in the ability of science to uncover the nature of the world, the secrets of nature and the mysteries of life and death (the elongated shape on the floor is a skull – perhaps suggesting Holbein's reservations about their quest). The original painting in the National Gallery in London has a small, discreet crucifix in the top left hand corner. Most reproductions of the painting fail to show this but it is vital in understanding Holbein's possible reservations about the scene he was portraying. Similarly the whole way of understanding the world in the enlightenment period is undermined by the findings of quantum science.

It is often thought that scientific conclusions about the world are based on observation. The scientist observes certain phenomena and then hypothesizes about what causes the phenomena to happen. The hypothesis is then tested by further observation and science advances with logical steady steps. This model of science has been challenged by observation of science at work. Science does not advance by steady progress. Thomas Kuhn argued that instead the scientific community work within a paradigm. The paradigm is the accepted way of understanding the world through a particular set of scientific theories. The paradigm is developed and then accepted but then a sudden shift of paradigm takes place, which is generally resisted by those in power in the scientific community. This is what happened with the overthrow of Newtonian science – indeed Einstein was a patent clerk, he was not a member of the normal academic, scientific establishment and when he first put his ideas forward they were largely dismissed or greeted with incredulity.

Scientists, Kuhn held, work within a given paradigm which is generally accepted and explored. A new paradigm represents a break with the existing understanding. It challenges many of the old ideas. It is not a development but a total shift of perspective and understanding. The shift from one paradigm, or way of understanding the world through a particular set of scientific theories, to another comes suddenly – as a result of an insight or intuition rather than progressive development. Both paradigms can make sense of the observations, but one will come to command wider acceptance and therefore will be adjudged "true." **Truth, then, in science is not an absolute – it represents the theories that are generally accepted as true at the time and these remain "true" until they are shown to be false.** The history of science is, thus, a long history of theories that were supposed to be true but were eventually found to be false. In *The Structure of Scientific Revolution* Kuhn put it like this:

"If anomalies become serious and numerous, a scientist will sense a crisis for the paradigm. Typically they will begin to lose faith and then to consider alternatives. They do not renounce the paradigm that has led them into crisis." (p.77)

"The scientist in crisis will continually try to generate speculative theories that, if successful, may disclose the road to a new paradigm." (p.87)

"A new paradigm emerges all at once, sometimes in the middle of the night, in the mind of a man deeply immersed in crisis." (p.90)

"When making the revolutionary change from one paradigm to another, scientists often speak of 'the scales falling from the eyes.'" (p.122)

Kuhn likens the shift from one paradigm to another as being like a religious conversion experience.

Most great scientific breakthroughs do not come from logic but from intuition. Einstein said that his theory of relativity arose from him imagining riding on a beam of light. Kekule, one of the greatest chemists, realized that benzene is a string-like structure through his famous dream in which he saw a snake holding its own tail.

The emergence of quantum physics can be seen as a complete shift in paradigm from Newtonian physics. The trouble with quantum physics is that it does not make sense in ordinary common sense terms. What is more, it is impossible to observe quantum events, since it is a fundamental principle of quantum physics that any observation of a quantum event changes this event. As Bohr said:

"Any observation regarding the behavior of the electron in the atom will be accompanied by a change in the behavior of the atom."

So it is IMPOSSIBLE to know the state of an electron as measuring it changes its state. What is more, there is nothing to know until it is measured. This seems ridiculous and Shroedinger put forward his famous example of the cat to disprove it[2] – he thought that this example was absurd and would show that quantum theory was false. The only trouble is that quantum theory IS absurd by any normal, common sense understanding – and yet it is true!

- *If quantum theory is true, particles can travel faster than the speed of light – but nothing can travel faster than the speed of light.*

- *If quantum theory is true, then a particle at one side of the Universe can affect a particle on the other side of the Universe even though there is no connection between them.*

- *If quantum science is true, there is no solid matter – just oceans of empty space interspersed by force fields.*

The word "chaos" first appeared in Hesiod's *Theogeny* (c700 B.C.E.) in Part I:

"At the beginning there was chaos, nothing but void, formless matter, infinite space."

Later in Milton's *Paradise Lost*:

"In the beginning, how the heav'ns and Earth rose out of chaos."

Both Shakespeare (*Othello*) and Henry Miller (*Black Spring*) refer to chaos. In these instances chaos was an undesirable disordered quality. Dictionaries defined chaos as turmoil, turbulence, and primordial abyss. Scientifically, chaos has traditionally implied the existence of undesirable randomness but chaos is, extraordinarily, not like this. The American historian Henry Adams (1858–1918) expressed the new scientific meaning of "chaos" succinctly:

"Chaos often breeds life, when order breeds habit."

At the edge of chaos is order – what is chaotic, random, and without pattern at one level is orderly at another. In fact the whole fabric of the Universe seems to be based on precisely this. Some indication of disorderly orderliness is given in fractals – these are incredibly intricate patterns generated by repeated plotting of mathematical equations. The pictures that result from such plotting has only been possible since computer technology made it practical. In recent years many mathematicians have been fascinated by the link between mathematics and beauty – for much longer than this there have been known links between mathematics and music, but fractals make an extraordinary new link (the picture is of possibly the best known fractal – the **Mandelbrot** set[4] – although there are innumerable others). Fractals have

also been closely linked to the relation between randomness and order in the natural world. For instance:

1. *Every drop of water in a rushing stream is, individually, a random drop with no way of predicting its movement, but the stream of which it forms part behaves according to predictable laws.*

2. *An avalanche is triggered by a small sound or a random fall of flakes of snow, but the way the avalanche moves is predictable once the movement has begun.*

3. *Every snowflake falls randomly based on innumerable forces that are in principle unpredictable, but the avalanche which may be triggered by an individual snowflake obeys clear laws.*

4. *An iceberg topples into the sea because of an unpredictable and random moment of evaporation but the laws that cause icebergs to topple are well known.*

There is order on top of chaos and this is part of what makes the quantum world so hard to comprehend. In fact we can now see that the whole Universe, which has chaos at its most fundamental level, is incredibly orderly. This is remarkable given the second law of thermodynamics, discussed in the previous chapter, which states that the whole world is being driven towards entropy.

STRANGENESS

We now know that the world is far more strange, far more complex, far more alien than anything any previous generations can have imagined. The current paradigm of science goes against everything our common sense tells us. Currency values in the area of common sense have been radically undermined.

What does this all mean for ideas about God?

It is now clear that the Universe has any number of dimensions and that the simple observations are inadequate to explain the phenomena of the world in which we live. In this sense our existence is much like the existence of the Flatlanders – we now know that it is not just that there is a fourth dimension (time) but there may be five, six, ten, eleven, or twelve dimensions. Most people will remain unaware of these dimensions and as human beings we do not have the sensory apparatus to experience them directly. In many ways quantum theory supports what the great theologians and philosophers have recognized throughout the generations – that we live in Flatland. They have attempted to talk about what lies beyond the narrow human horizons which limit people in their perception of reality. They have wrestled with complexity even though they knew that they could not understand this complexity. The theologian would argue that God as creator of the whole Universe is the creator of all dimensions – if understanding these dimensions and the quantum world is hard, how much harder will it be to understand or to talk of God? Even without knowledge of quantum physics theologians argued that "Flatland" language can only be used to refer to God with very great difficulty, because the concept of God is of One who is so radically other – but if it is difficult to talk about quantum how much more difficult is it to talk of God?

Plato's god, the Demiurge, brought order out of chaos – Plato considered that God did not create chaotic matter, but he ordered this matter like a sculptor molds the clay or bronze he or she uses to make a statue. The raw matter is disorderly, but God brings order out of this. Aristotle's God was more remote – contemplating God's self – yet although Aristotle considered that the Universe was without beginning, the orderliness of the Universe was central to his understanding. Christians, Jews, and Muslims drew on both these understandings as well as their convictions of the unity of God. They have always considered that God is a mystery. As we saw in chapter 4, the Jewish philosopher, Moses Maimonides, argued that God was so radically Other that silence was the only form of worship. St. Thomas Aquinas built on the work of Islamic and Jewish theologians and, as described in chapter 6, his *Five Ways* of attempting to prove the existence of God sought to arrive at "that which explains the Universe." God, for Aquinas, is *de re* necessary – necessary in and of God's self. The Five Ways are different but they have one thing in common. They attempt to establish that there is a referent, X, such that this X explains the existence of the Universe. If you like, this X may be referred to as "Mystery" or, as Karl Rahner SJ does, as Holy Mystery. To this X, or to this Mystery, which is largely unknowable, Aquinas gives the name God. Victor White, in *God the Unknown* puts it this way:

"St. Thomas' position differs from that of modern agnostics because while modern agnosticism says simply 'we do not know and the Universe is a mysterious riddle,' a Thomist says 'we do not know what the answer is, but we do know there is a mystery behind it all which we do not know, and if there were not, there would not even be a riddle. This unknown we call God. If there were no God, there would be no Universe to be mysterious, and nobody to be mystified."

This is important and profound. It represents the fault line between atheist and believer. The believer maintains that:

1. *This unknown Holy Mystery not only exists but creates and sustains the Universe.*

2. *This Holy Mystery brings order out of chaos and puts in place the mechanisms in the Universe including the precise conditions necessary for the singularity that is the Big Bang – see previous chapter.*

3. *This Holy Mystery is the explanation why evolution takes place and why Gaia can engineer and manipulate the conditions for life on Earth,*

4. *More than this, this Holy Mystery is interested in every individual, and the Universe was brought into being in order that human beings should be created and should be able to identify the Holy Mystery that brought it about and to enter into a reciprocal relationship of love with this Mystery.*

5. *Love lies at the heart of the Universe. Although human beings have evolved, they are distinct from other animals in that they are able to reason and to love and, more than this, they will survive death.*

The affirmation of the Holy Mystery that emerges in the great world religions is also an affirmation that there is more to life than that which can be observed. World religions all claim that there is a greater reality than it is possible for the Flatland world, in which humans being live, to be able to grasp. This other reality is where the ultimate purpose of life, and the Universe, is to be found. It cannot be denied that the world's great faith traditions have many differences BUT, in spite of these differences, the extent of the unity underlying the great traditions is profound – they all see the Universe not as an accident, they all see human beings having a high and noble purpose, and they all reject the idea that truth is merely something human beings construct.

Of course, they could be mistaken. Any religious believer has to admit to this possibility. However, most will see their beliefs and commitment to God as providing meaning, hope, and purpose in a world which would otherwise be devoid of any of these, and furthermore quantum theory opens up the possibility of God in a way that Newtonian physics did not and philosophy has been very slow to work with the new possibilities.

PHILOSOPHY AT THE BUFFERS

Philosophy, the search for wisdom, understanding, and truth begun by the ancient Greeks, has run into the buffers. Originally philosophers were scientists and scientists were philosophers. Aristotle's philosophy underpinned all science until the time of Copernicus and, later, Galileo. The empirical observations after the enlightenment forced everyone to recognize that Aristotle's science, whilst brilliant at the time, was mistaken and science had to find its feet independent of philosophy. Philosophy has since gone its own way but has remained shackled to old ways of understanding. Its methodology is essentially unchanged since the time of the Greeks. It has not been forced to come to terms with the new world presented by quantum theory. Many modern philosophers do not even understand quantum theory and, of the few who do, fewer integrate it into their philosophy. The result is that most philosophers still work in Flatland and do not see beyond this. Many are closet verificationists[5] and the result is seen in countless philosophy departments in the Western world where even philosophy of religion is regarded as a marginal and sidelined subject and, within philosophy of religion, only the logic of Flatland is acceptable.

There is a need to open philosophy to the broader dimensions represented by the quantum world and to the possibilities to which quantum science gives rise. This affects the issue of God in various ways:

1. *The existence of God becomes far more of a possibility than most philosophers considered feasible ten, fifty, or a hundred years ago. The Gaia hypothesis, the reversal of the Second Law of Thermodynamics, and quantum theory all point to a reality beyond that which can be observed and to the existence of an ordering force in the Universe.*

2. Religious experience, as reported by so many people (see p.89), can no longer be dismissed but can be understood, at least partly, as an apprehension of a vastly more complex reality that we inhabit without realizing it. Such experiences may sometimes be a temporary ability to experience dimensions beyond Flatland due to the agency of God or other transcendent agencies dependent on God.

3. Life after death, and the idea of a quantum consciousness (p.147) is now a live hypothesis and challenges the materialistic view of the Universe. Evidence is pointing away from the idea that human persons are just material objects who live and die like any other animal and away from the idea that consciousness is simply a material brain state which will inevitably come to an end when the brain dies.

4. Miracles can no longer be dismissed as divine actions contrary to firm and inviolable laws of nature (chapter 9) but as part of the outworkings of a much stranger world where there are no absolute natural laws.[6] Exceptions to the approximations which natural laws represent are perfectly consistent with quantum theory and, assuming there are a range of other dimensions and that God is not in Flatland but controls all dimensions, then what human beings see as breaches of natural law are perfectly coherent and possible. To those in the Flatland world, a sudden intervention into their world from another dimension would be ridiculous and to be dismissed out of hand but once multiple dimensions are conceded then these interventions are perfectly plausible. The fact that these interventions do not conform to Flatland science does not undermine their veracity in the way that David Hume argues – rather it may point to their transcendent[7] origin.

5. If at the quantum level a particle can be in two places at once and fulfilling two different functions, and if at the quantum level a particle can impact on other particles at the other end of the Universe, then when one person prays for another it is conceivable that at the quantum level something is happening. Prayer becomes a way of recognizing the transcendent aspect of existence and, in the case of petitionary prayer, of seeking God's intervention in the world which God has made. No Christian, Jew, or Muslim would consider that all prayers will be granted – indeed at the heart of Christian prayer is the idea of "Thy will be done," but the possibility of a transcendent action having an effect in our world is perfectly coherent.

If the Flatland analogy is taken seriously, then the great religious traditions share another insight – that although human beings are born and live in Flatland, their final destiny does not lie here. Talk of "heaven," the Beatific Vision of God or the after-life are all attempts to stammer about the reality that is affirmed after death when no one has any experience of what this reality is. These are the attempts of Flatlanders to comprehend what lies beyond their comprehension.

Bringing the threads together

Theology used to be regarded as the queen of the sciences because it integrated other disciplines within it – today the great insights of the past remain valid but need interpretation in the light of our changing under-standing of the world. God has become a derided and dismissed word by many in our modern, post-modern, culture yet the yearning for meaning and for an understanding of the depth and relevance of human existence has never been more apparent in all societies.

Martin Buber was one of the great Jewish theologians in the first half of the 20th century. He tells the story of staying at an old castle and getting up early one morning to read the proofs of a book he had written. Downstairs he met a venerable old man and, when he explained what he was doing, the old man asked him to read the proofs out loud to him. Buber did so, and after a time the old man suddenly intervened with some vehemence:

"How can you bring yourself to say 'God' time after time? How can you expect your readers will take the word in the sense that you wish it to be taken? What you mean by the name God is something beyond all human grasp and comprehension, but in speaking about it you have lowered it to human conceptualization. What word of all human speech is so misused, so defiled, so desecrated as this! All the innocent blood that has been shed for it has been used to cover and has effaced its features. When I hear 'God' it sometimes seems blasphemous."

Buber says he sat, silent. Then he felt as if a power from on high entered into him and what he then replied he says that he can only indicate. It was as follows:

"Yes, it is the most heavy-laden of all human words. None has become so soiled, so mutilated. Just for this reason I may not abandon it. Generations

of men have laid the burden of their anxious lives upon this word and weighed it to the ground: it lies in the dust and bears their whole burden. The races of men with their religious factions have torn the word to pieces: they have killed for it and died for it, and it bears their finger-marks and their blood. Where might I find a word like it to describe the highest? If I took the purest, most sparkling concept from the treasure chambers of the philosophers, I could only capture thereby an unbinding product of thought. I could not capture the presence of Him whom the generations of men have honored and degraded with their awesome living and dying. I do indeed mean Him whom the hell-tormented and heaven-storming generations of men mean. Certainly they draw caricatures and write 'God's' name. But when all madness and delusion fall to dust, when they stand over against Him in the loneliest darkness and no longer say 'He, He' but rather sigh 'Thou,' shout 'Thou', all of them with one word, and when they then add 'God,' is it not the real God whom they implore, the One living God, the God of the children of man? Is it not He who hears them? And just for this reason, is not the word 'God' the

word of appeal, a word which has become a name, consecrated in all tongues for all times? We must esteem those who interdict it because they rebel against the injustice and wrong which are so readily referred to 'God' for authorization. But we may not give it up. How understandable it is that some should suggest that we should remain silent about the 'last things' for a time in order that the misused words may be redeemed! But they are not to be redeemed thus. We cannot cleanse the word God and we cannot make it whole: but, defiled and mutilated as it is, we can raise it from the ground and set it over an hour of great care."

The old man got up, came over to Buber and laid his hand on his shoulder and said, "Come, let us be friends."

'God' has, indeed, become a defiled and mutilated word but Buber is right – it is a word we cannot abandon. This book has attempted to explore some of the issues related to God today. It has attempted to show the depth and profundity of thought that characterizes the great philosophers and theologians of the past. Yet, in the final analysis, the question of God is a question for each of us. It is possibly the most profound question each person has to face. Does the world have any meaning? Has life any significance? Is death the end? Does God exist? These are not simply academic questions as they will affect and possibly transform our lives. Reading books is one thing but responding to these questions is at a deeper and more significant level. These are questions we have to address when we are alone at 2.00 in the morning and when we come to die – the answers we give should also transform the way we live. However, only you, the reader, can answer these questions for yourself – just as only you can decide how the answers will affect your life.

Notes

[1] *By the end of the 19th century science had discovered gaps in the Newtonian theories – which were explained as anomalies. One of these was that a purely black object absorbed all frequencies of light and should, therefore, have radiated all frequencies, but it does not. It emits lower range frequencies which only slowly increase as the heat is increased. If all frequencies of light were to be emitted (as Newton's theories led one to suppose) then we would suffer ultra-violet burns when we sit in front of a fire, and this does not happen. It was Max Plank who discovered, in 1900, what was actually going on. Planck showed that the size of the quanta varied in proportion to the frequency of the radiation – this gave rise to the theorem which is as famous as Einstein's $E=MC^2$ namely $E=hv$ where E is the energy value of the quantum and v is the frequency of the radiation. The h is a constant known as "Planck's constant" – which has a miniscule value just above zero BUT the point is that there IS a value! However, it is only the existence of this constant that means that higher frequency quanta require more energy – thus avoiding ultra-violet radiation which would kill us. No one believed Planck at first, but five years later Einstein confirmed Planck's findings. Even then, most of the scientific community refused to accept it.*

Neils Bohr (1885–1962) contributed more to an understanding of quantum physics than even Einstein. He was not only a great scientist but also a philosopher and his philosophic work anticipated some of that of Ludwig Wittgenstein. For instance, he wondered how a word could describe both a mental state and also a series of actions (e.g. drunkenness, joy, etc). These words were, he said, ambiguous as they applied at two different levels with two different meanings.

The same applied in mathematics and this began his understanding that conflicting interpretations can exist at the same time. Interestingly, other scientists were also prompted by philosophers. Thus Einstein was greatly influenced by David Hume's questioning of cause and effect and others' studies such as Kant's views on space and time. Science and philosophy were seen as complementary – not as rivals.

[2] *Imagine a live cat placed in a box with a radioactive source which has a precise 50% chance of emitting a radioactive alpha particle in 60 seconds. If the particle is released, it will trigger a hammer to hit a vial of deadly poison which will kill the cat contained in the box. The box is then sealed. Common sense says that either the cat will be alive or it will be dead at the end of 60 seconds even though, as the box is closed, we may not know which is the case. Quantum theory, however, says that the release of the quantum particle depends on observation and, therefore, at the end of a minute the particle has both been released and not released and, accordingly, the cat is both alive and dead – which is the case will depend on the observation. This seems to be absurd but it is actually the case.*

[3] *The maths is not difficult. If you have some x-and-y equations, any value for x gives you a value for y. On a graph you would plot the point where it's right for both x and y. Then you take the next value for x which gives you another value for y, and when you've done that a few times you join up the dots and this becomes the graph of whatever the equation is. Fractal patterns emerge when an algorithm is iterated; every time the value for y is worked out it is used as the next value of x. And so on.*

[4] *Mandelbrot sets were developed as a part of the fractal geometry of Benoit Mandelbrot. Fractal geometry deals with the formalization of irregularity. Many natural phenomena posses a scaling property. This occurs when subsections of an object are similar in some sense to the whole of the object. If regions are subdivided into smaller and smaller parts, there is no loss of detail. The set is connected by fine tendrils. While this does naturally occur in nature, for instance in the fjords of Norway, the Mandelbrot sets are a mathematical phenomenon. In the images of the set, detail continues to an infinitesimal scale and is infinitely repeated no matter how far the picture is analyzed.*

[5] *See p.233.*

[6] *Natural laws are now accepted as being, at best, approximations of general patterns of order in the Universe. According to chaos theory, randomness lies at the heart of the Universe and although, at the macro level, there is a degree of predictability represented by our understanding of natural laws, these are in no sense absolute and exceptions to them are perfectly possible.*

[7] *The very word "transcendent" points to a reality beyond the Flatland world. God has always been held to be a transcendent agent, yet an agent that is also imminent in the world God creates. Once multiple dimensions are accepted, then God's ability to be both transcendent and imminent, being within the dimensions of Flatland yet also transcending these, is perfectly possible.*